Lovecraft's "The Bride of the Sea" and the Uses of Bathos

Manuel Pérez-Campos

I. A Poetic Challenge

In a December 8, 1914, letter to Maurice W. Moe, Lovecraft wrote he had learned through a third party that Moe wanted to see Lovecraft try his hand at verse forms other than heroic couplets. Defending his choice of heroic couplets on the basis of long-standing habit and antiquarian outlook, Lovecraft offered an analogy: "As the strength of Antaeus depended on his contact with Mother Earth, so does any possible merit to my verses depend on their execution in this regular and time-honoured measure (*SL* 1.3).

It would be almost a year before Lovecraft elaborated another response to that challenge. The result—included in a September 30, 1915, letter to Rheinhart Kleiner—was "Unda; or, The Bride of the Sea." By then Lovecraft had already gone through a heated dispute with James Ferdinand Morton, conducted in the sphere of amateur journalism, for coming to the defense of Charles D. Isaacson after he was lambasted by Lovecraft for championing the modernist aesthetic of Walt Whitman in his journal, *In a Minor Key*. In his July 1915 riposte essay, "In a Major Key," Lovecraft described Whitman's verbal art as bathetic: "Whose fever'd fancy shuns the measur'd pace, / And copies Ovid's filth without his grace" (*CE* 1.56, ll. 3–4), and "Scorning the pure, the delicate, the clean, / His joys were sordid, and his morals mean" (ll.11–12). And he fulminated against Whitman's muse (*CE* 1.57, ll. 17–18): "Would that his Muse had dy'd before her birth, / Nor spread such foul corruption oe'r the earth." But Lovecraft seems to have been particularly energized by Isaacson's promoting Whitman as a poetic voice for racial equality.

Consequently, he also contrarily extolled racial prejudice on the grounds that it was "intended to preserve in purity the various divisions of mankind which the ages have evolved" (CE 1.57).

Lovecraft composed "Unda," a poem cast in the modernist mold to fulfill Moe's curiosity, in September 1915. It came right after he had completed another poem titled "The Isaacsonio-Mortoniad," in which he engaged in ad hominem vitriol against Isaacson and Morton for their rebuttal of "In a Major Key." However, according to Joshi, Lovecraft "wisely" never sought to have it published (AT 493). This was probably due to the realization that "The Isaacsonio-Mortoniad" might earn him Morton's enmity. But Lovecraft was not interested in going that far; intrigued by Morton's erudition and stimulated by his personality, he preferred instead to remain on a good terms with him.

"Unda" was in many respects a continuation of Lovecraft's "Isaacsonio-Mortoniad," albeit on a more subdued and artistic note. This continuation may be appreciated in the way poetical devices and imagery from "The Isaacsonio-Mortoniad" are echoed in "Unda."

Lovecraft starts off "The Isaacsonio-Mortoniad" with an apostrophic invocation: "Wake, Heav'nly Muse!" (AT 208, l. 1). He is referring to the muse of sublimity: if she needs to wake, it is so that she may be on his side when he criticizes Isaacson and Morton. In a similar manner, "Unda's" narrator, in the first stanza, engages in associational thinking, using as his prompt a seashore setting. The associational thinking succeeds in evoking a muse (this is a modernist—given it is psychologically oriented—equivalent of an apostrophic invocation), only in this case the muse is that of the anti-sublime. This is the same muse to whom Isaacson and Morton, as Lovecraft taunts in "The Isaacsonio-Mortoniad," are in thrall, and the one Moe has wanted him to pursue. "Dim are the pathways and rocks that remind me" (AT 211, l. 3), he says, and the rest of the poem is about this muse, personified in the character of Unda, who leads him to a tragic end.

Secondly, "Unda's" epigraph, "I, a dog, sing at the moon," is a parody of "The Isaacsonio-Mortoniad's" epigraph, "Of arms and men I sing" (in turn a parody—cf. Joshi in AT 493—of Virgil's opening line in the Aeneid, "Of arms and the man I sing").

THE LOVECRAFT ANNUAL

Edited by S. T. Joshi   No. 4 (2010)

Contents

Abbreviations used in the text and notes:

AT   *The Ancient Track* (Night Shade Books, 2001)
CE   *Collected Essays* (Hippocampus Press, 2004–06; 5 vols.)
D   *Dagon and Other Macabre Tales* (Arkham House, 1986)
DH   *The Dunwich Horror and Others* (Arkham House, 1984)
HM   *The Horror in the Museum and Other Revisions* (Arkham House, 1989)
LL   *Lovecraft's Library: A Catalogue* (Hippocampus Press, 2002)
MM   *At the Mountains of Madness and Other Novels* (Arkham House, 1985)
MW   *Miscellaneous Writings* (Arkham House, 1995)
SL   *Selected Letters* (Arkham House, 1965–76; 5 vols.)

Copyright © 2010 by Hippocampus Press

Published by Hippocampus Press, P.O. Box 641, New York, NY 10156
http://www.hippocampuspress.com

Cover illustration by Allen Koszowski. Hippocampus Press logo designed by Anastasia Damianakos. Cover design by Barbara Briggs Silbert.

Lovecraft Annual is published once a year, in Fall. Articles and letters should be sent to the editor, S. T. Joshi, c/o Hippocampus Press, and must be accompanied by a self-addressed stamped envelope if return is desired. All reviews are assigned. Literary rights for articles and reviews will reside with *Lovecraft Annual* for one year after publication, whereupon they will revert to their respective authors. Payment is in contributor's copies.

ISSN 1935-6102
ISBN13: 978-0-9844802-5-8

And thirdly, there are two passages, one in "The Isaacsonio-Mortoniad" and one in "Unda," in which sky-related phenomena are used to imply bathos. In "The Isaacsonio-Mortoniad," Lovecraft writes: "Thus from the window, undisturb'd and warm, / We safely view the grandeur of the storm" [AT 211, ll. 121–22]. The storm in question, of course, is the difference of opinion that he, Isaacson, and Morton have been sharply exchanging. The storm is bathetic because it has consisted of an intermingling (as far as Lovecraft is concerned) of the points of view of those who tout the anti-sublime with his, who espouses the sublime. Similarly, in "Unda," Lovecraft has his narrator cry out, "Lo! the red moon from the ocean's low hazes / Rises in ominous grandeur to view" [AT 213, ll. 45–46]. The "red moon" is described in the same manner as the storm, that is, as evoking a sense of terrifying "grandeur" because it is an event one is powerless to control. The moon is bathetic because the narrator is looking to it superstitiously for a sign that Unda, his lover, will return to him, and what he will get from it instead is a sign to commit suicide.

And yet, "Unda" was addressed to neither Isaacson nor Morton, but to Moe. Though never part of Lovecraft's amateur journalism debate over modernist poetry, Moe had unwittingly became part of it simply by wishing to see poetry from Lovecraft in a modernist vein. "Unda" was not as potential a disruptor of an interpersonal relationship as "The Isaacsonio-Mortoniad" because, even though in it he sought to belittle the modernist aesthetic further, it did so in a veiled manner. Still, it had that potential. In the context of their fledgling friendship, Moe might construe it as contentious, even confrontational. And Lovecraft, who at that time certainly had a greater emotional investment in Moe than he had in Morton, was not willing to take that risk. From the onset, Lovecraft must have had misgivings over the way Moe would take "Unda." And so, though ostensibly addressed to Moe, it was Rheinhart Kleiner to whom Lovecraft initially sent it—not Moe.

II. Paratextual Devices

As "Unda's" recipient, Kleiner was its actual addressee; and Moe, to whom it was addressed but not sent, its pseudo-addressee. Lovecraft prefaced "Unda" with preambles or paratextual devices, some of which remained constant, and some of which changed each time he changed its actual addressee, which happened a total of three times—to Kleiner, to the *Providence Amateur*'s readership, and to Moe.

Taken together, these paratextual devices—their generic types have been identified by Gérard Genette—consist (aside from the double title) of a dedication, advertising matter, authorial disavowal, epigraph, postscript, epilogue, patronymic or pseudonym, and public epitext.

Lovecraft's manipulation of these paratextual devices was not whimsical. It was in order to effect a measure of control over "Unda's" perlocutionary force on Moe. That is, he did not want Moe to take "Unda" as a rebuff, which might have meant the end of their friendship, then fledgling: Joshi and Shultz (169) date their friendship from "no later than the end of 1914." The paratextual devices thus had a blocking and obfuscatory function: they were intended to keep Moe from figuring out that "Unda" was a peremptory dismissal of modernist poetry and—if this was not to be had—to attenuate any impression it was intended as a personal attack.

The dedication Lovecraft used when he sent "Unda" to Kleiner, "Respectfully Dedicated without Permission to MAURICE WINTER MOE , Esq." (*SL* 1.14; *Letters to Rheinhart Kleiner* 22), suggests that Lovecraft had qualms about showing the poem to Moe. But it also shows that he was determined to give Moe recognition for having given him the impetus that led to it.

The advertising matter—"A Dull, Dark, Drear, Dactylic Delirium in Sixteen Silly, Senseless, Sickly Stanzas" (*AT* 211)—signals, with its excessive alliteration, that the poem will be executed in an infelicitous manner. It imparts an air of triviality to the poem, tagging it as a sophomoric exercise.

Though Lovecraft did not use a pseudonym with Kleiner, he did use—just this once—an authorial disavowal. It is ironic: "$5000.00 Reward for the Apprehension, Alive or Dead, of the Person or Persons who can prove that This is the Work of HOWARD PHILLIPS LOVECRAFT" (*SL* 1.14). Betraying mock-anxiety over the poem's alleged low quality, this pronouncement serves to further his disqualification campaign for the poem, begun in the advertising matter. Unintentionally, however, it also reveals genuine anxiety, expressed here indirectly to Kleiner, at having Moe link him to "Unda."

The Latin epigraph, "Ego, canis, lunam cano" ("I, a dog, sing at the moon"), suggests that the poem will be a mockery of a Romantic cliché—a mortal fascinated by the unattainable. In the context of his relationship with Moe, however, this may be taken as Lovecraft announcing that he is willing to go along with pretending to be the "dog" Moe wants him to be—that is, a poet for whom sublimity is unattainable. Lovecraft is taking a one-down stance before Moe by admitting he is not competent outside of heroic couplets. He is also implying for Moe to be careful what he asks of him, as he may like the result even less than what he was complaining about. But there is ambiguity here as well: for he could very well be saying that to venture into the territory of modernist poetry is by definition to be doomed to be such a "dog." Lovecraft attributed the epigraph to Maevius Bavianus, a fictive author he invented by combining the names of two personages of the Augustan era—Bavius and Maevius (*AT* 493 [Joshi's note]). Nothing is known of this duo other than that they ridiculed Virgil and Horace as hack poets, each of whom returned them the favor—the former as evidenced by *Eclogue* 3 (Lemprière 128), the latter in writings that do not survive. In the *Dunciad Variorum* (1729), in which Lewis Theobald appeared as anti-hero, as well as in *The Dunciad* (1742–43), in which he was replaced by Colley Cibber, Alexander Pope singled out Bavius as the envoy of the goddess Dulness, chosen to corrupt the literary language of England. This fictive author functions to mark the poem—like the advertising matter and the disavowal before—once more as aesthetic junk, though this time through another ruse. By having Bavius and Maevius conflated as one identity, he renders the worthlessness of their implicit endorsement of his poem doubly potent.

In the postscript—written as a quatrain—Lovecraft takes ownership for "Unda" by saying tongue-in-cheek that Moe should now be satisfied, as Lovecraft has granted him his wish. However, though Lovecraft tries to sound conciliatory, he does not entirely succeed. The tone seems one of resigned annoyance: Lovecraft seems to be hinting that he has violated his own standards of poetry in order to please Moe. And now that he has done so, "Let me again as a poet be rated" (*AT* 214, l. 3), he proclaims. Here the humor—especially because it is self-deprecating—seems a polite mask for censure.

On this occasion the paratextual devices, of course, could not have their intended effect. Lovecraft was being cautious, and using Kleiner to gauge from his reaction if it would be appropriate to send Moe the poem.

When the poem was published in the *Providence Amateur* in February 1916, it was as by Lewis Theobald, Jr. Lovecraft also suppressed all the paratextual devices he had included when he sent it to Kleiner. Whether Moe knew at the time that this pseudonym belonged to Lovecraft is uncertain. Lovecraft may have intended the pseudonym as a distancing mechanism, communicating reluctance over taking ownership of the poem, or in order to mark the poem as a playful utterance (especially as his pseudonym was taken from the King of Dunces in Alexander Pope's *Dunciad*). And he offered a review of it in the *United Amateur* 15, No. 9 (April 1916): "In 'The Bride of the Sea', Mr. Lewis Theobald presents a rather weird piece of romantic sentimentality of the sort afforded by bards of the early nineteenth century. The metre is regular, and no flagrant violations of grammatical or rhetorical precepts are to be discerned, yet the whole effort lacks alertness, dignity, inspiration, and poetic spontaneity" (*CE* 1.106). (Genette [351–53] calls this type of auto-review a public epitext and considers it a paratextual device.) This praise of its metrical perfection was an in-joke, however, for by pointing this out Lovecraft was also ironically identifying himself as its author—in view of the fact that he had written a July 1915 essay called "Metrical Regularity" (*CE* 2.11–13). By condemning its content, however, he was laying the groundwork for a future occasion when Moe might see the poem.

In 1917, Lovecraft sent Moe the poem as part of a poem-cycle dubbed "Perverted Poesie; or, Modern Metre" (a jocular allusion of his initial disclaimer to Moe that he was hesitant to undertake poetry outside heroic couplets lest he make a poor showing), as by Humphrey Littlewit, Esq., of Grubstreet Manor. This new pseudonym was appropriate because it too suggested—though less obviously—that the poem-cycle was bathetic. Lovecraft seems to have derived the pseudonym from a dramatic comedy, *Bartholomew Fair* by Ben Jonson (1572–1637). It combines the name of its protagonist, a middle-class proctor and amateur playwright called John Little-Wit, and that of his servant, Humphrey Waspe. Lovecraft may have found much that resonated with him in *Bartholomew Fair*. The play centers on a visit to Bartholomew Fair by two groups, one headed by Little-Wit, the other by Adam Overdo, an upper-class judge. But in the carnivalesque atmosphere of Bartholomew Fair, the rules of society at large are in abeyance. As a result, the two groups suffer a series of mishaps that force them to act out roles they would normally regard as either beneath them or above them. Bartholomew Fair is the locus of bathos: in that space the elite and the disadvantaged intermingle in ways Jonson presents as daft and preposterous. It is a microcosm of society at large in Jacobean England, in which the transition to a capitalist economy was creating a similar social chaos (Zumack 3; Cantor 11; Sutherland), much in the same manner Lovecraft complained was happening in his own era, due to industrialization.

But the play also has other elements that must have appealed to Lovecraft. Little-Wit's mother-in-law, for example, is a widow called Dame Purcraft—a near-cognate of Lovecraft's own surname—as well as that of his mother, who is similarly a widow. Waspe, tasked with extricating Little-Wit from problems Little-Wit creates through his own stupidity, strongly disapproves of drinking, just as Lovecraft did. (Hence, for example, in Act 4, Scene 4 [Jonson 417], he says, with regard to ale, "Nay, it is no sweet Vapour neither. Sir, it stinks, and I'll stand to't.") In Act 5, Scene 5, a character says, "Down with Dagon," and another, a hypocritical Puritan preacher, says that he will "remove Dagon"—the god of the Philistines—from the play that is being enacted by puppets at Bartholomew Fair. This play, authored by Little-Wit (who styles himself, like Lovecraft, an amateur when it comes to writing), is about puppets who are cross-dressed, just as Lovecraft was as a child—and who, when accused of encouraging licentiousness, bare themselves to reveal they have no sex—which is similar to the claim, by Lovecraft, that he was fundamentally asexual. (As a further point of interest, the play retells a story of heroic friendship, viz. that of Damon and Pythias, but mixing it up with that of Hero and Leander: Lovecraft may have recalled this when using this pseudonym with Moe, as it was a perfect analogy of the lengths to which he was going to ensure his friendship with Moe remained intact.) In conclusion, Lovecraft's use of this pseudonym may have been expressing subconsciously his anxiety about "Unda," for he, like Little-Wit, had created a potential predicament through his own "stupidity" that now required him to be rescued from it, only in his case his recourse was to a pseudonym instead of a servant.

By bundling "Unda" with other poems ("The Introduction," "Pacifist War Song—1917," "A Summer Sunset and Evening," and "The
Peace Advocate"), Lovecraft de-emphasized its importance. These
poems were intended to give Moe a sample of his poetic skills as a
modernist poet. But they also served to normalize "Unda," creating a
less serious set of expectations around it. By now Lovecraft's friendship with Moe had also grown, and he seems to have felt secure
enough to tease him. Thus, in "The Introduction" he makes the
pseudo-complaint that in following Moe's "Advices" anent venturing
outside of heroic couplets, his pieces have become steeped in bathos—"Whene'er I write I seek the Trite, / And sing but idle Chat-
ter" (AT 230, ll. 23–24)—and takes a jibe at modernist poetry: "But
since you say the Papers / Wish most for common Musing, / Tho'
Classics quake my Lyre I take, / Each modern Measure using!"
(ll. 25–28). In "Pacifist War Song—1917" and "The Peace Advocate,"
he holds forth, rather conventionally, that pacifism is unpatriotic.
And in "A Summer Sunset and Evening," a pastoral, he gives Moe an
inkling of the Arcadian vision he considered sublime. Moe was a
theist, and Lovecraft tried to enlist his sympathy by making the ending line, "For Deity's in all, and all in Deity!" (AT 290, l. 26).

When it came to "Unda," Lovecraft restored the advertising matter, the epigraph, and the postscript, but not the authorial disavowal
(which was unnecessary). He also modified the dedication, making it
"with permission." Through a minimalist rearrangement of these
paratextual devices, Lovecraft shifted the frame around "Unda" from
condescension—as seen in the Kleiner version—to deference. Joshi
guesses that Lovecraft also added an epilogue to "Unda" at this time
(AT 494). The epilogue served to bolster this deference: it offered an
alternative allegory to "Unda," one Lovecraft must have hoped would
cover up the original one. The epilogue cast "Unda" as a cautionary
fable about "our youth, inflam'd by tempters fair" (AT 213, l. 67). And
it offered a moral: if a man cannot relate to a woman in a way that
does not deprive him of his virility or sanity, he would be well ad-
vised to "to take a rest" from the pursuit of romantic liaisons—a rest
to be had, it is implied, among "brothers." The epilogue, moreover,
had an added virtue: it could also be construed as an apologetic
statement, useful in case Moe was not deceived by these ruses. For if
the "tempters" were seen as proxies for the muse of the anti-sublime,

then the epilogue was actually telling Moe something different: namely, that their friendship was more important to him than being right or wrong about issues such as modernist poetry.

III. *Structure and Synopsis*

"Unda" consists of sixteen stanzas, each a quatrain with an *ABAB* rhyme scheme. The metrical pattern, adhered to throughout, is rare: every *A* consists of two dactyls followed by a trochee; every *B* of two dactyls followed by a choriamb. Additionally, every *A* ends always in as feminine rhyme (or pendant), and every *B* in a masculine rhyme (or blunt). All this is a subtle prosodic reinforcement of the theme of a lovers' dialogue gone awry: not only does Lovecraft correlate each sex with a rhyme, but he assigns to it a distinctive rhythm. Given that dactyls are the common denominator of *A* and *B*, they may be said to be the metrical foot that is most characteristic of "Unda," just as they are in classical hexameter.

"Unda" can be summarized in terms of plot. In the following synopsis, each bracketed number refers to the corresponding stanza:

[1] An unnamed narrator recalls feelings of rapture he associates with a seaside cliff as opposed to feelings of anguish he associates with the strand beneath it.

[2] He used to walk the strand with Unda.

[3] He was young and infatuated, and so was she.

[4] Taking each other at face value, they never asked questions of each other.

[5] One night they stood on the seaside cliff while the moon was out.

[6] The waves changed her demeanor.

[7] She rebuffed him without explanation and descended to the strand, and he, shocked and distraught, did not follow her.

[8] The sea grew less tumultuous as she greeted its waves, then she beckoned to him and vanished.

[9] He searched for her in the strand until morning, but to no avail.

[10] He searched for her all over the world and, during a storm at sea, caught a glimpse of her face in a wave.

[11] Discouraged, exhausted, and at a loss as to her whereabouts, he returned to the strand.

[12] He saw the moon rising up over the horizon across the sea.

[13] He saw a bridge of light on the waves, stretching from the strand the moon.

[14] He fancied she was out in the distance on the bridge of light and began to walk on it.

[15] He advanced until he was out in the open sea.

[16] He sank and as he drowned she appeared to him in a vision, and now he no longer seeks her because, having become a part of the sea, he is now with her.

What makes the poem parody as opposed to pastiche is the paratextual devices on the one hand and its elliptic and intentionally recherché symbolism on the other. Joshi observes that "Unda" is a spoof of the sort of poetry produced by "Thomas Moore and other late Romantics" (*AT* 493). Although true, Lovecraft, seems to owe more to Thomas Moore (1779–1852) than generic inspiration. There are striking parallels—thematic as well as imagistic—between "Unda" and Moore's six-stanza "By That Lake, Whose Gloomy Shore" to suggest he may have creatively drawn from it.

Moore's poem relates an incident from the life of an Irish saint, Kevin of Glendalough (d. 618) (Attwater and John 219). To avoid further harassment from a female stalker infatuated with him, Kevin withdraws to the top of a lakeside cliff and takes a nap. Undeterred, the woman discovers his hiding place. When he wakes up he becomes so irate at finding her there he pushes her off the cliff. He then feels regret and prays—rather arrogantly for a Christian role model—not for forgiveness for murder, which ecclesiastical doctrine declares is a capital sin, but for her soul's salvation. Her ghost—it is smiling sadly—is then seen strolling on the lake to celestial music. The notion of a saint who is a killer is, of course, farcical. And yet Moore's tone remains incongruously respectful, and his treatment of the moral seriousness of the incident doggedly lighthearted. These considerations make the poem an exemplar of bathos, and is perhaps the reason Lovecraft used it as his model. (The fact that the saint in question is Irish may have also compounded the bathos for Lovecraft, given his prejudiced attitude against the Irish.)

Following is a list of the similarities between Moore's poem and Lovecraft's:

(1) Unda as well as the woman infatuated with Kevin follow the same trajectory: from the top of a cliff to the bottom of a body of water. (The means by which they accomplish this are, however, the opposite of each other: Moore's character is pushed toward its destination, Lovecraft's is pulled.)

(2) Moore's Kevin goes to sleep at the top of a cliff, and Lovecraft's Unda goes into a trance—popularly regarded as a form of sleep—at the top of a cliff. (Once more, there is a reversal: Kevin is male, Unda female.)

(3) In Lovecraft's poem a narrator (apparently a man) goes out walking on a body of water; in Moore's, it is a female ghost. In each instance, this takes place toward the end of the poem. (The reversals here are twofold: Lovecraft's character is male and embodied, Hood's female and discarnate.)

(4) In Moore's poem a woman is killed by a saint, a supernatural man, while in Lovecraft's a water elemental—that is, a supernatural woman—drives a man to kill himself. (Again, reversals are at work: In Moore's poem, the one in league with the supernatural is male, in Lovecraft's female; in Moore's poem the saint becomes homicidal; whereas in Lovecraft's obsession with a water elemental induces a man to become suicidal.)

IV. Lovecraft's Familiarity with Bathos

Lovecraft probably felt that when Moe was disparaging heroic couplets, he was by extension discounting their foremost exponent, Alexander Pope. As a result, he decided, when complying with Moe's request, to give Moe a taste of the type of poetry Pope had disapproved of. It was a joke, his way of pretending to have Pope indirectly reply to Moe. To accomplish this, he constructed his poem in accordance with the guidelines Pope had facetiously set down for creating such poetry.

Peri Bathous; or, Of the Art of Sinking in Poetry was a satirical inversion of the precepts expounded by Longinus' first century C.E. treatise, *Peri Hypsous* (*On the Sublime*). Although it is recognized as a collaborative effort of the Scribblers Club (comprised of John Arbuthnot, Jonathan Swift, John Gay, Thomas Parnell, Robert Harley, and, to a lesser degree, John Morphew and Francis Atterbury), Pope is recognized as its chief author. A hodgepodge of rhetorical principles and

techniques aimed at insuring tawdriness in poetry, *Peri Bathous*, rife
with logical lacunae and explanatory lapses and elliptically and ob-
scurely argued, is, by design, itself an example of the sort of vulgarized
art it is peddling. Playing on the fact that the term "bathos" in Greek
means "depth," as well as "sinking," Pope avers, "I grant, that to excel in
the Bathos a Genius is requisite; yet the Rules of Art must be allow'd
so far useful, as to add Weight, or as I may say, hang on Lead, to facili-
tate and enforce Descent, to guide us to the most advantageous De-
clivities, and habituate our Imagination to a Depth of thinking" (394).
Peri Bathous proposes the natural and the rhetorical anti-sublime as
the new ideal for poets. Pope's political sympathies were Tory, and
Peri Bathous was a snipe at the Whig interpretation of sublimity in
poetry. The difference between these factions was significant.
Whereas Whig poets strove to break new ground both in terms of
subject matter and disregard for rules, Tory poets admired the pol-
ished upholding of these conventions (Williams 199).

Lovecraft may have cast himself as being in an analogous situation
with regard to free verse: one month after finishing "Unda," he wrote a
poem in heroic couplets called "The State of Poetry," a sardonic critique about modernist poetry. Bewailing the aesthetic of bathos most
contemporary poets had subscribed to, it shows Lovecraft taking a
stance against the art perversely touted in *Peri Bathous*. His epigraph, a
quote from Ovid's *Metamorphoses* ("The discordant seeds of things not
well joined" [*AT* 215]), tallies with the sardonic instructions given in
Peri Bathous: "He [the poet] is to mingle Bits of the most various, or
discordant kinds, Landscape, History, Portraits, Animals, and connect
them with a great deal of *Flourishing*, by *Heads or Tails*, as it shall
please his Imagination, and contribute to his principal End, which is to
glare by strong Oppositions of Colours, and surprize by Contrariety of
Images" (395). Lovecraft goes on to condemn "lofty coarseness" (*AT*
216, l. 40) and lackluster subject matter such as "mills, and mines, and
shops" (l. 58). And he laments: "When verse ideal brings the vulgar
smile / And honest words are slighted for the vile" (ll. 65–66).

Lovecraft's "The Brief Autobiography of an Inconsequential
Scribbler" links him to *Peri Bathous*. The phrase "Inconsequential
Scribbler" evokes Martinus Scriblerius, *Peri Bathous'* fictitious au-
thor and champion of the inconsequential in literary art.

Lovecraft aligns himself in this essay with the reformative intent of Pope, who, despite seeming advice to the contrary, was really advocating the aesthetics of the natural and the rhetorical sublime. Thus: "I have endeavoured to . . . aid in a revival of that conservatism and classicism which modern literature seems dangerously prone to reject" (CE 5.144). He adds that his periodical, the *Conservative*, is a venue for this project—a sign of how important this revival is to him. And he concludes in a tone of mock-humility, declaring that the story of his life has been one of "Boeotian mediocrity." In antiquity the Boeotians, citizens of a city-state close to Athens, were renowned as being boorish and smugly indifferent to the arts (Mish 360). But Lovecraft is being ironic. What he means is that the revival to which he has dedicated his life may seem retrograde in light of the modernist Zeitgeist, but is actually indicative of his sophistication. He is playing the same game Pope is playing in *Peri Bathous:* calling things the opposite of what they are, as if he were living in mundus inversus.

"The Poe-et's Nightmare" (*AT* 18–25), a 1916 poem about Lucullus, a grocer's clerk, who suffers from gluttony and aspires to become a poet of the sublime, is a wacky indictment of the aesthetic of bathos. Lovecraft here follows the *Peri Bathous* injunction that the poet must "debase the high and raise what is base and low" (Pope 426). Thus the poem ends with the grocer's clerk disqualifying the sublimity of his cosmologic dream by attributing it to indigestion (*AT* 25, l. 267), and by giving up being a poet in favor of being a grocer's clerk, which, he realizes, is more spiritually fulfilling (ll. 286–87). But if Lovecraft carries out this injunction, it is to make fun of modernist poets who strive for sublimity while their fundamental orientation is to consumerist values. It is thus not whim on Lovecraft's part that Lucullus' vice is gluttony, nor that he is a grocer's clerk. And it his consumerist values that prevent him from becoming a poet. He may experience the natural sublime by way of a dream, but he only has the language and the preconceptions of the marketplace in which to express it: he is lacking in the rhetorical sublime and will continue to be lacking in it until his fundamental orientation shifts.

The dream is written in blank verse, once considered ideal for expressing sublimity. It is framed by two sections, each consisting of heroic couplets (a favorite with satirists in the eighteenth and nineteenth centuries) and devoted to the pathetic tribulations of Lucullus' waking life. Lovecraft has intentionally created a "sandwich" structure as a metaphor of the consumerist values he is criticizing. The dream, he is saying, exists for Lucullus not for its own sake, but to be exploited, to be devoured. Lovecraft uses foreshadowing early in the poem to indicate Lucullus' fate. When he talks of "those who dine not wisely, but too well" (*AT* 26, l. 58) he is alluding to Act 5, Scene 2, ll. 343–46 of Shakespeare's *Othello: The Moor of Venice* (c. 1603): "Then must you speak / Of one that lov'd not wisely but too well; / Of one not easily jealous, but being wrought, / Perplex'd in the extreme." This is uttered by Othello, a general of Arabian-Semitic ethnicity born in Africa, after he has smothered his wife, a Caucasian aristocrat, on a suspicion of infidelity—a situation created by the machinations of Iago. And Lovecraft is drawing a bigoted comparison between this interracial marriage and Lucullus' goal of mastering the rhetorical sublime: he is hinting that Lucullus, like Othello, will not succeed.

V. Peri Bathous' Rules of Art in "Unda"

Lovecraft's allusion to bathos begins with the first word of the title, "Unda," a Late Latin word meaning "wave." In his 1652 treatise *De Nymphis* ("On Elemental Spirits"), Paracelsus gave this word new currency, albeit modified as "undine," which he applied to signify a water elemental, irrespective of gender. It was also in this treatise that Paracelsus started the literary convention of having a male mortal victimize a female water elemental (an undine can gain a soul by a bearing a child to a mortal, but also stands to lose that soul if her lover is unfaithful, which he invariably is), which would be followed in several nineteenth-century Romantic works. The most relevant of these, in terms of their influence on "Unda," are Baron Friedrich H. C. de la Motte-Fouqué's novella *Undine* (1811) and Oscar Wilde's fairy tale "The Fisherman and His Soul" (1892). Lovecraft owned a copy of *Undine* (*LL* 513), calling it, in his 1927 monograph "Supernatural Horror in Literature," the "most artistic of all the Continental weird tales" (*CE* 2.97).

Lovecraft satirized this literary convention in "Unda" by inverting it. In so doing he may taken a cue from Wilde, who in "The Fisherman and his Soul" has the eponymous fisherman lose his soul when he decides to cohabit with a mermaid. And yet, because the soul is negatively connoted by Wilde, who makes it a representative of bourgeois values, he gives one to understand that the fisherman is better off without his soul. Thus in "Unda," the male mortal also chooses to lose his soul. In contrast to Wilde tale, however, the soul—that is, the ability to experience and express the sublime—is in this instance positively connoted.

The fundamental assumption of the rules of art in *Peri Bathous* is to avoid common sense, which undermines wit and elegance: the poet must therefore cultivate a taste founded in the grotesque: "He is to consider himself as a *Grotesque* Painter, whose works would be spoil'd by an Imitation of Nature, or Uniformity of Design," and in "a most *happy, uncommon, unaccountable Way of Thinking*" (Pope 395). That is, in order to surprise the reader one must present "Circumstances" that are "far-fetch'd, or unexpected, or hardly compatible" (404).

The most obvious point that violates common sense in "Unda" is that the narrator has drowned, yet he is speaking. This type of flagrant contradiction—known in logic as the liar's paradox—is at the basis of the poem and serves to create the confusion and uncertainty Pope purports to be advocating. Is it true he has drowned, or is he lying? Is he perhaps speaking metaphorically, in which case the issue of veracity is irrelevant? Or is he subscribing to a false belief, maintaining he is no longer alive when he in fact is? Why has he—like Poe's narrator in "Annabel Lee"—returned (whether in the flesh, as a ghost, or through memory is not clear) to the physical setting in which he had his affair? Could it be that, his claim of happiness at the end of the poem notwithstanding, he actually regrets having gone to his doom and is therefore mourning his own death—whether literal or figurative—and the hopelessness of changing it? Or could it be that, being psychologically "dead," he is reminiscing in the hope that he can awaken his desire for her once more, and thus get to "live" again? In speaking out, is he addressing someone among the living, someone in the afterlife, or himself? These questions are ultimately unanswerable; and the reader, led to entertain all these scenarios as equally valid, ends up, as Pope recommends, thoroughly perplexed.

In Chapters X and XI of *Peri Bathous* Pope makes a list of tropes and figures that are especially conducive—if misused as he proposes, that is—to the stylistic awkwardness that accompanies bathos. Love-craft seems to have drawn from this list when creating "Unda."

Pope says *metonymy* leads to fustian when an item is not entirely synonymous with the item it is being called on to replace. This happens when causes are referred to as effects, inventions by the names of those who invented them, and so on (Pope 411). Lovecraft does this with the term "wave," for which he deploys a variety of substitutes. Thus he offers "Soft laps the ocean" (*AT* 211, l. 6); "Unda" (which is a proper name; l. 8); "billows" (*AT* 212, l. 17); "surges" and "waves" (ll. 21, 23); "regions" (l. 8); "tumultuous beating" and "ripple" (ll. 29, 30); "wavelets" (*AT* 213, l. 50); and "currents" (l. 57). Love-craft undermines the synonymity of these terms in a subtle manner. "Soft laps the ocean" depicts a wave as the *effect* of an action performed by the sea. So do "regions," "ripple," "wavelets," and "currents." But this is at odds with terms like "billows," "surges," "waves," and "tumultuous beating," which describe the wave as having initiative, that is as being a *cause*. Moreover, "Unda" belongs to both sets of terms and is thus sui generis. She behaves like a cause in that it is she who leaves the narrator, yet she behaves like an effect in that she does so under a compulsion instigated in her by the sea. (Incidentally, this erratic multiplication of synonyms parallels the ad infinitum dividing and re-dividing of the waves that separate the narrator from Unda.) Another family of metonymies involves the term "sea." It is variously referred to as "ocean" (*AT* 211, l. 5); "brine" (l.10); "waters" (*AT* 212, l. 18); "where the wide waters rumble" (l. 43); "vast reaches of sparkle and blue" (*AT* 213, l. 48); and "murmuring waters" (l.61). Here the three everyday nouns "ocean," "brine," and "waters" are cast into complex equivalence with three epithets glorifying the same object: a set of terms that refer to the sea in a way that is commonplace are blocked together with a set of terms that, contradictorily, refer to the sea in lofty diction.

Pope advocates using *synecdoche*—eliciting a whole by mentioning one of its parts—to suggest bathos. Calling attention, for example, to an objectionable part has the effect of degrading an otherwise desirable whole. Conversely, calling attention to a desirable part creates the illusion that an objectionable whole is, by virtue of this exception, meritorious. This latter usage of synecdoche is in evidence in the poem: Lovecraft posits Unda as desirable, yet she belongs to the sea, a medium that the narrator, a terrestrial creature, cannot live in.

"Bright was the morn of my youth when I met her; / Sweet as the breeze that blew o'er the brine" are *hackneyed*, an example of Pope's tongue-in-cheek lauding of "Mediocrity in the *Thought*" (Pope 401).

Expletive, extending the sense unnecessarily for the purpose of rounding out a line, is also used: "Swift was I captur'd in Love's strongest fetter, / Glad to be hers, and she glad to be mine" (*AT* 212, ll. 11–12). "Glad to be hers," however, is unnecessary: it is a given, if he is as infatuated as he claims to be. The only justification for this phrase is as filler. On a separate note, these two lines, which start off oddly, with the word, "Swift," appear to be a punning allusion to the Brobdingnag episode in Swift's *Gulliver's Travels*, in which Gulliver falls in love with the giant Queen and she with him. Swift, as already mentioned, was a member of the Scribblers Club and probably had a hand in creating *Peri Bathous*. And Unda, construed as a projection of the sea on land, certainly qualifies as a giant Queen. Moreover, in *Gulliver's Travels* this love is bathetic: for it coexists with repulsion, both from Gulliver with respect to the Queen because her size exaggerates her physical imperfections, and vice versa, because the inhabitants of Brobdingnag have a more developed sense of ethics than human beings, and she is appalled at the tales he relates of life back in England. Another example of expletive is "All the wide world have I search'd for my darling, / Scour'd the far deserts and sail'd distant seas" (ll. 37–38). Line 38 adds nothing to what has been already said: it is merely a restatement of line 37.

Lovecraft's narrator also becomes *infantine*—"This is when a Poet grows so very simple, as to talk and think like a Child" (Pope 417). He confesses that he and Unda never asked normal questions adults would ask of each other, and that, "Happy as children, we thought not nor ponder'd" (*AT* 212, ll. 13–16). Lovecraft may have been inspired at this point by the same conceit as used by Poe in "Annabel Lee," who has his narrator proclaim, "She was a child and *I* was a child, in this kingdom by the sea, / But we loved that was more than love— / [. . .] / With a love that the wingèd seraphs of heaven / Coveted her and me" (Poe 102, ll. 7–12).

Aposiopesis—rhetorical speechlessness—occurs when the narrator overreacts to Unda's capricious departure by remaining literally dumbstruck (*AT* 212, ll. 25–28). In failing to challenge her verbally when most pressing, his faulty command of language is revealed.

Hyperbole—or undue exaggeration—is woven in to convey the narrator's angst. Thus: "Still ach'd my soul with its infinite pain" (*AT* 212, l. 36); "All the wide world have I searched for my darling" (l 37); "Ever in restlessness" (l. 41); "as my tortur'd eye gazes" (*AT* 213, l. 47); "Her whose sweet beckoning hastens my tread" (l. 56).

An example of both *catachresis*—the wrong use of a word—as well as of the *mixture of figures*—that is, of juxtaposing figures in such a way that a clashing effect is obtained, so that the figures undermine each other (Pope 410)—occurs when the narrator says, "while the tempest was snarling, / Flash'd a fair face that brought quiet and ease" (*AT* 212, ll. 39–40). Here "snarling," which is more properly and typically said of a beast in an aggressive attitude, is applied to a tempest—an example of catachresis. And the effect is outlandish, because it is such an atypical usage it readily lends itself to mockery. Moreover, these two lines incorporate a mixture of figures: the way the tempest is described in the line 39 bleeds over into the way Unda's face is described in line 40. To achieve this, Lovecraft manages to separate "a fair face" from "snarling" by just one word. Blocked together, the effect is bizarre and unsettling: "snarling, / Flash'd a fair face . . ." And it is also absurd if not humorous because he then claims it "brought quiet and ease."

Lovecraft makes creative use of *pleonasm*—redundancy—by way of punctuation marks. He sets up two exclamation points— there are no others in the poem—to mark by way of hysterical emphasis Unda's physical disappearance, "Beckon'd to me, and no longer was there!" (*AT* 212, l. 32), as well as her psychological disappearance—"Lo! The red moon from the ocean's low hazes / Rises in ominous grandeur to view" (*AT* 213, ll. 45–46). Though the physical disappearance is obvious, the psychological disappearance is not. Therefore, an explanation is in order. If the moon "Rises in ominous grandeur," it is because it is divested of Unda. In "Annabel Lee" (elements of which Lovecraft seems to have playfully rewritten as "Unda" to render it bathetic), Poe's narrator exclaims, "For the moon never beams without bringing me dreams / Of the beautiful Annabel Lee" (Poe 103, ll. 34–35) But here, in this realm of bathos, the moon has no such power, and Lovecraft's narrator, who has "read" the moon—that is, has understood its import—is shocked. If not by looking up, where is Unda then to be found? Lovecraft gives a sly clue, for "Lo!" has a homonym in the same line: "low." The interjection, functioning as a deixis, thus points to the adjective that describes Unda's new place of residence: the depths of the sea. Furthermore, Lovecraft also uses a question mark—the only one—to signal her reappearance. "What is yon face in the moonlight appearing; / Have I at last found the maiden that fled?" (*AT* 213, ll. 53–54). The fact that he is driven to ask means that he is now uncertain as to whether he still considers her a symbol of the sublime. Moonlight serves to reaffirm her link to the sea, for it is the moon that induces the ebbing and flowing of the tide. When Unda left the narrator, it was in the moonlight, and it is in the moonlight that she comes back to him. Moonlight thus rightly confuses the narrator: it is not, as in "Annabel Lee," an unambiguous sign—quite the contrary.

The *vulgar*—the reduction of nobly motivated to coarsely motivated action—also makes its way into the poem. The narrator avows he is "half panting, half praying" (*AT* 213, l. 59). "Half panting," a double entendre, signals prurience, and thus contaminates "half praying." (Additionally, Lovecraft may have further intended the phrase "half panting" as an allusion to a style of bathos called "the Alamode" in *Peri Bathous* [Pope 425], whose hallmark is to talk about any topic in terms that denote prurience.)

Lovecraft transforms the phrase "the lost nevermore" (*AT* 211, l. 4) into a complex *pun*. The lost nevermore refers on the one hand to the narrator's own life, which he has lost by drowning and is therefore irretrievable; and it also refers to the happiness he could have had with Unda—for, being dead, he can no longer miss her. In this sense, then, the phrase may be read as "that which is never again to be experienced has been truly lost." But the phrase may also be read alternatively as "that which was once truly lost will now be never again lost." That is, it also admits the possibility that the narrator is speaking from a postmortem condition in which he has achieved a type of happiness he could not have in life.

Additionally, this phrase also works as a punning allusion to Poe's "The Raven." Lovecraft is through this means giving to understand that his narrator's mental state is similar to that of Poe's, who is deluded. Poe's narrator is taking his game of having a pretend dialogue with a raven about the inaccessibility of the loved dead with escalating seriousness, until, suffering a lapsus, he forgets that it is a game. Unda's narrator, on the other hand, is playing the same game: for he is searching for one who, having merged with the vastness of the sea, is just as inaccessible. And, like Poe's narrator, he too undergoes a lapsus—for he ceases speaking about the moonlight on the waves *as if* it were a bridge and begins speaking about it instead *as* a bridge. Thus "the lost nevermore" can also refer to that condition of sanity which both Poe's and Lovecraft's narrators cannot regain (and to which Lovecraft also points to in his subtitle by way of the term "Delirium").

Another punning allusion is "Down, ever downward, half gliding, half creeping" (*AT* 212, l. 27), said of Unda, who is in a trance, and leaving the narrator. Lovecraft is here recycling in altered fashion an epigraph from Horace's *Ars Poetica* that he used in his January 17, 1915, amateur journalism column, "Concerning "Persia—in Europe." This column was part of his clash with Morton, as in it as he castigated Morton for an inconsequential error made when arguing against him in *In a Minor Key*. Joshi translates the epigraph as: "I am outraged when good Homer nods; but it is allowable for sleep to creep upon [the poet] in a long work." In Lovecraft's utilization of this epigraph, Unda's trance is a humorous dramatization of the lapse in poetic judgment Horace is referring to; the fact that this lapse, contrary to Horace's stipulation, is here taking place in a short as opposed to a long work makes it doubly reprehensible. Lovecraft redefines this lapse as bathetic by making the direction Unda is heading toward downward. And he adds another feature of the bathetic to the description of her descent: he says it proceeds through a blend of "gliding" and "creeping"—code for that indiscriminate mix of sublime and anti-sublime that characterizes the bathetic.

Pope also speaks of a "Florid Stile [i.e. style]" to achieve the effect of bathos. He means this literally: a florid style, for him, is one which makes frequent mention of flowers, especially those which are gaudy and thrive in the lowest of places, such as "Ponds and Ditches" (Pope 423). Lovecraft shifts into the Florid Stile when his narrator rhapsodizes, "Bound was her hair by a garland of willows, /

Pluck'd by the fount in the bird-haunted wood" (*AT* 212, ll. 19–20).
As a symbol of the Florid Stile, the willow is doubly appropriate: its
branches are droopy rather than upright, and its flowers sprout in
catkins, which also tend downward. Recalling Pope, Lovecraft adds
that the "willows" came from the area adjacent to a fount, which
may be said to fall in the category of "Ponds and Ditches," only he
outdoes Pope, because a fount is also an artifact, that is, anti-natural.
The garland on Unda's head may be taken as *a serpent biting its own
tail*, that is, as Ouroboros, a symbol of the sea. And it is also an allusion (especially considering that the garland came from a "*bird*-
haunted wood") to a Latin phrase in *Peri Bathous* by which Pope
sums up his mock-thesis that a poet should strive for incongruity in
his imagery: *"Serpentes avibus geminentur, tigribus agni."* Or: "Ser-
pents couple with birds, lambs with tigers" (Pope 395n7).

VI. "Unda" and Hermann's Bridge

In "Unda," Lovecraft created an allegory that correlated bathos, es-
poused by modernist poetry, with the downfall of classical hexameter (or, to give its technical name, dactylic hexameter catalectic)—
the verse form of choice in Graeco-Roman culture for producing
epic poetry, regarded then as the epitome of sublimity. The allegory
hinges on a concept known as Hermann's Bridge, a distinctive feature of classical hexameter.

Hermann's Bridge was discovered in 1805 (West 223) by Johann
Gottfried Jakob Hermann (1772–1848), a German philologist who
studied grammar and meter in classical poetry. According to Ross
(155), "Hermann's Bridge—the avoidance of caesura after the fourth
trochee . . . has an important history in both Greek and Latin hexameter verse. Homer violated this bridge once in every 1000 lines,
but Callimachus invariably respects it. The Latin poets, however,
with some notable exceptions, are indifferent to it, though a strong
stop or sense break was avoided at this point in the line. . . . Virgil
. . . has it once every 28 lines in the *Eclogues*, every 32 lines in the
Georgics, and every 31 lines in the *Aeneid*." Moreover, maintaining
the integrity of Hermann's Bridge can be used as a criterion of sublimity: "Hermann's Bridge can be used to distinguish between canonical epic verse and certain forms of epigraphic hexameter
'doggerel.' It can thus function as a device for making cultural can-

ons and distinguishing their core from their periphery" (Kahane 75).

(Another well-known bridge in classical hexameter, Meyer's Third Law, is not as significant because less consistently adhered to. Actually, it is so hit-or-miss that it should be considered more of a heuristic. As an example of this, West [225] points out that in the *Iliad*'s opening line Homer breaks not just this Third Law, but Meyer's First and Second as well. This lax rule, and the relative obscurity of its formulator, Wilhelm Meyer of Speyer [1845–1917], when compared with Hermann, makes it unlikely that Lovecraft was referring to this bridge in "Unda.")

Moreover, in classical hexameter, an end-stopped line is a faux pas; lines are typically enjambed, which lends the verse form an unrestricted flow that makes it easier to declaim.

Lovecraft deployed three strategies to allude to the corruption of classical hexameter. The first was to depict, by way of imagery, the failure to maintain Hermann's Bridge. The second was to make the end-stopped line a mainstay of the poem: thus out of a total of 64 lines, 55 are end-stopped. This was done to insinuate that the narrator is trapped in a realm in which bathos prevails; and also to emphasize the hopelessness he faces when attempting to regain a sense of sublimity (which in his case turned into self-deception when he projected it on to Unda). The third was to use enjambment at critical points to remotivate the narrator: enjambment is an antidote to hopelessness, used to get him to move on to the next line with the least of obstacles: the enjambment is thus tantamount to giving the narrator a taste of sublimity so as to lure him on and keep him moving toward disaster.

The first and third of these strategies will now be reviewed in turn.

When the narrator sets out to cross the sea on a "bridge"—an illusion created by moonlight on waves—he hopes it will take him to Unda. This "bridge" mirrors the concept of Hermann's Bridge: it transposes it into the poem in visual terms. Unable to follow the bridge to its conclusion, the narrator sinks and drowns. At that moment he has literally lost his breath; that is, he has, metaphorically speaking, introduced a full stop (more objectionable than a caesura, which, after all, is transient) into the poem at a point where none ought to exist. In this manner Lovecraft recapitulates the thesis that it was the non-observance of formulaic conventions such as Hermann's

Bridge that corrupted all classical hexameter, precipitating its obsolescence. And he was also, through this allegory, telling Moe that free verse, the antipode of classical hexameter, was by definition bathetic. The irony is that the narrator, who is courting Unda, the muse of bathos, in the mistaken belief it will lead him to sublimity, is intended to represent a free verse poet. In making the bridge in "Unda" a correlate of Hermann's Bridge, Lovecraft has created a pun: for it is *her man's* bridge, that is, the poetic rules he decides to abide under the sway of whim as opposed to tradition, that leads to his downfall.

(As a final note, the imagery of walking on water may be a parody of Matthew 14:22–33, in which Jesus of Nazareth purportedly did the same in order to rescue his disciples, who were on a ship during a storm. When Jesus got close to the ship, Peter asked him if he could go out to meet him by walking on water too, and Jesus assented. Peter had not gotten very far, however, when he began to sink. Jesus clasped him by the hand and pulled him up, and told him he was lacking in faith. Lovecraft's narrator can be seen as Peter, but Unda, who is in the role of an anti-Jesus, does not [as befits the muse of bathos] have the power to save him from the depths, only that of joining him there.)

In "Unda" Lovecraft uses enjambment to signal an occurrence of peripeteia, a turning point in the plot. When the narrator says, "Dim are the pathways and rocks that remind me / Sadly of years in the lost nevermore" (*AT* 211, ll. 3–4), the story goes from being a simple description of a littoral topography, that is, of his external circumstances, to a re-enactment of his relationship to Unda.

"Calm grew the sea, and tumultuous beating / Turn'd to a ripple as Unda the fair / Trod the wet sands in affectionate greeting" (*AT* 212, ll. 29–31). These lines present Unda interacting with the sea in a supernatural manner; they offer the narrator, although misguidedly, the impression that Unda partakes of sublimity. This is necessary so that when in the next line (l. 32) she gestures for him to seek her out and then vanishes, he will be sufficiently moved to do so.

In stanza 6, the narrator registers an awareness that Unda might be bathetic. When she gazes out at the sea, he notices that she does so "strangely" and that she acquires a "wild aspect," as if excited by the prospect of visiting the depths of the sea. Yet he has been trying to deny it ever since. This awareness, however, sets the stage for the psychological insight that takes place in the next two enjambments and which impels him to commitment himself to bathos. Thus when the narrator says "Lo! The red moon from the ocean's low hazes / Rises in ominous grandeur" (*AT* 213, ll. 45–46), he is indirectly admitting that Unda might not be the muse of sublimity he has made her out to be. He does this by creating a metaphor: by appearing to rise out of the sea, the moon seems to become tainted with the quiddity of the sea. But then he can deny it no longer, and makes a decision: he will pursue Unda, even if she is the muse of bathos; and he transfers his attention to her domain: "Strange is its face as my tortur'd eye gazes / O'er the vast reaches of sparkle and blue" (ll. 47–48).

"Straight from the moon to the shore where I'm sighing / Grows a bright bridge" (*AT* 213, ll. 49–50): through this enjambment, Lovecraft extends an illusion to his narrator—namely, that he can tread on the waves without sinking, that is, that he can pursue sublimity in her domain. This illusion gains strength in the next enjambment: "Out on the beam-bridge my footsteps are nearing / Her whose sweet beckoning hastens my tread" (*AT* 213, ll. 55–56).

The illusion, however, does not last. Stanza 15, in which all the lines are end-stopped, is a litany of the troubles he runs into. Then, in stanza 16, the narrator sinks. Reconciled to his own mediocrity ("done are my trials," *AT* 213, l. 63), he deceives himself into believing that he has found sublimity in bathos: "my heart is reposing / Safe with my Unda, the Bride of the Sea" (ll. 63–4).

VII. Bathos in Lovecraft's Works

For Lovecraft, the most commendable effect a literary artist could attain was to suggest the natural sublime in a language in keeping with the rhetorical sublime—like James Thomson in *The Seasons*, a poem whose influence Lovecraft counted as formative (*SL* 3.317–18). But in the society in which he belonged, dominated by the ethos of laissez-faire capitalism—which decreed that no human experience or part of the natural world was immune to debasement through commodification—this was no longer possible. In Lovecraft's estimation, bathos, the opposite of the rhetorical and the natural sublime, had now become the accepted standard—by the mainstream—of poetic practice.

The central problem posed by Pope in *Peri Bathous* was the disconnect between the natural sublime and the rhetorical sublime. His proposed mock-solution was to transfer the respectability commanded traditionally by both to their antithesis, bathos.

Lovecraft brought Pope's satire into the twentieth century by pretending to take this at face value. Typically, his characters are engaged in a struggle to deny bathos in their own lives. (Lovecraft, however, connoted this bathos not as a matter of jest, as Pope, but of horror.) His tales can be grouped into four broad types, each reflecting a unique outcome of this struggle. Thus his narrators—or some character in whom they are emotionally invested—can either: (1) suffer transformations or revelations that render them personifications of the ludicrous, grotesque, ineffectual, or vulgar (e.g., "The White Ship"; "The Doom That Came to Sarnath"; "The Statement of Randolph Carter"; "The Terrible Old Man"; "The Tree"; "The Cats of Ulthar"; "The Temple"; "Facts concerning the Late Arthur Jermyn and His Family"; "The Street"; "The Picture in the House"; "The Nameless City"; "The Quest of Iranon"; "The Moon-Bog"; "The Outsider"; "Herbert West—Reanimator"; "Hypnos"; "The Hound"; "The Lurking Fear"; "The Horror at Red Hook"; "He"; "In the Vault"; "Cool Air"; "Pickman's Model"; "The Colour out of Space"; "The Dunwich Horror"; "The Whisperer in Darkness"; "The Shadow over Innsmouth"; "The Dreams in the Witch House"; "The Thing on the Doorstep"; "The Evil Clergyman"; "The Shadow out of Time"); (2) try to defend themselves against being ridiculed or otherwise disqualified for their tasteless, lurid, or implausible confessions (e.g., "The Tomb"; "Polaris"; "The Temple"; "From Beyond"; "The Music of Erich Zann"; "The Unnamable"; "The Festival"; "Under the Pyramids"; "The Call of Cthulhu"; *At the Mountains of Madness;* "Through the Gates of the Silver Key"); (3) be reduced to fragmentary and incoherent speech by the presence of bathos (e.g., "Dagon"; "The Transition of Juan Romero"; "Nyarlathotep"; "The Other Gods"; "The Rats in the Walls"; "The Haunter of the Dark"); or (4) manage to dissociate from (or suppress) bathos—or, its corollary, to effect a journey to the realm of the natural sublime in the language of the rhetorical sublime (e.g., "Celephaïs"; "The Shunned House"; "The Silver Key"; "The Strange High House in the Mist"; *The Dream-Quest of Unknown Kadath; The Case of Charles Dexter Ward*).

Additionally, Lovecraft's cosmicism (Joshi 260–65) may be con-strued as an expanded definition of the natural sublime based on a reframing of Pope's false directives so that, when followed, it would yield not bathos, but the natural sublime. Hence when Pope called for an art that, like that of "Harlequins and Magicians," presents the illusion of a break away from "natural Things" (395), his real pur-pose was to encourage bathetic poets to turn away from the gran-deur of nature—that is, not to take on a subject they lacked the skills to write about. But Lovecraft, while pretending to go along with Pope's charade, must have wondered what kind of break from "natural Things" could lead to the natural sublime (as Pope was claiming to arguing it would). His conclusion: that it was not a break from natural things themselves that could yield this outcome, but rather a break from *the class of natural things*—that is, from the order of the phenomenal realm—or as he put it, it was laudable to strive to achieve "the illusion of some strange suspension or viola-tion of the galling limitations of time, space, and natural law which for ever imprison us" ("Notes on Writing Weird Fiction," CE 2.176). Pope gave the would-be practitioner of this art facetious instruc-tions on how to accomplish this illusion: "He ought therefore to render himself Master of this happy and anti-natural way of think-ing to such a degree, as to be able, on the appearance of any Object, to furnish his Imagination with Ideas infinitely below it" (396). Lovecraft creatively reinterpreted this to mean that our knowledge (especially of the complex matter-energy-spacetime vastness of the universe) is, given our built-in sensorial and cognitive constraints, *infinitely degraded*—another tenet of his cosmicism. And because any object has the potential, under the right circumstances, to sur-prise, to reveal aspects of itself to which we are ordinarily oblivious, it is this intrinsic faultiness of human knowledge that should be the basis of any break from these "galling limitations." Pope furthermore counsels that "his Eyes should be like unto the wrong end of a Per-spective Glass [a telescope], by which all the Objects of Nature are lessen'd" (396). That is, he is ironically advocating that the grandeur of nature should be drastically reduced when appraised so that it may be grasped by the imagination. Lovecraft, however, finds a way of following this injunction so as to bring back the grandeur of na-ture: he does so by replacing the conceit of the "wrong end of a Perspective Glass" with that of deep time. This allows him to consider "all the Objects of Nature," from galaxies to humanity, as "lessen'd," that is, as *trivial events within the context of deep time*—a notion found in his cosmicism.

Lovecraft incorporated the "lessons" of *Peri Bathous* in other ways as well. His underground and underwater imagery, for example, may be seen as an extension of Pope's rhetorical query—"There is an Art of sinking in Poetry. Is there not an architecture of Vaults and Cellars as well as of Domes and Pyramids?" (394)—and thus as generally indicative of the condition of being claimed or subjugated by bathos. But it was early in his literary career, in "Unda; or, The Bride of the Sea," that Lovecraft first hinted—by way of a sophisticated exploitation of intertextuality—at the extent of his indebtedness to Pope's *Peri Bathous*.

Works Cited

Attwater, Donald, and Catherine Rachel John. *Penguin Dictionary of Saints*. Harmondsworth: Penguin, 1995.

Boerem, R. "The First Lewis Theobald." In *Discovering H. P. Lovecraft*, ed. Darrell Schweitzer. Holicong, PA: Wildside Press, 2001. 35–38.

Cantor, Paul A. "The Law Versus the Marketplace: Spontaneous Order in Jonson's *Bartholomew Fair*." *Ludwig von Mises Institute*. 2008. http://mises.org/journals/scholar/Jonson.PDF.

Genette, Gérard. *Paratexts: Thresholds of Interpretation*. Trans. Jane E. Lewin. New York: Cambridge University Press, 1997.

Jonson, Ben. *Bartholomew Fair. The Holloway Pages: Ben Jonson: Works (1692 Folio): Bartholomew Fair*. Ed. Clark J. Holloway. 2003. 17 March 2010. http:// hollowaypages.com/jonson1692bartholmew.htm.

Joshi, S. T. *A Subtler Magick: The Writings and Philosophy of H. P. Lovecraft*. 1996. Berkeley Heights, NJ: Wildside Press, 1999.

Joshi, S. T., and David E. Schultz. *An H. P. Lovecraft Encyclopedia*. Westport, CT: Greenwood Press, 2001.

Kahane, Ahuvia. *Diachronic Dialogues: Authority and Continuity in Homer and the Homeric Tradition*. Lanham, MD: Lexington, 2005.

Lempriere, John. *Bibliotheca Classica*. London: T. Cadell, 1788.

Lovecraft, H. P. *Letters to Rheinhart Kleiner*. Ed. S. T. Joshi and David E. Schultz. New York: Hippocampus Press, 2005.

Mish, Frederick C. *The Merriam-Webster New Book of Word Histories*. Springfield, MA: Merriam-Webster, Inc.

Nelson, Dale J. "Lovecraft and the Burkean Sublime." *Lovecraft Studies* No. 24 (Spring 1991): 2–5.

Poe, Edgar Allan. *Poetry, Tales, and Selected Essays*. Ed. Patrick F. Quinn and G. R. Thompson. New York: Library of America, 1996.

Pope, Alexander. *Poetry and Prose of Alexander Pope*. Ed. Aubrey Williams. Boston: Houghton Mifflin, 1969.

Ross, David O. "The Roman Poetic Traditions: The Neoteric Elegiacs and the Epigrams Proper." In *Catullus*, ed. Julia Haig Gaisser. New York: Oxford University Press, 2007.

Sutherland, Keston. "The Trade in Bathos." *Jacket Magazine* No. 15 (December 2001). February 04, 2010. http:// jacketmagazine.com /15/sutherland-bathos.html.

West, Martin. "Homer's Meter." In *A New Companion to Homer*, ed. Ian Morris and Barry B. Powell. Leiden, Netherlands: Koninklijke Brill, 1996.

Williams, Abigail. *Poetry and the Creation of a Whig Literary Culture, 1681–1714*. New York: Oxford University Press, 2005.

Zumack, Martha. "The Threat of Social Inversion from Economic Changes." *John Brown University—Academics*. Ed. Kendra Mullison. 2009. February 04, 2010. http://www.jbu.edu/acadmeics/journal/2009/files/marthazumack.

Briefly Noted

AudioRealms.com, a company that has an extensive line of audiotapes and CDs of horror, supernatural, and science fiction literature, has now produced six full-length CD packages of works by Lovecraft, all of them read effectively by Wayne June. The series, titled *The Dark Worlds of H. P. Lovecraft*, is produced and directed by Fred Godsmark, and the volumes range from 2 hours and 41 minutes (3 CDs) to as long as 4 hours and 45 minutes (4 CDs). Of ancillary interest are volumes of work by Algernon Blackwood (*The Empty House and Other Ghost Stories*; 6 hours) and Clark Ashton Smith's *The Double Shadow* (3.5 hours), a recording of the 1933 booklet. For further information, see www.AudioRealms.com.

Following "The Ancient Track"

Jonathan Adams

I began setting "The Ancient Track" for mixed chorus and piano in December 2009. I had previously written a set of short, a cappella carols on Lovecraft's incidental Christmas poems and as I worked on the carols, I began to see the heartfelt sentiment expressed in the poetry. I had just finished reading S. T. Joshi's wonderful biography, *H. P. Lovecraft: A Life*, so I felt I had come to a more complete picture of Lovecraft the man and the writer than I had previously had. I contacted Joshi to tell him how much I enjoyed the book and found out that he and his wife sing in the Northwest Chorale in Seattle, a large choir that specializes in performing major works with orchestra. I was concerned about copyright issues, as I try to publish as much of my work as I can, and Hal Leonard or Santa Barbara Music are not interested in dealing with copyright lawsuits to protect themselves or composers who didn't check to see whether the poem they set was in the public domain or not. Joshi told me to go ahead and set one to music because he didn't believe copyright on the poetry was a issue. I was looking at "The Rutted Road" and "The Ancient Track." The latter won out.

"The Ancient Track" was originally written in early December 1929 and was published in *Weird Tales* in March 1930. This poem was part of Lovecraft's outburst of poetry that began in November 1929 and ended in early February 1930 and included the well-known *Fungi from Yuggoth*. As I read the poem over several times, as I usually do before starting on the music, I was stuck by the imagery, or rather the transformation of the scene. As the narrator goes farther down the path, the stranger the scene becomes until he finally passes (I believe) into oblivion. As I studied, I realized just how much Lovecraft influenced modern weird writing. The narrator passes suddenly from the familiar into a "valley lost and dead" that should not even exist in this place. He introduces the supernatural or *supernormal*, the narrator enters it, and Lovecraft doesn't feel the need to explain it rationally or apologize for it. This was one aspect of the poem that I found I could use as a turning point within the music; in other words, everything would change when the narrator reaches the crest of Zaman's Hill. Another interesting facet of the poem is the repetition of the line, "There was no hand to hold me back . . .," which I could also use as a musical "marker" to keep my thematic material organized.

The dilemma in setting a poet like Lovecraft was the same problem I had faced with my choral settings of Edgar Allan Poe. His poetry and stories were so established in pop culture and had been used as lyrics by so many rock musicians that it might be difficult for "legitimate" musicians to take me seriously. This was even more of a problem with Lovecraft, as his poetry was only originally published in the pulp magazines, amateur journals, or newspapers, if he allowed it to be published at all. Poe was an established poet, albeit somewhat underappreciated (Ralph Waldo Emerson called him "the jingle man" after the publication of "The Bells"), but Lovecraft's reputation as a poet was almost nonexistent and his poetry was generally panned by critics and scholars alike. I think this began with Lovecraft's own constant disparaging of his own poetry and Winfield Townley Scott's conception that "to scare is slim purpose in poetry," although many great poems deal with comparatively weird themes. With the new interest in Lovecraft's tales and so much scholarship having taken place in the last thirty years, I felt I was justified in beginning the first "classical" treatment of Lovecraft's poetry since the 1930s. I know nothing about Harold S. Farnese's settings of two poems from the *Fungi from Yuggoth*. His idea of Lovecraft writing an operatic libretto was interesting, if extremely impracticable in reality, as Lovecraft knew nothing about the composition of a libretto.

As with any poem I set to music, I try to remain true to the original. Many composers alter poetry so that it works better with some aspect of the music, or completely rewrite a poem for no aesthetic reason. My mentor, Alfred Skoog, always told us that the best choral music remains true to the poetry, therefore achieving a true union of music and literature. I could have shortened "The Ancient Track" (and many may say that I should have), but I felt no need to do so. The composition became sort of a personal challenge to me over the next couple of months. As I actually started work, I had to take up Lovecraft's own dictum of composition without thought of publication. When I had written "Annabel Lee," the first editor to whom I submitted it said he would publish it, but it would have to be severely abridged. I wondered why you would want to sing a "Reader's Digest Condensed Book" version of one of the most well-known poems in the English language. I also remembered reading that Lovecraft had no interest in contemporary music of the period and at a literary gathering would only sing songs from the 19th century. That gave me a reference point: to use a melody that might sound as if it were a Victorian parlor song.

As a composer, I love a rapid, sixteenth-note introduction. I had used something like this in my setting of Poe's "Hymn" and also in a commission I had written for the Arkansas All-State Mixed Choir, entitled "All Men Dream," with the text from T. E. Lawrence, better know as "Lawrence of Arabia." I wanted to set a mood I felt appropriate—somewhat melancholy but with a feeling of impending menace. I felt the sixteenth notes hammering constantly in E minor during the introduction would give the audience the mood I wanted to convey. I also felt that this sixteenth-note pattern, coupled with contemporary harmony in some sections, would give me a kind of a combination of styles that would be somewhat unique.

Now I had to deal with the action in the poem, the constant upward trodding of the narrator. The most obvious way to do this was "word painting," in which the melody or melodic fragments would constantly ascend. The problem with this vocally is that singers can only sing so high and you run out of vocal range at a point, so I tried to solve this dilemma by using a melodic and harmonic fragment over several times but constantly moving without modulation to unrelated keys. In the end, I believe this to be one of the better features of the piece, as the constant shifting of the tonal center at short intervals keeps the listener from ever getting comfortable in a key area and, I believe, contributes to the overall weirdness of the music. So by constantly shifting the tonal center suddenly, usually up a minor third in this case, and by doubling back on the key areas, I was able to preserve the constant feeling of ascent with out literally running out of vocal range and forcing the sopranos to scream higher and higher!

Yet more word painting occurs with the lines, "There was no hand to hold me back / That night I found the Ancient Track." I used a repetitive descending motive that matches the theme found in the introduction. This would be obvious to the listener, and as one of the few descending lines in the piece it would help to mark the "frame" device in the poetry and the frame in the music. I had used these basic ideas with my setting of "Annabel Lee" and it seemed to work effectively. I chose to use the exact melody as the ending, without any bizarre chords or odd effects, because I felt the piece should end with simple dignity. I also used as few authentic cadences as I could within the piece (or as few as I felt I could get away with) so that I could keep a lot of the harmony up to date. The sheer modality of the melody helps eliminate the need to define the areas where the music stays within key area for more than a few measures. One thing that I attempted to do was to write something that was common sounding melody yet using several different devices (instantaneous key changes, minimalist-like repetition, odd chromatic harmony) to meld the commonplace and the odd or, for lack of a better phrase, to write a "pulp" choral piece. I had read Robert Bloch's introduction to a Lovecraft collection, where he referred to "Lovecraft's distaste for music as dissonance" in "The Music of Erich Zann," and so with that in mind, I tried to keep harsh dissonance infrequent until the chromatic climax two-thirds of the way through the piece. In the end, I could not know what would have appealed to Lovecraft (maybe a barbershop quartet with the melody in the first tenor!), so I could only philosophically write it for myself and stay as true to the poetic roots as I could.

I didn't start with the idea of writing a mythical pulp piece or even know where I was going when I initially started writing. The piece has gone through three rewrites and many corrections to finally get it where it is now, and after all that the time has come to call it finished. It is an extremely long work for me at five and a half minutes in length and 85 measures on paper, but I can say I have thoroughly enjoyed working on it, which brings me back to my first dilemma: Why write a choral setting of H. P. Lovecraft's poetry?

First of all, in comparison to modern song lyrics or even texts used by or even written by some choral composers, much of Lovecraft's better poetry, especially "The Ancient Track," "The Wood," and the *Fungi from Yuggoth*, hold up extremely well, if slightly antiquated in their style. Secondly, because as a teenager, I began reading his tales and loved the density of the style and his treatment of dark themes and now, as an adult, I am still fascinated by his writing and philosophy of art as denoted in his letters. His statement that "There are probably only seven persons, in all, who really like my work; and they are enough" (CE 5.53) is as good advice to a writer or composer as I have ever heard. Last of all, it was a joy to try to bring it to musical life, and if only seven people like it, that is good enough.

> Pleasure to me is wonder—the unexplored, the unexpected, the thing that is hidden and the changeless thing that lurks behind superficial mutability. To trace the remote in the immediate; the eternal in the ephemeral; the past in the present; the infinite in the finite; these are to me the springs of delight and beauty.
>
> From "In Defence of Dagon" (CE 5.53)

TO S. T. JOSHI

THE ANCIENT TRACK

H. P. LOVECRAFT

JONATHAN ADAMS

The Ancient Track

was no hand to hold me back that night I found the an-cient track o-ver the hill and strained to see the fields that teased my mem-o - ry. This tree that wall-I knew them well, and all the roofs and or-chards fell fa- mi - liar - ly up - on my mind as from a past not far be-hind. I knew what sha - dows

Jonathan Adams

The Ancient Track

would be cast as the late moon came up at last from

back of Za - man's Hill and how the vale would shine three

hours from now, and when the path grew steep and high and

The Ancient Track

seemed to end a - gainst the sky, I had no fear of

what might rest be - yond the sil - hou - et - ted crest. Straight

on I walked, while all the night grew pale with phos - phor -

Jonathan Adams

The Ancient Track

e - scent light, and wall and farm - house ga - ble glowed un -

earth - ly by the climb - ing road. There was a mile - stone

that I knew "Two Miles to Dun - wich" now the view of

The Ancient Track

Lyrics under the staves:

dis - tant spires and roofs would dawn with ten___ more up - ward

pa - ces gone.

There was no hand to hold me back that night I found the an-cient track, and reached the crest to see outspread a

Jonathan Adams

The Ancient Track

val-ley of the lost and dead; and o-ver Za-man's Hill the horn of a ma-lig-nant moon was born, the

light the weeds and vines that grew on ru-ined walls I ne-ver knew. The fox-fire glowed in

field and bog, and un - known wa - ters spewed a fog whose

8   # The Ancient Track

curl - ing ta - lons mocked the thought that I had e - er

known this spot. Too well I saw from the mad scene that

my loved past___ had ne - ver been nor was I now up -

Jonathan Adams

The Ancient Track

on the trail de - scend - ing to___ that long dead vale. A -

round was fog a - head the spray of star - streams in the

Milk - y Way. There

The Ancient Track

10

was no hand to hold me back that night I found the an- cient track,

Feb. 5, 2010, revised April 24, 2010

Letters to Carl Ferdinand Strauch

H. P. Lovecraft

Edited by S. T. Joshi and David E. Schultz

Carl Ferdinand Strauch was born on September 25, 1908 in Lehighton, Pennsylvania, the son of Henry and Anna Margaret (Foesch) Strauch. He attended Allentown High School (1922–26), then attended Muhlenberg College in Allentown, receiving his B.A. in English in 1930. He did graduate work at the University of Pennsylvania (1930–31), Lehigh University (1933–34; M.A. in German), and Yale University (1937–39), receiving his Ph.D. in English in 1946. His Ph.D. dissertation was "A Critical and Variorum Edition of Emerson's Poetry" (1946). Ralph O. Orth, an authority on Emerson, writes in the preface to *The Poetry Notebooks of Ralph Waldo Emerson* (Columbia: University of Missouri Press, 1986): "Carl F. Strauch . . . forty years ago undertook the first significant modern research into the tangled skein of [Emerson's] poetry notebooks and showed the way to the present volume."

Strauch was assistant librarian at Muhlenberg College from September 1930 to June 1933. Shortly after this time he wrote an article, "A College Library Goes Regionalist," for the *Wilson Library Bulletin* (December 1933). In September 1934 he became an instructor in the English department at Lehigh, where he remained for the rest of his career. In 1941 he became an assistant professor, in 1946 an associate professor, and in 1953 a full professor. In 1962 he received the Lindback Award for distinguished teaching. In 1968 Emma Richards, one of his graduate students, endowed the Carl F. Strauch Fund to support the purchase of books in American literature for the Lehigh University Library. Strauch retired in 1974 as Distinguished Professor Emeritus of English. The previous year he received an honorary Doctor of Humane Letters from Muhlenberg College.

Strauch's first published book was *Twenty-nine Poems* (Boston: Bruce Humphries, 1932). He was the editor of *Style in the American Renaissance: A Symposium* (Hartford: Transcendental Books, 1970) and *Characteristics of Emerson, Transcendental Poet* (Hartford: Transcendental Books, 1975) and served on the editorial board for the *Collected Works of Ralph Waldo Emerson* (Harvard University Press, 1971f.) and of *ESQ* [*Emerson Society Quarterly*]. He published poems in the *American Poetry Journal, L'Alouette, Wings,* and the *Galleon,* and articles in the *English Journal, PMLA, Philological Quarterly, Modern Language Notes, New England Quarterly, Harvard Library Bulletin,* the *Personalist,* and other scholarly journals.

Strauch was married to Helen Dery, who predeceased him. He had one daughter, Helen. He died on November 13, 1989.

Carl Ferdinand Strauch is not a familiar name in Lovecraft studies. He escaped the attention of the editors of Lovecraft's *Selected Letters,* and indeed he is mentioned only very briefly in Lovecraft's published letters. We are fortunate indeed that Strauch's letters were deposited among the Lovecraft papers at the John Hay Library in Providence.

Lovecraft's and Strauch's mutual friend Harry K. Brobst, like Strauch a native of Allentown, PA, had suggested that Strauch write Lovecraft. The two maintained a prolific correspondence for nearly two years, and Strauch visit Lovecraft in Providence in September 1932, staying at a vacant room in Lovecraft's residence at 10 Barnes Street. Lovecraft clearly enjoyed Strauch both as a correspondent and a visitor. He wrote to August Derleth:

> I reached home just in time to welcome young Strauch, who had come from Allentown to visit Brobst & me. He is a delightful youth—slim, dark, handsome, & extremely brilliant—& I believe he will go far in the poetic field. I showed him the historic & antiquarian high spots of the town, & took him through the famous Harris Collection of Poetry in the Brown Univ. library. He is now in Boston visiting friends. I was extremely sorry he could not spend a longer time here.[1]

1. Letter to August Derleth, 12 September [1932]; *Essential Solitude: The Letters of*

And when Robert Bloch asked Lovecraft in the summer of 1933
who might be "promising correspondents in the weird," Lovecraft
suggested Strauch:

> Strauch, Carl F., 812 Washington St., Allentown, Pa. Age 24. Poet
> with one published book to his credit. Bosom home-town friend of
> Harry Brobst.... Graduate of Muhlenberg College & has acted as
> assistant librarian there. Authority on Pennsylvania folklore with
> weird Hexerei beliefs. Working on a realistic novel. Delightful & af-
> fable—he visited Providence last summer & will probably come
> again this September. Enthusiast in Germanic literature. Rather
> anti-scientific by temperament—affording material for heated & in-
> teresting arguments with Brobst.[2]

Although Lovecraft never addressed Strauch less informally than
"My dear Strauch," his letters were not merely polite replies. The
early exchange of letters focused primarily on their common interest in weird fiction, but expanded into many other subjects including general literature, Lovecraft's travels and antiquarianism,
Providence architecture, folklore, and others. Yet their correspondence ended abruptly around August 1933 and Strauch did not visit
Lovecraft again. The exact reason for the dissolution of their friendship is unknown, for Lovecraft does not seem to have mentioned
the matter in his letters to others, but three conjectures may be
postulated: (1) the critical comments made by Lovecraft and others
on a story written by Strauch may have severely discouraged the
would-be writer, (2) his interest in weird fiction may have waned,
as evidenced by the literary interests of his later years, and (3) his
post-graduate work beginning in late 1933 may initially have ham-
pered continued correspondence.

The twenty-nine surviving letters and postcards from H. P.
Lovecraft to Strauch are not abundant with new facts about or insights, but they strengthen our grasp of Lovecraft's psychological

H. P. Lovecraft and August Derleth, ed. David E. Schultz and S. T. Joshi (New
York: Hippocampus Press, 2008), 2.500.
2. Letter to Robert Bloch, [c. late June 1933]; Letters to Robert Bloch, ed. David E.
Schultz and S. T. Joshi (West Warwick, RI: Necronomicon Press, 1993), 24.

make-up and numerous interests and augment the vast knowledge already gained from the tantalizing yet fragmentary *Selected Letters*.

Acknowledgments: The editors wish to thank Dr. Harry K. Brobst, Professor Edward J. Gallagher of Lehigh University, and Ruth L. Seither, Office Coordinator of Alumni Relations at Muhlenberg College, for information concerning Carl F. Strauch. In addition, they wish to thank the John Hay Library of Brown University for permission to publish the letters to Strauch.

Abbreviations

ALS   autograph letter, signed
ANS   autograph note, signed
SHL   "Supernatural Horror in Literature" (in *The Annotated Supernatural Horror in Literature* [New York: Hippocampus Press, 2000])
WT   *Weird Tales*

Editors' Note

Except for notes pertaining to type of manuscript, postmarks, postscripts, and enclosures, square brackets within the text of Lovecraft's letters are Lovecraft's. The letters are printed with as little alteration as possible, and the editors have retained Lovecraft's idiosyncrasies of usage and occasional spelling errors or slips of the pen. No omission has knowingly been made

———————

[1]   [ALS]

10 Barnes St.,
Providence, R.I.,
Septr 20, 1931

My dear Mr. Strauch:—

I was glad to receive yours of the 16th, since I had heard of you & your work very favourably from our friend Brobst. I hope to see a copy of your book when it is out[1]—for I appreciate poetry despite the mediocrity of my own attempts in that medium.

I am glad that you have found some of my efforts worth read-ing—especially "The Strange High House", which I wrote five years ago, when strongly under the influence of Dunsany.[2] Other things of mine in that semi-poetic medium have been more mawkish & un-satisfactory—for in the long run I think a style of greater objective simplicity is my really natural mode of expression.

I heartily agree with you regarding the lame inadequacy of nearly everything that passes for weird fiction in the popular magazines—to say nothing of more pretentious specimens. Poe had an inherent convincingness & brooding menace of style & atmosphere which no one has been able to duplicate, though many living writers have surpassed him in width of cosmic outlook & originality of bizarre invention. Of later weird material I would tend to say that Alger-non Blackwood, (despite a wretched style) Arthur Machen, Lord Dunsany, & Montague Rhodes James furnish the greatest abundance of really fine examples. Robert W. Chambers' early "King in Yel-low" has a certain sombre convincingness, as have several things—notably "Seaton's Aunt"—by Walter de la Mare. I do not care much for May Sinclair[3] or Fletcher,[4] & believe that Doyle's[5] flat style spoils many tales which would otherwise be extremely powerful. A few years ago I wrote a longish article on the history of the weird tale, which appeared in a magazine (a venture called *The Recluse*, which did not survive its first issue) privately printed by a friend.[6] If I can resurrect a copy, & if it would interest you to see it, I will give you a look at that sketch. If I had more energy I might revise & expand it, & try to get it published as a small book.[7]

Weird fiction is necessarily a minor field of art, since it confines itself to one narrow side of the human personality—the subjective image-building tendency which speculates beyond the realm of the visible & creates a natural rebellion against the inexorable limita-tions of time, space, & cosmic law. But at the same time it is silly to deny that it is art at all; for the instinct on which it is based is a genuine one, & there is art in any well-presented & sincere manifes-tation of a genuine human impulse. Like you, I regard the current depreciation of weird writing as a lamentable & conspicuous exam-ple of academic pedantry based on artificial standards; & believe that an artist of the right skill & endowments might readily create work of the highest aesthetic quality in the medium.[8] Of modern authors, Blackwood is the only one who treats the unreal with suitable seriousness—& he unfortunately has a crude style & lack of self-criticism (as witness the endless volumes of namby-pamby inanity which he grinds out in addition to masterpieces like "The Willows") which will always prevent him from attaining the heights. The supreme weird writer has yet to appear—& meanwhile Poe still holds first place.

With best wishes, & hoping that I may some day get around to see you & your interesting group (of whose discussions Brobst has sometimes written), I am

Yrs most cordially & sincerely,

H. P. Lovecraft

Notes

1. *Twenty-nine Poems* (Boston: Bruce Humphries, [1932]).

2. "The Strange High House in the Mist" (*WT*, October 1931). HPL wrote "The Silver Key," "The Strange High House in the Mist," and *The Dream-Quest of Unknown Kadath* in 1926–27, when the Dunsany influence on his stories was not nearly so strong as in 1919–21.

3. May Sinclair (1863–1946), *The Intercessor and Other Stories* (New York: Macmillan, 1932; LL #803). HPL cites her *Uncanny Stories* (1923) in SHL (58).

4. Perhaps J. S. Fletcher (1863–1935), primarily a detective writer but author of a few weird novels at the turn of the century.

5. I.e., Arthur Conan Doyle (1859–1930). HPL had three collections of Doyle's tales: *The Mystery of Sasassa Valley* [etc.] (1900?; LL #260), *Tales of Long Ago* (1922; LL #261), and *Tales of Twilight and the Unseen* (1922; LL #262); the latter is predominantly weird.

6. W. Paul Cook published a single issue of the *Recluse* in August 1927. A second issue was planned and was partially typeset, including HPL's "The Strange High House in the Mist"; it was also to include several stanzas from HPL's *Fungi from Yuggoth*.

7. A revised version received incomplete serialization in the *Fantasy Fan* (October 1933–February 1935). Cook had intended to publish SHL in book form, but it was August Derleth who secured its publication by Ben Abramson in 1945.

8. Cf. the opening paragraph of SHL.

[2]   [ALS]

10 Barnes St.,

Providence, R.I.,

Octr 10, 1931.

My dear Strauch:—

Your letter of the 4th proved exceedingly interesting to me, & I was delighted with all the poems—especially the
autumn piece. Of your poetic gifts there can be no question, & I am
sure that Allentown must be a notable abode of the Muses if it can
produce many genuine rivals! You have the true poet's sense of sym-
bols & images, & a highly enviable command of the right words &
rhythms for their aptest conveyance. I have often tried to express in
verse the various moods evoked in me by various phases of beauty,
but never get very far in that direction. Enclosed is a typical bit of my
metrical tripe—a rhymed protest against the wanton destruction of a
splendid row of ancient brick warehouses along the Providence waterfront a couple of years ago.[1] Unfortunately the protest did not succeed in its object—which was a pity, because the old buildings
formed a priceless link with early maritime days, & gave the central
square of Providence a rich quaintness unique among cities of equal
size. I possibly mentioned in my former letter that I am an inveterate
antiquarian, whose greatest delight is in recapturing the past through
contemplation of its architectural vestiges. This is reflected in the
bookplate I had designed a few years ago[2]—a typical old Providence
doorway—a specimen of which I will enclose.

I trust you have been able to take all the rural rambles you promised yourself—surely the genial weather of last week was favourable
enough to such a design! Yes—Brobst has often confirmed my long-
standing impression of the beauty of your region, so that I am quite
anxious to see it for myself. Rural landscapes exert a very potent
charm upon me—being on a parity with colonial architecture in this
respect. Fortunately my own section is very beautiful scenically, & I
have always been within walking distance of the woods & fields. Indeed, my birthplace[3] was so close to what was then the edge of
Providence's settled residence district, that in boyhood I was as much
a ruralite as an urbanite. I have always felt very close to the ancient
cycle of New England agricultural life with its various seasonal manifestations; so that today I am acutely conscious of belonging to the

vanishing rural-minded civilisation rather than to the coming age of machinery and urbanisation. Every sunny day in summer I take my work out to the open fields & woods in a black enamel-cloth bag, & see just as little as possible of paved streets & modern houses. Last week I had a splendid taste of autumn scenery by virtue of a dual trip to neighbouring parts of New England. First I went to Massachusetts on a pleasure jaunt—taking in the unspoiled region south of Boston, (ancient Hingham with its "Old Ship Church" built in 1681 &c) & the exquisite Merrimack Valley (containing the ancient city of New-buryport) to the north. Then, upon returning home, I found a tele-gram summoning me to Hartford, Conn. to confer about a book revision job I am performing for the Stephen Daye Press of Brattle-boro, Vt.[4] I had, curiously enough, never been to central Connecticut before; close though it is to my own doorstep—hence was eager to sample the scenery along the route. It proved surprisingly fine, & an ideal day shewed it at its best. On the return trip I chose—for vari-ety's sake—an indirect route passing through Norwich & Plainfield, & found the scenery even lovelier than on the direct route. Bold hills & valleys—gleaming lakes—breath-taking panoramas—everything to enchant the imagination. The old town of Norwich, where I stopped for a thorough exploration, is ineffably quaint—being built on the steep terraces that rise above a bend in the river Thames.

About that anthology—it has only *one* of my stories, albeit one that is quite a favourite of mine. There are other pieces of much greater merit by other writers, so that the book is most distinctly worth buying. It is called "Creeps by Night", is edited by Dashiell Hammett, & published at $2.50 by the John Day Co.[5] I haven't seen a copy yet—am waiting to see if the publisher gives me one free. There is no published collection of my stuff, though various things of mine are included in anthologies. My "Call of Cthulhu" is in "Be-ware After Dark", edited by T. Everett Harré & published by the Macaulay Co., & the British "Not at Night" collections[6] (published annually) usually include me among their contents.

I have seen reviews of the work of Egon Friedell,[7] & am inclined to agree that his is one of the profoundest philosophic minds of this generation. I must certainly get hold of his "European Culture" sooner or later. Spengler is already a standby of mine[8]—whom I hailed upon his first appearance as a scholarly confirmer of ideas I had long held in my fumbling & unscholarly way. You are right, I think, in emphasising the indispensably encyclopaedic quality of German scholarship. Indeed, I fancy that history & philosophy would still be painfully primitive but for the contributions made by the relentlessly thorough Germanic mind.

I am aware that your part of Pennsylvania is rich in folklore & superstitions—but was surprised when Brobst told me of the prevalence of weird beliefs in the cities as well as the rural districts. Such superstition as New England still retains is confined wholly to the remotest backwoods—even the ordinarily populous farming districts being to a great extent rational & disillusioned in their dominant attitude. Most certainly, Pennsylvania folklore ought to be better represented in literature than it so far has been—though a few books have centred to some extent around it. In the 18th century Charles Brockden Brown touched this region in what was virtually the first American novel—"Wieland; or, The Transformation"—& in the present generation there has been a rather mediocre book by Prof. Fred Lewis Pattee—"The House of the Black Ring"—covering the same ground.[9] I realise, though, that these things have scarcely scratched the surface. As for the distinction between Pennsylvania "Dutch" & other Germanic elements—the only one I know is that the former have been settled in the Pennsylvania countryside for over two centuries, developing localisms in dialect & folkways, whereas other U.S. Germans date from 1848 & later, & have not formed such a differentiated nucleus—keeping closer to the European German type until absorbed into the Anglo-Saxon cultural stream. I believe, also, that the old Pennsylvania Germans came chiefly from the Palatinate & South Germany—thus being perhaps of a more specialised type than latercomers who hailed in more equal proportions from all parts of the Germanic world. The principal differentiation, I take it, is due to the long isolation of the Pennsylvanians in a remote region where ancestral superstitions were nurtured & magnified rather than weakened by time. This isolation would perhaps account for the element of cruelty or the sinister which you remark—but which I never heard of before. It is paralleled by certain characteristics of back-country people everywhere. The "hex" anecdote you cite is certainly unique—& all the more impressive because of its un-theatrical homeliness. Certainly, the minds of the people are open to all sorts of suggestions; so that every opportunity is offered for the practice of delusive phenomena according to ancient & half-submerged patterns.

This kind of thing ought to be studied soon, I imagine, if it is to be encountered in its pristine purity; for a generation or two of modern standardised life with radios, cinemas, tabloids, & cheap magazines will leave very little of the ancient folk-heritage.

With best wishes, & again expressing my appreciation of the poems sent, I remain

Yrs most cordially & sincerely,

H. P. Lovecraft

Notes

1. "The East India Brick Row," *Providence Journal* (8 January 1930): 13.

2. By Wilfred B. Talman c. 1929.

3. 194 (later 454) Angell Street.

4. Leon Burr Richardson, *History of Dartmouth College* (Hanover, NH, 1932; 2 vols.). The Stephen Daye Press was managed by HPL's friend Vrest Orton.

5. *LL* #394 The book contains HPL's "The Music of Erich Zann."

6. *Not at Night* (1925; *LL* #879) with "The Curse of Yig"; *You'll Need a Night Light* (1927) with "The Horror at Red Hook" (*LL* #882); *By Daylight Only* (1929) with "Pickman's Model" (*LL* #876); *Gruesome Cargoes* (1928; *LL* #878); *Switch On the Light* (1931) with "The Curse of Yig" and "The Rats in the Walls" (*LL* #881); *Grim Death* (1932; *LL* #877); *Terror by Night* [1934] with "The Horror in the Museum"; *The "Not at Night" Omnibus* (1936) with "The Curse of Yig," "Pickman's Model," and "The Horror in the Museum" (*LL* #880). All edited by Christine Campbell Thomson (1897–1985) and published by Selwyn & Blount, London. HPL ghost-wrote some of the stories cited.

7. Egon Friedell (1878–1938), German historian and philosopher. HPL evidently refers to Friedell's *Kulturgeschichte der Neuzeit* (1927–31; 3 vols.), Friedell's only work to be translated into English; as *A Cultural History of the Modern Age: The Crisis of the European Soul from the Black Death to the World War* (New York: Knopf, 1930–32; 3 vols.).

8. Oswald Spengler (1880–1936), *Der Untergang des Abendlandes* (1918–22; 2 vols.); tr. as *The Decline of the West* (1922–26; 2 vols.). See *SL* 2.120–21 and 4.323.

9. Charles Brockden Brown (1771–1810), author of *Wieland; or, The Transformation* (1798) and other novels, generally regarded as America's first professional novelist; Fred Lewis Pattee (1863–1950), *The House of the Black Ring* (Harrisburg, PA: Mount Pleasant Press, 1916; *LL* #679). Pattee later reviewed the Ben Abramson edition of SHL in *American Literature* (May 1946).

[3]   [ALS]

Guy Fawkes' Day
[5 November 1931]

My dear Strauch:—

Very glad to hear from you, & sorry your eyes have been bothering. It pays to rest one's vision all one can, for a tremendous amount depends on that one delicate sense. I had some severe eye strain last winter, but my long spring & summer trip in the South set things right again.

You have my sympathy regarding the tutoring—but it helps, at least, if the subjects are willing & earnest. I don't think I'd make a good tutor in any subject, for I haven't the concise expository faculty which I notice in many.

Good luck with the novel—which, with your general talent, ought to be successful if you stick close to nature for your material. Hawthorne's general type of atmosphere ought to be as effective today as in his own time, though I imagine that a Dickensian treatment of character would need many modifications. I never could abide Dickens—finding him a peculiarly wearisome mixture of hollow sentimentality & grotesque exaggeration. None of his characters ever impressed me as in the least like a human being. But then, I seem to find all Victorian literature alien. I like either the present or the 18th century—anything except the artificiality of the 19th. I see no reason why you should not fulfil your literary ambitions, & expect to hear of you in the course of time as a recognised poet—& perhaps novelist. With such a start at your age, everything is in your favour.

About "Creeps"—amusingly enough, Benét's contribution is unqualifiedly & indisputably the worst thing in the book! It is an attempt to be comic—& succeeds about as well as Poe's similar attempts. To my mind, the best thing is Ewers' "Spider".[1] Most of the stuff, unfortunately, lacks real atmospheric weirdness—but belongs more to the genre of the mere *conte cruel*. There is too much artificial cleverness—I found it easy to predict the outcome of most of the tales at a relatively early point in their structure.

Herbert Asbury edited the pirated American "Not at Night" anthology (containing my "Horror at Red Hook") which Macy-Masius withdrew from the market rather than pay royalty or damages to

Weird Tales. I don't recall whether or not he ever contributed to the magazine. He is rather clever, & his "Gangs of New York"[2] has become almost a folklore classic. I make no attempt to keep up with contemporary books—for how much of every year's output is really worth reading? A retrospective glance at the best sellers of 1926 or 1921 is sardonically illuminating—how many have really survived?

Glad the material I enclosed proved of interest, & that the verses did not seem too irredeemably flat. Here are a couple of cards reflecting my antiquarian wanderings of last week—my final excursion of the season, since temperature conditions now begin to preclude comfortable travel. I visited four of my favourite ancient towns—Portsmouth, N.H., & Newburyport, Salem, & Marblehead, Mass.[3] Portsmouth & Newburyport are almost solidly archaic, but Salem has a brisk modern life besides its antiquities. Marblehead—now that the herd of summer visitors has dispersed—is like a deserted museum. There is nothing else like it in the U.S. You can see by the enclosed view that it is absolutely an unchanged & miraculously preserved seaport of the 18th century—a tangible bit of the past which makes no demands on the imagination.

With best wishes—

        Yrs most cordially & sincerely,

        H. P. Lovecraft

[Enclosures: two postcards ("A quaint old street in Marblehead, Mass." and "Old Witch House, After 1780, Salem, Mass.").]

Notes

1. Stephen Vincent Benét, "The King of the Cats"; Hans Heinz Ewers (1872–1943), "The Spider." The Ewers story clearly influenced HPL's "The Haunter of the Dark."

2. Herbert Asbury (1891–1963) ed., *Not at Night!* (New York: Macy-Masius [The Vanguard Press], 1928; *LL* #44); *The Gangs of New York: An Informal History of the Underworld* (New York: Knopf, 1928).

3. This trip influenced the composition of "The Shadow over Innsmouth" in the weeks following.

[4]   [ALS]

10 Barnes St.,

Providence, R.I.,

Novr 17, 1931.

My dear Strauch:—

Glad you found the postcards interesting. I think I told you that I am something of an amateur antiquarian whose chief delight is to visit ancient towns. If you'd like, I can send you views of other old places, both in New England & the South. Trout Hall must be a very interesting place, & I am glad Allentown has preserved at least that much linkage with the past. As for material comforts & cleanliness—I probably agree largely with you that their citation as a criterion of civilisation is distinctly childish & absurd. Yet on the other hand I think they are so eminently desirable that I wouldn't encourage any attack on them in the manner of G. K. Chesterton—who backs up his ostentatious mediaevalism to the extent of lecturing in visibly soiled linen. (Recalling, no doubt, Dr. Johnson's dictum—"As for clean linen, why, Sir, I have no passion for it!'") Every advance in the standard of neatness & immaculateness is an aesthetic asset, & is intrinsically good. The only silly thing is to magnify these background details into major objects & criteria. They ought, rather, to be understood & taken for granted—for when they are overstressed we have a suspicion that they are rather recent & not quite assimilated acquisitions. When a man talks too much about taking a bath each day, we are inclined to suspect that he did not always do so! But all the same, I'd rather he would take it & talk about it than *not* take it. Ah, me—what a complex fabric is life! New England has much of Pennsylvania's emphasis on cleanliness, though I don't think it wholly displaces an interest in the intellectual & aesthetic. It seems to be an ingrained instinct of the Nordic race—as comparison with our Mediterranean, Slavic, & Semitic newcomers vividly demonstrates. One finds it equally developed among the Dutch families (real Holland Dutch) of the New-Netherland region—New York & New Jersey—of whom more remain than is commonly supposed.

I envy you your sight of Quakertown with its quaint tombstones. My familiarity with the Pennsylvania-German culture is limited to Germantown—the suburb of Philadelphia—but that delightful place has nothing as quaint as what you describe. Germantown, indeed, was never truly rustic—being only 4 miles from the colonial metropolis. Its houses—even back in the 1690's—were solidly & tastefully built, & the gravestones (in Dunkard, Quaker, & Moravian churchyards) quite devoid of the autobiographical & anticipatory features you cite. It was in Germantown, by the way, that the Bible was first printed in the present area of the U.S.—by Christopher Sauer, in 1740-something or other, in the German language. Germantown (as you may perhaps know from first-hand observation) is still one of the most picturesque & unspoiled places in America, with a vast number of the old stone houses (late XVII & XVIII cent.) still standing in & near the long main street. Wyck—a fine old manor-house of 1690 or so—is in splendid condition & frequently photographed for books on architecture, & several homesteads of the celebrated Wistar or Wister family remain in excellent shape. A good number of the present inhabitants are descended from the old families, & their Site & Relic Society (housed in a fine old 18th century mansion in a small park) has done much to keep the traditions of the past alive. I never visit Phila. without taking a stroll through Germantown. By the way—there is a fine set of rooms from a typical Pennsylvania-German farmhouse (unaffected by British influence) in the new Philadelphia Art Museum—furnished with appropriate material. Also—in Fairmount Park there is a reconstructed stone farmhouse of the 18th century (moved from Frankford) illustrating the transition period when German families near Philadelphia began to speak English & adopt Georgian motifs to some extent in interior architecture.

Oh, yes—we have the usual community chests hereabouts, & I don't doubt but that they are necessary during the present bewildering period when actual industrial & social conditions are out of touch with the available political & economic machinery. Owing to the mechanisation of industry, a vast number of persons are now hopelessly unemployable—& there seems to be nothing to do but to feed them until somebody thinks up some sort of industrial adjustment which can reabsorb a good proportion of them. It is not within the capacity of fumbling, groping human nature to keep basic institutions in step with the rapidly changing conditions of the present. People reared in a simpler age cannot think in terms of this—hence the acute strain for a full generation or two. No perfect social balance, of course, ever has been or ever will be possible; but in time the danger of an unfed mass will probably be recognised enough to bring about a modified set of conditions—employment of large numbers at shorter hours & with sufficient remuneration to remove violent suffering & discontent. Whether such changes will come voluntarily from large industrialists, or whether they will be imposed politically by a more or less fascistic government, still remains to be seen. But I think the solid sense of the Nordic race can be depended on to make the transition of Western Europe & North America less violent & destructive than that of upheaved Russia. In the case of that hapless region the remedy seems worse, from the point of view of a liberal & individualistic civilisation, than the original disease. Meanwhile—in the absence of other machinery for quick equilibration—charity is an absolute necessity as a palliative. This year the chest business in Rhode Island seems fairly well devoid of absurd frills, & the primary relief objects are not so much the scouts, Y, &c., as the actually homeless & foodless. This state is also about to assess special taxes for the aid of the unemployed.

I think I can agree with you on the merit of Hawthorne's style—but somehow I lack the ability of Machen & others to find anything really solid or magical in Dickens.[2] The "immense gusto for living" which many praise in novels of the Dickens type seems to me a sort of insincere & artificial excrescence—something essentially tawdry & detracting from the really impartial & artistic delineation of human life. I recognise the merit of Fielding & other 18th century English writers, yet on mature reflection cannot help thinking that the French novel tradition is at bottom rather sounder than ours. There is more honest objectivity, less irrelevant digression, less meaningless sentimentality, & less traditional hokum disguised as profundity. Less humour, too—a good thing, since much of our overrated humour is at bottom a mere superficiality depending on false, artificial standards & limited insight. Of course the French miss certain atmospheric overtones which only the poetic sense of a northern race could supply—yet even so, I think their assets outweigh their liabilities. But of course, this applies only to serious fiction. In *poetry*, the Northern races hopelessly outclass the precise, logical Gaul from the very start. The same also goes for *weird fiction*, which is in essence a branch of poetry in disguise. Yes—I like Jane Austen, though for personal enjoyment I prefer my homely realism & gentle irony in moderately small doses. Good luck, by the way, with your own novel. Brobst has outlined some of his ideas to me, & I have thought them all excellent. He ought to write a few out in story form—either alone or in collaboration. W.T. once discussed a book of my stuff, but gave up the idea in the end.[3] They prefer to feature popular writers like Otis Adelbert Kline.

Best wishes—

Yrs sincerely,

H. P. Lovecraft

Notes

1. James Boswell quotes Johnson as saying: "[Christopher Smart] did not love clean linen; and I have no passion for it." *Life of Johnson* (1791), 24 May 1763.

2. Arthur Machen (1863–1947) wrote extensively on Dickens, including the essay "The Art of Dickens" (1908), rpt. in *The Shining Pyramid* (1923), and the introduction to *A Handy Dickens* (1941). Dickens is also discussed in Machen's *Hieroglyphics: A Note upon Ecstasy in Literature* (1902; *LL* #571).

3. The earliest of several inquiries (c. 1926) about publishing a collection of HPL's stories (cf. *SL* 2.53), the *WT* book, to have followed A. G. Birch et al., *The Moon Terror* (Indianapolis: Popular Fiction Publishing Co., [1927]); HPL's preferred title for it was *The Outsider and Other Stories* (HPL to Farnsworth Wright, 22 December 1927; Arkham House Transcripts).

[5]   [ALS]

10 Barnes St.,

Providence, R.I.,

Decr. 8, 1931

My dear Strauch:—

Yes, indeed—G K C is an odd case, & very amusing if one does not accept him seriously as an explainer of the universe. A match between him & Darrow is really a farcical thing to consider; since the well-meaning Clarence is so relatively naive & primitive in his emotions & attitude toward life. A far better opponent would have been H. L. Mencken or Bertrand Russell or George Santayana. The modern civilised man accepts a purposeless & imper-

sonal cosmos of electrical energy as a matter of course, & does not
bother to proclaim & preach his doctrines. Religion will die a natural
death among the intelligent in time, while the herd will always believe in some sort of supernatural machinery. Propaganda is singu-
larly futile one way or the other—for it doesn't make the least bit of
difference whether the majority believe in gods & devils or not.
Human actions, in the main, are very largely what glandular physiology & environmental accident make them. People don't mould their
actions according to their beliefs, but concoct their beliefs to justify
or explain their actions. The one way to head off a theistic believer
is to ask him what shred of evidence there is, in the universe as now
understood, to justify the invention of any such gratuitous & unmotivated improbabilities as a cosmic consciousness & purpose, a condition of "spiritual" entity, a personal immortality, & so on. Today
these assumptions are grotesque & puerile—& all the more so because psychology & anthropology can now account for the religious
"intuitions" formerly cited as theistic evidence. We can see that religion was an inevitable phenomenon among primitive men—but must
also perceive that every apparent evidence which once suggested it
is now destroyed. Only blind tradition causes anyone today to be
predisposed toward such a superseded concept. In the universe
around us, as now interpreted, there is nothing at all to indicate the
existence of the beings & values & purposes postulated by the obso-
lescent mythologies. When one pulls this truth on a theist, he is
forced into defences so absurd & far-fetched that his case suffers before an impartial judge.

Glad you've seen the Philadelphia Museum—whose extension, by
the way, as seen atop its Acropolis down the length of the Parkway, is
to my mind the most fascinating modern urban vista in America. I am
intensely fond of Old Philadelphia anyway. You must see Germantown some time—it is an ineffably quaint & attractive place, with a
surprising proportion of the old stone houses still in excellent preservation. Just south of it is the superlatively exquisite wooded gorge of
the Wissahickon Creek, (of which Poe wrote an appreciation)[1] in one
of whose tributary ravines is the old stone mill where the eminent as-
tronomer & mintmaster David Rittenhouse was born two centuries
ago. These snatches of Pennsylvania countryside which I have seen
around Philadelphia make me anxious to see wider & less suburban

stretches. I don't think I've seen more impressive scenery than the Wissahickon gorge.

I'd be very grateful for postcards of the Pennsylvania landscape with its characteristic architecture, & will send you some of New England when I can get hold of some good rural specimens. No—our barns have no embellishment, since in the last two centuries Yankees have taken their traditional superstitions very lightly indeed. Our houses & farm buildings are almost always of wood, & tend to be low & spreading, in harmony with the gently rolling landscape. They are very simple—with a simplicity that makes for beauty—& blend admirably with the surrounding orchards, rambling stone walls, & glimpses of distant village steeples. If climatic-physiological reasons ever force me to move southward, I shall be more homesick for this exquisite type of pastoral landscape than for anything else. I am very fond of the country, & seek out a rural spot every sunny afternoon in summer, carrying reading & writing materials in a bag. Those "hex" circles on your barns are intensely interesting—& I had never heard of them before. I certainly must see this region some day. Incidentally— that anecdote of the sheriff is remarkable in the highest degree.[2] Probably the wizard repeated ancient formulae which the sheriff knew of old, & in which he believed, so that the result was equivalent to actual hypnosis. Primitive groups have many seemingly magical practices of this sort; which appear quite effective, & which depend on the perfect credulity of the victim. Africa, the West Indies, & Polynesia supply analogues.

I wish the editor of W.T. shared your point of view regarding a book of my stuff, but unfortunately he seems to have given up the idea. Possibly the indifferent success of other books published by the firm was a deciding factor. However, I don't let the matter worry me.

I trust you managed to secure a good rest during the vacation season. I am a nocturnal bird myself—but I normally make up the sleeping time the next day, since my programme is of my own dictating nowadays. I can concentrate for thinking & writing much better in the dead of night when all the objective world is effaced in darkness & silence. Unmotivated speed & meaningless activity are as irritating to me as to you—leading me often to recall the query of your friend Emerson's—"Why so hot, little man?"[3] Loafing surely is the finest of all arts—the art of being, as opposed to the meaningless treadmill of doing. I love to idle through scenes of quaintness & beauty, letting the atmosphere of accumulated ages filter into me unforcedly & unsystematically. ¶ Best wishes—

Yrs most cordially & sincerely—
H P Lovecraft

Notes

1. "Morning on the Wissahiccon," also known as "The Elk."

2. Cf. HPL to A. W. Derleth, 10 December 1931: "I find that there is still a whole region in the U.S. where witchcraft is believed as uniformly & implicitly as in the Salem of 1692. It is the Lehigh Valley region of Pennsylvania, where the 'hex' murders attracted attention a few years ago. I thought those a rather isolated vestigial case, but I now have two bright young correspondents in Allentown who (themselves as sceptical as I) indicate a widespread surviving belief. 'Hex' doctors have a strong hold on the imaginations of the people; & only last week one of them kept at a distance, by some quasi-hypnotic psychological menace, a sheriff who wanted to search his garage. The country folk paint on their barn gables great circles filled with labyrinthine lines—to entrap any 'hexes' who may have designs on their livestock & grain" *Essential Solitude: The Letters of H. P. Lovecraft and August Derleth*, ed. David E. Schultz and S. T. Joshi (New York: Hippocampus Press, 2008), 1.428.

3. The quotation has been variously given as "Why so hot, my little man?" or "Why so hot, little sir?" It cannot be definitively found in Emerson's writings and may have been uttered in conversation.

[6]   [ALS]

10 Barnes St.,
Providence, R.I.,
Dec. 23, 1931.

My dear Strauch:—

I am certainly learning a vast amount of contemporary folklore these days! As I recently wrote Brobst, I had no idea that so much literal witch-belief survived on the surface of American life today. New England affords no parallel for things like cowbelled Fords, hieroglyphed barns, barrier-raising wizards, & the like—all our real superstition being in the past, & surviving only in legend & balladry. Pennsylvania's unique cases of survival must be due to special local causes, (isolation, &c) since I don't think German settlements elsewhere have anything approaching them. Wisconsin, with its almost solid German rustic population of the 1848 migration, presents no such baffling anachronism. I must ask my correspondents in that region (especially August W. Derleth, whose work in W.T. you probably know) whether there is much superstition under the surface.

Thanks exceedingly for that Molly Maguire cutting. I do indeed know of the institution referred to, though I had no idea its echoes lasted so long. The *original* Molly Maguires, so named because of the custom of the cutthroats to disguise in women's clothes, came into being in Ireland around 1843. Their object was to injure & intimidate rent collectors—it being a part of the same Irish resistance to landlordism which later appeared in the lawless Sinn Fein & cognate organisations. The outbreak in Pennsylvania in 1875 was engineered wholly by Irishmen familiar with the tactics of the Mollies in the "Ould Counthry". I'm not very certain about the precise cause of the local trouble, but I think it was both industrial & agrarian—hinging on the relation of Irish coal-miners to the companies that employed them & owned their homes. The victims—corresponding to the landlords & rent collectors in Ireland—were mine-owners & overseers. Probably the primary motive in all the murders was intimidation. Many modern strikes produce phenomena roughly comparable to the activities of the Mollies. The attempted suppression of their history is surely a phenomenon of vast interest—& I suppose the active factors are their descendants—or rabid Irish "patriots". Your family is surely lucky in having a copy. There is a vast fascination in the idea of some episode of history so horrible that it is expunged from the books & records of a nation. I have used it in fiction myself.[1] The legend of the hand print is an added feature of interest.

I have heard, though not in detail, of the beauty of Mauch Chunk,[2] & have meant to include it in some future trip when I feel like sparing enough time from the antiquarian to include the purely scenic. I did not know of the Switchback, but hope I may eventually take a ride over it. I am really a tremendous enthusiast for fine scenery, though my extreme antiquarianism & sadly slender purse combine to steer most of my trips to regions where architectural reliques are exceptionally thick. I shall most certainly appreciate any views you may send.

Brobst tells me you have been proofreading your coming book lately—a trying process, though eminently worth enduring in view of results. Typographical errors exasperate me, & I am willing to do anything to forestall them. I hope to see the book when it is out—let me know its price & where to get it. Just now I am on a job worse than proofreading—the revision of crude verse.[3] The only thing worse than this is doctoring up a rotten piece of fiction.

With best holiday wishes, & thanking you again for the cutting, I remain

Yrs most cordially & sincerely—
H P L

Notes

1. In "The Rats in the Walls" (1923) and *The Case of Charles Dexter Ward* (1927). Cf. "The Haunter of the Dark" (1935): "The Pharaoh Nephren-Ka … did that which caused his name to be stricken from all monuments and records" (*DH* 106).

2. Mauch Chunk, now called Jim Thorpe, is a resort area in the Blue Mountains northwest of Allentown.

3. Possibly Eugene B. Kuntz's *Thoughts and Pictures* (Haverhill, MA: Cooperatively published by H. P. Lovecraft and C. W. Smith, January 1932). Kuntz was an old-time amateur journalist.

[7]   [ALS]

Feby. 16, 1932

My dear Strauch:—

Very glad to hear from you! I expect Brobst over here tomorrow evening, & will tell him how much he is missed at home. Last Saturday afternoon—which fortunately was a fine warm day—I took great pleasure in showing him over the quaint & ancient parts of Providence; largely the picturesque hill which forms the keynote of local topography. We saw the place where Roger Williams landed in 1636, (now being made into a public park)[1] the old colony house built in 1761,[2] the 1775 church,[3] the 1773 market house,[4] the 1770 college edifice,[5] the hidden hillside churchyard of St. John's,[6] the "haunted" Halsey Mansion[7] & other fine Georgian residences, the home of Mrs. Whitman where Poe used to call,[8] the old Golden Ball Inn[9] where Washington stopped in 1790, the Sign of Shakespeare's Head where the old Providence Gazette was printed in 1762 & onward,[10] & the historic Athenaeum,[11] where Poe & Mrs. Whitman used to ramble through the book alcoves. At this latter place I had an attendant show Brobst the pencil signature which Poe affixed at Mrs. W's request to the anonymous text of "Ulalume" in the American Whig Review.[12] Mrs. Whitman, ignorant of the authorship, had been praising the poem—when Poe very proudly announced that it was his. Mrs. W. then declared that he ought to sign the copy in the library, which he did casually on the spot. This anecdote floated about orally in Providence folklore for 60 years, though no one had even bothered to verify it. Then—in 1909, at the time of the Poe centenary—Dr. H. L. Koopman, head of the John Hay Library of Brown University, determined to track it down. Going through the old Athenaeum files, he found the issue of the review containing "Ulalume"—& there, surely enough, was the faint pencil signature "Edgar A. Poe" beneath the printed verses. Ever since then many visitors have asked to see the signature. I suppose you know that the last stanza of this early version was subsequently removed—at the excellent critical suggestion of Mrs. Whitman.

I think Brobst will like his new work very much. He is in a ward of very high-grade patients—largely A.M.'s & Ph.D.'s—including my own old high-school principal.[13] The medical staff is of very high repute—the superintendent, Dr. Ruggles, having a wide reputation as a psychological authority. The place & landscape setting are very pleasant.

I am glad you found my descriptive letter of interest. It was written in haste, & probably doesn't amount to much as to form; but the facts are probably reasonably accurate. Hope you can get around yourself during the coming summer, as Brobst said you might manage to do. Brobst's advent is a highly pleasant circumstance—for I find him as brilliant & delightful in person as his letters led me to expect. In time I think he will turn to writing—a field in which he ought to make considerable success.

Glad Derleth sent you *The Midland*. I rather liked "Old Ladies",[14] which is part of a loosely-strung Proustian reminiscence or quasi-novel to be called "Evening in Spring." I have read the other parts, & think the massed effect is really remarkable. Derleth has had no novel published as yet, but I believe he will make great progress in the future. He has all the solid groundwork of real literary substance & poignancy—though he is only 23.

Thanks very much for the Bechtel cuttings. Tragedies of this sort—with cabalistic wounds—are like fragments of fiction out of Machen or Blackwood. It really seems incredible that such dark phantasy can persist till the present day!

Yes—an old & not especially notable tale of mine—"In the Vault"—will appear in the next W.T. My best recent stuff has been rejected.[15]

It turned cold here Sunday, but I hope for early abatement.

With best wishes—

Yrs most sincerely,

H P L

P.S. Brobst & I are going to try to find some decently representative postcards of Providence to send you. It is provokingly hard to get anything really satisfactory.

Notes

1. The Roger Williams National Memorial Park at 150 North Main Street.

2. The Old State House (1762), 150 Benefit Street. Rhode Island declared its independence from England in the Providence Colony House two months before the Declaration of Independence.

3. The First Baptist Meeting House, 75 North Main Street.

4. On Market Square.

5. University Hall, "The College Edifice"—the original, and for fifty years the only, building at Brown University.

6. St. John's Episcopal Church (1810), 275 North Main Street. The churchyard is mentioned in "The Shunned House" (1924) and "The Messenger" (1929). It was there HPL wrote his Poe acrostic, "In a Sequester'd Providence Churchyard Where Once Poe Walked" (1936).

7. The Thomas Lloyd Halsey House (c. 1800, c. 1825), 140 Prospect Street; the home of Charles Dexter Ward in HPL's *The Case of Charles Dexter Ward*. See HPL to A. W. Derleth (10 December 1931): "In the 1850's this fine old brick house was actually feared by the ignorant." *Essential Solitude* 1.422n.

8. The John Reynolds House (c. 1785) at 88 Benefit Street. Sarah Helen Whitman (1803–1878) lived at the house when it was owned by Samuel

Hamlin, a Providence pewterer. HPL mentions Poe's romance with Mrs. Whitman in "The Shunned House."

9. Only the Golden Ball Inn Ell (1784 et seq.) stands today at 17–23 South Court Street. In HPL's time, the four-story Golden Ball Inn stood across from the State House (150 Benefit Street) and stable (160 Benefit Street). The main portion of the house was demolished in 1941.

10. The John Carter House (1772), 21 Meeting Street. William Goddard published the *Providence Gazette and Country-Journal* (est. 1762) in a shop marked by the sign of Shakespeare's Head on North Main Street. John Carter joined the paper in 1767 and by 1768 was sole proprietor. He and his wife moved the business into the house they built on Meeting Street.

11. 251 Benefit Street.

12. The journal was in fact the *American Review* for December 1847. On this matter see *Collected Works of Edgar Allan Poe*, ed. Thomas Ollive Mabbott (Cambridge, MA: Belknap Press of Harvard University Press, 1969), 1.413, 423. Cf. Will Murray's interview of Harry K. Brobst, *Lovecraft Studies* Nos. 22/23 (Fall 1990): 40–41.

13. Charles E. Dennis, Jr., principal of Hope Street High School.

14. August W. Derleth, "Old Ladies," *Midland*, 19, No. 1 (January–February 1932): 5–9. Rewritten and incorporated into *Evening in Spring* (New York: Charles Scribner's Sons, 1941) in the section "Take Arms!"

15. *WT*, April 1932. The story was previously rejected in October 1925, but was accepted upon later submittal by August Derleth.

[8]   [ALS]

Feby. 25, 1932

My dear Strauch:—

Glad to see that your book is out, & many thanks for the notice. I shall try to invest in a copy before long, when I can see a little more financial daylight. Hope it will have a good sale & receive some favourable reviews in important quarters. I suppose the publishers attend to the distribution of review copies.

By all means try to get around this way in the summer—for both the Providence & the Boston zones cannot fail to contain much of genuine interest to you. Possibly Brobst has told you of the quaint & spectral hidden churchyard down the hill not so very far from this house—a picturesque backwater which seems to have especially captivated his own imagination.[1] Unfortunately we could not get the postcards I spoke of—both places I had in mind having given up their sale. Rhode Island is very imperfectly covered by pictorial & guide material—a contrast to the well-exploited historic towns of Massachusetts.

Hope you can get to Baltimore to pay your respects at the tomb of Poe. I have seen it once,[2] & have been meaning to stop off & revisit it some time. It is now well marked & cared for in a corner of the yard of Westminster Presbyterian Church, though unfortunately the neighbourhood is now a slum. Providence is rich in Poe memories—the hidden churchyard mentioned above being a favourite haunt of the bard during his local sojourns.

Your southward travels must have been delightful, & I hope I can some day get a look at the regions involved. I have not seen much of Virginia west of the tidewater region & the main route south, though I once took an excursion from Washington to the Endless Caverns[3] near New Market, which gave me a brief glimpse of the Blue Ridge & Shenandoah Valley. I am anxious to see Charlottesville & the U. of Va. where Poe studied in 1828. I also wish to see your own state—both the weird & historic Lehigh Valley, & the wilder central portions you refer to. Incidentally—Rhode Island, small as it is, is so highly urbanised that much of the back country is left in total isolation. There are places where one might wander indefinitely without sight of a human habitation, & it is a mathematical fact that the state has the greatest proportion of woodland of any of the 48 commonwealths. Deer are increasingly numerous.

Sorry to hear that another witch-cult murder has occurred in Pennsylvania. That is certainly a high price to pay for the picturesque backwater traditionalism which makes such things possible! Probably a few more generations of compulsory education, radios, & the like will eradicate the more extreme phases of this phenomenon—though superstitions are certainly very persistent whenever a population remains rural. Even among urban populations such things are tenacious enough, as witness the almost incredible survival of occultism, astrology, & similar delusions in the most surprisingly informed & prosperous circles. Indeed, the very native credulity which keeps any sort of religion alive guarantees a certain amount of life to less orthodox & disciplined aspects of supernatural belief.

Cold days have been increasingly present of late—though at worst, spring is not far off now. Thanks again for the book list—&

renewed congratulations on the appearance of your volume. With best wishes—

Yrs most sincerely,

H P Lovecraft

Notes

1. St. John's Churchyard.

2. In July 1928; cf. "Observations on Several Parts of America" (1928) in *CE* 4.28–29. The travelogue is a letter to M. W. Moe.

3. See "A Descent to Avernus," *Bacon's Essays* (Summer 1929); *CE* 4.287–88, and *SL* 2.246.

[9]   [ALS]

[New Orleans]
June 7, 1932

My dear Strauch:—

Yrs. of 19th ult. was duly forwarded to me in the course of my annual travel outbreak, & I greatly appreciated hearing from you. I left home May 18th, & stopped a week in New York visiting Frank B. Long & seeing other members of the local crowd. Then—on the 25th—I hopped off for the journey proper. For the first time in my life I traversed the entire length of the Shenandoah Valley—Winchester—Staunton—Lexington—Roanoke—& was utterly enthralled by the beauty of the Blue Ridge landscape. Then came Knoxville, Tenn., & a ride across country to Chattanooga. Here once more I was reduced to breathless admiration; for the beauty of the Cumberlands—& of the river-bluff environs of Chattanooga in particular—surpassed every possible expectation. I ascended Lookout Mountain & revelled in the marvellous view of the outspread river, town, countryside, & hills—& also descended into the mountain's vast chain of caverns, including the great vaulted chamber (discovered 1930) wherein a 145-foot waterfall roars ceaselessly amidst eternal night. The ride from Chattanooga to Memphis (this whole trip is by 'bus) took me through a continuation of this mountainous wonderland—along what is locally known as the "Grand Cañon of the Tennessee." At Memphis I saw the lordly Mississippi for the first time, & was duly impressed. Then "down de ribber" through the flat delta cotton country, & finally up the bluffs of picturesque & historic

Vicksburg. Between there & Natchez I began to encounter signs of
the real far South—gnarled live-oaks with tangles of Spanish moss, &
similar forms of luxuriant vegetation. In general, I think the Natchez
country has the finest subtropical scenery I have ever beheld. It reminds one of the landscapes delineated in the "Atala" of Chateaubri-
and—who, indeed, once visited in Natchez.[1] The roads, owing to the
soft & friable nature of the local yellow clay, are all deeply sunken
below the level of the surrounding terrain; & present a weirdly impressive appearance with their high vertical walls overrun with vines
& the roots of ancient oaks & cypresses. These great trees, arching
overhead & draped with grotesque festoons of Spanish moss, keep
the scene shrouded in a perpetual green twilight.

Natchez itself is a stately old town where the past still lives—a
quiet backwater with but little physical change since the early 19th
century. Few places can be more fascinating to the historically-
minded. The settlement was founded by the French in 1716, as the
military & trading post of Fort Rosalie. Ruins of the fort still exist on
the high bluff. In 1729 the Natchez Indians massacred all the garrison,
but the post was regarrisoned & maintained. In 1763, by the treaty of
Paris, the whole region passed to Great Britain as part of the new
Providence of West-Florida, & Natchez became Fort Panmure. In
1779 the Spaniards then controlling Louisiana invaded the territory &
held it till 1798, when it was ceded to the U.S. Many houses of Spanish design attest the solid nature of this occupation. When the
Americans came, the great days of Natchez began. It was a logical
port for the abundant cotton of the newly-developed delta country,
& the rising Mississippi traffic made it a predestined commercial centre. It became, likewise, a town centre for the wealthy Louisiana
planters across the river. From about 1810 onward Natchez filled up
with stately mansion-houses of the pillared classic-revival type—
most of which remain to this day in every stage of preservation from
perfect maintenance to utter ruination. The town proper lies atop the
great bluff, while on the narrow shore strip at the foot of the 200-
foot precipice are the wharves—not quite deserted yet, since steam-
boats can still carry cotton more cheaply than railways can. Around
the wharves cluster the ancient brick houses of what is called
"Natchez-under-the-Hill"—once a roaring haunt of roystering sea-
men, but now a squalid abode of niggers, occasional mills, & desola-

tion. I spent two full days in Natchez, thoroughly absorbing its atmosphere & hating to leave it when the time came. Finally, however, I had to continue "down de ribber." Louisiana is flatter than the Mississippi bluff country, & the soil is grey instead of yellow. I did not pause at Baton Rouge, for this town—the La. state capital—has been disconcertingly modernised. South of there the ground falls to river level & below—giving me my first glimpse of the vast levee system. The great artificial bank slopes very gradually upward from the land level for a long distance, & then drops much less gradually to the river—or to some frequently inundated alluvial flat bordering on the river. It is all these titan embankments can do to control the caprices of Father Mississippi, & they frequently have to be relocated by means of giant steam shovels. The older ones are overgrown with grass & form an occasional pasturage for cattle. At one point there is a monstrous spillway under construction—to relieve pressure during extreme flood conditions like those in 1927.

At length New Orleans was reached—& after settling down at a modest hostelry I proceeded to explore the town & its environs. N.O. was founded in 1718 by the French-Canadian officer Jean-Baptiste Le Moyne, Sieur de Bienville, & was first peopled rather heterogeneously by the dupes of John Law's famous real-estate racket—the Mississippi Bubble.[2] In 1763 it was passed to Spain, though still remaining French in language & institutions. The great fire of 1788 destroyed nearly all of the old French town, but the area was at once rebuilt—very solidly, & in a predominantly Spanish style—with the aid of government engineers. It is this really Spanish town of arcaded, galleried brick houses with inner courtyards or patios which survives to this day, almost unchanged physically, as the "Vieux Carré" or "old French quarter. This quarter represents the original extent of the town as laid out by Bienville— & as fortified by Carondelet in 1794. It is now, of course, only a tiny speck in the spreading expanse of modern New Orleans—clinging tenaciously to its place at a bend in the river. In 1803 the city & province passed to the U.S., & the new American town grew up outside the walls of the older Latin city. Prosperity came, & little by little the Creoles & Americans fused; but still certain essential distinctions remained. French is still spoken in parts of New Orleans, & the modern Creoles build houses with curious affinities to certain of the ancient Creole types. Outside the Vieux Carré, the American city was very ambitiously laid out. Draining of the low land was accomplished by means of open canals in the middle of certain inordinately broad streets—& in later years these canals were roofed over one by one to form great boulevards with car tracks in the centre. Of these, the main business artery Canal St. is the most famous. Only one or two of the open canals still remain to hint at the original aspect of the American city. Commerce & prosperity tended, from the very first, to centre in the new town outside the ancient area, so that the latter—a parallelogram bounded on the north by Esplanade Ave., on the west by Rampart St., on the south by Canal St., & on the east by the river—had little reason to replace the bulk of its old Spanish buildings with their arches, patios, sidewalk arcades, & wrought-iron galleries. There they stand today as a living reminder of old times, together with a few still earlier buildings (such as the Ursuline Convent of 1734) which escaped the Great Fire. The cathedral of 1794, the old Spanish Cabildo or Government House of 1795, & other quaint edifices still look down on the sleepy old Place d'Armes—now called Jackson Square & boasting an equestrian statue of the intrepid old warrior. The whole "Vieux Carré" or ancient section is a perfectly preserved 18th or early 19th century city, vying for architectural honours with Charleston & Quebec. In its day it has been a slum, & it is now slightly touched with the Greenwich-Village atmosphere—studios & antique shops. For this reason it has not quite the utter charm of quaint Charleston & Quebec, which are still leading their simple old lives in unbroken organic continuity with the past. But for all that it's a great old place, & I'm certainly having the time of my life drinking in its archaic colour & getting set on my feet by its life-giving tropic warmth. My hotel is outside the Vieux Carré, but I spend each day in that centuried backwater—wandering through the narrow old streets with no modern impressions intruding upon me, & doing my reading & writing on a bench in old Jackson Square .... where the silver chimes of the old cathedral float on the air each quarter-hour. Of late years much tasteful restoration has taken place within the Vieux Carré, so that today even the old small lamp-posts have been put back—albeit with electric lights inside. The fantastic old *cemeteries* of N.O. deserve a word for themselves.

On account of the shallow soil all burials are above ground. The wealthy lie in fantastic tombs, while less opulent citizens are enclosed in oven-like vaults along the ten-foot-thick brick walls of the necropolis. Of all these grotesque ossuaries, the old St. Louis cemetery outside the Vieux Carré is undoubtedly the most interesting.

I'm here for over a week, & have seen the modern as well as the ancient city. I have also looked up such old plantation-houses as are near to (or overtaken by & imbedded in) the growing city. Of these country houses there are two general types—the older Creole sort with steep slant roof & dormers, & the early 19th century American type, massive in proportions & of pillared classic-revival architecture. Both of these types can also be found in & around Natchez. From here I shall go to Mobile, Ala., & after that my plans will depend upon finances. I have a *very faint* hope of getting to Charleston, which is still my favourite among towns. New Orleans is quite subtropical in vegetation, being well below the 30th parallel of latitude. The change from Natchez is noticeable; for whereas that town has only a few tiny scrub palmettos carefully nurtured in gardens, New Orleans is crowded with tall Washington Palms & opulent Brazilian date-palms.

But I can see from your epistle that spring in the North also has its idyllic aspects! I can well appreciate such days as you describe, & am always to be found outdoors upon them. The only trouble is that they are so few—& so interspersed with days of chill & raw wind. And our northern nights are always so shivery except in the very middle of summer. I have no real comfort in the north except from about the middle of June to the middle of August. It is tragic to waste so much of each year—but when one is attached to the landscape & architecture of his native region it is hard to break away permanently.

Yes—the love of green Nature—field & hedge, brook & wood—is certainly one of the typical attributes of the British race & its literature. I feel the ancestral impulse strongly, & am never under a roof in summer except when I have to be.

The "hex" story you mention sounds very interesting indeed, & I hope to be able to get hold of a copy sooner or later. It is easy to understand the difficulty in reproducing a regional dialect, when so much depends on inflection & intonation, but one can at least try to capture the grammatical idiom. I'd like to see that sinister "Hex-

enkopf" some day. Haunted mountains are right in my line! No—I
have never heard of the equivalent of an "Hexenbanner" in New
England. Our systematic belief in witchcraft hardly survived the 17th
century, & there was very little consistency or main-stream traditionalism in such furtive, feeble whispers as survived among the il-
literates of the back country. The great Salem upheaval of 1692
more or less purged the atmosphere of witchcraft-belief so far as we
were concerned. Moreover—Rhode Island in particular never had
any witchcraft beliefs except among the Indians & the negro slaves
on the King's County plantations. (We had the only northern
equivalent of the Southern plantation system, but the Revolution
ruined it) Our colony was, indeed, a sort of protest or reaction
against the macabre puritanism which (in common with superstitious popery) inclines the mind to such credences of the supernatural. It is for this reason that I can never feel anything really sinister
in Rhode Island's past, but am forced to go across the line into Massachusetts to find a site for any morbidly brooding fictional com-
munities of Arkham, Kingsport, Innsmouth, & so on.

Derleth is right in thinking that many of Brobst's ideas would go
splendidly in fictional form, & I surely wish that B. would work up
some of them as stories. As you are aware, however, he is reluctant to
try his hand at an art for which he has had no special preparation. I
agree that the "Hexenbanner" would form a fine & unhackneyed subject for weird tales. Probably you'll get around to this sort of thing in
the course of time—for after all, you know the country & its rich
folklore, & to an objective artist it doesn't matter very much whether
or not he feels personally identified with the background he depicts.
The main thing is to *know* it well. So far as that goes, I really feel very
little personal kinship with the sombre Massachusetts types I depict.
My paternal line is close to *Old* England by way of New York State,
& does not include the New England tradition at all. But I know the
country, & am perhaps all the more fascinated by it because a good
part of me is able to look upon it with an outsider's dispassionate eye.
Yes—I think Brobst's excursion into the outside world will prove a
good thing for his perspective, & I am very glad to note that he feels
himself very congenially placed in Providence & amidst his new & ar-
duous duties. If he ever wants to write, he surely has all the equip-
ment—the question now is to convince him that he wants to!

Glad you enjoyed your New York week-end. I suppose Allentown must wear sometimes on its own inhabitants—though a newcomer might like it very well. No—I've never read von Masoch's "Venus in Furs"[3]—which has done so much to enlarge the vocabulary of psychology. Neither have I perused the equally famous & nomenclaturally potent—though psychologically opposite—works of the late Marquis de Sade.[4]

Your woodland verses are very clever, & form quite a testimonial to your versatility & mastery of light forms. Hope the book is going over well. Here is a card describing the magazine I spoke of.[5] As you see, Derleth is among the contributors. I also enclose a poem by Loveman—one of the editors—which ought to appeal to you.

Best wishes—

Yrs most sincerely—

HPL

Notes

1. François-René de Chateaubriand (1768–1848), *Atala* (1801), a romance based in large part upon a visit that Chateaubriand had taken to wild and uninhabited regions of the American continent. Chateaubriand made use of the bluffs of Natchez, Miss., in his novel (see *SL* 4.41).

2. The Mississippi Bubble refers to the disastrous attempt by the Scotsman John Law to exploit the resources of French Canada. He established a trading company at New Biloxi, MS, in 1719, and aggressively promoted the company's stock, leading to wild speculation. The stock collapsed in December 1720, and many of the colonists of New Biloxi died.

3. Leopold von Sacher-Masoch (1835–1895), *Venus im Pelz* (1870); first Eng. tr. as *Venus in Furs* (1921). Cf. *SL* 3.108.

4. E.g. *Justine; ou, Les Malheurs de la vertu* (1791) by Donatien Alphonse François, marquis de Sade (1740–1814); first Eng. tr. as *Justine; or, The Misfortunes of Virtue* (1889). Cf. *SL* 3.106.

5. I.e., *Trend*.

[10]   [ALS]

10 Barnes St.,

Providence, R.I.,

Aug. 13, 1932

My dear Strauch:—

Your recent outing along the dry river-bed

sounds highly idyllic, & I am sure the attendant antics were no more absurd than any of mankind's accustomed releases for surplus energy. You are fortunate in having such a pleasant countryside within reach—& in having the taste to enjoy it.

I don't wonder that "Vathek" impressed you—or that you found the dark & sanguinary character more likeable than otherwise. Beckford certainly was a singular character—with his fantastic "Fonthill", his travels, his books, & his sundry eccentricities—& it is not the least of his caprices that he composed "Vathek" entirely in French—the existing version being a translation by the Rev. Samuel Henley.[1] As you are probably aware, Henley published the translation prematurely, causing Beckford to hurry out the original French text at once, omitting the extra episodes he had designed for insertion. These episodes, coming to light only in modern times, are to me well-nigh as fascinating as the book itself. Many members of our group have thought of preparing an ending for the unfinished third episode—& I really think that Clark Ashton Smith could do it justice.

I did indeed enjoy your poems—as did my recent guest James F. Morton, (about whom Brobst will tell you) who read some of them here. In time I trust you will assemble another collection. You have the genuine vision of the poet, & I am sure that time will bring you a more than local recognition.

The other day I felt rather pleased at receiving a letter from a Los Angeles composer—Harold Farnese, Asst. Director of the Inst of Musical Art & graduate of the Paris Conservatory (whose 1911 prize for composition he won)—asking permission to set two of my weird sonnets (which appeared in *Weird Tales*) to music.[2] Naturally, I promptly accorded the desired permission—& am now rather curious to see what he will do with my bizarre images. Another moderately pleasing occurrence is the appearance of an article in the July *American Author*—"What Makes a Story Click", by J. Randle Luten—in which the work of Clark Ashton Smith & myself is favourably cited & quoted in connexion with certain problems of narration.[3]

I have been to Newport several times on account of the reduced boat fares—& may go again today. At the end of the month I hope to get north of Boston (though not necessarily in the Maine belt of maximum duration) to see the total eclipse, & afterward I hope to take a cheap rail excursion to Montreal & Quebec. I have never seen Montreal, though Quebec is one of my favourite cities—without doubt the most beautiful city I have ever seen or ever will see unless I get across to Europe.

Brobst has been over twice since his return, & I was surely glad to see him again. He thinks he will be able to get an entire day off before long—on which occasion I'll be able to show him some scenic & antiquarian high spots he has not seen before. Hope you'll be able to get around this way before the summer is over. I can assure you that the region won't disappoint you.

With every good wish—

Yrs most cordially & sincerely—
H P L

Notes

1. William Beckford (1759–1844), *The History of the Caliph Vathek*, Printed Verbatim from the First Edition, with the Original Prefaces and Notes by Samuel Henley (1786; New York W. L. Allinson, [1868? or 188-?]; *LL* #74).

2. HPL gave Farnese permission to set "Mirage" and "The Elder Pharos" (*WT*, February/March 1931) to music. We know that Farnese wrote music for at least "The Elder Pharos" in 1932 (see *SL* 4, page of sheet music facing p. 159), but HPL never saw or heard the completed score for either poem.

3. J. Randle Luten, "What Makes a Story Click?" *American Author* 4, No. 4 (July 1932): 11–13.

[11]   [ALS]

Aug. 22[, 1932]

My dear Strauch:—

I'll *certainly* be back from my trip by Septr. 10, hence urge you to come to Providence if you possibly can. Brobst & I will be delighted to see you, & there are amply enough sights to keep you busy. Keep me posted on when to expect you. Wish I could offer hospitality, but as a mere congested roomer can do no better than steer you to modest lodgings. The Crown Hotel in Weybosset Street is good—& reasonable—& I'll also see if the landlady at my own joint has any space for an orderly & prepossessing transient. Will send a later bulletin on that point.

My own trip will begin a week from tomorrow, when I go to Boston to meet my friend W. Paul Cook. The ensuing day he & I will go to Newburyport or Portsmouth to see the total eclipse—probably stopping in Haverhill to add an 80-year-old friend to the party.[1] On Friday Septr. 2 I hope to entrain for Montreal—going thence to Quebec & being back in Boston on the 6th. Thus I'll be in Providence again well before the 10th.

Glad indeed that one of Muhlenburg's serious & devout youths[2] found pleasure in my frivolous tale of Cthulhu, as well as in other products of my less than pious pen! Glad also that you found the effort acceptable. Cthulhu isn't one of my worst stories, though it doesn't come up to my "Colour Out of Space" or "Erich Zann." By the way—the Hammett anthology containing the latter has just been republished in England.[3] It goes in for older & more standard work as a general thing, & has some exceedingly powerful items. Benson's "Negotium Perambulans" is great. By the way—if you liked "The White Powder" you ought to read all of Machen's "Three Impostors", of which this episode forms a part. I can lend it to you if local bibliothecae have it not.[4]

Glad you've had a good outdoor week. I've been keeping in the air pretty well myself—am there now, in fact, writing these lines on my favourite wooded river-bluff. Saturday I went to Newport again—to celebrate my 42nd birthday—& took the *entire* walk along the famous cliffs for the first time in my life. The remoter sections are really much more picturesque than the better-known stretches—offering magnificent vistas of seaward rocks & reefs. You ought to devote a day to Newport when you visit R.I. The sail down the bay alone is worth the price of the trip—& coming back there are delightful sunset vistas. Brobst hasn't taken this trip yet. I hope the boats won't have stopped running by the second week in September.

Well—I'll have to close, for golden sunset has turned to purple twilight. Today has been delightfully hot—weather after my own heart.

With best wishes, & hoping to see you in about three weeks, I remain

  Most cordially & sincerely yrs
  —H P L

[On envelope:] P.S. Donald Wandrei is now in N.Y. & will get around to Providence some time in September. ¶ I must get hold of the translation of that Perutz novel[5]—many have praised it to me.

Notes

1. Charles W. Smith (1852–1948), editor of the *Tryout*.

2. Muhlenberg College was associated with the Lutheran Church in America, Southeastern Pennsylvania, Slovak Zion, and Northeastern Pennsylvania Synods.

3. Dashiell Hammett (1894–1961), ed., *Modern Tales of Horror* (London: Victor Gollancz, 1932; *LL* #395); see n. 13.

4. Arthur Machen, *The Three Impostors* (1895; New York: Knopf, 1930; *LL* #578).

5. Leo Perutz (1884–1957), *Der Meister des jüngsten Tages* (1923); tr. as *The Master of the Day of Judgment*, tr. Hedwig Singer (London: Elkin Mathews & Marrot, 1929; New York: Charles Boni, 1930; *LL* #687). Cf. *SL* 4.91.

[12]   [ALS]

August 28[, 1932]

My dear Strauch:—

Good news! The landlady *can* give you a room at 10 Barnes, so come right up here when you strike town. If by any chance I'm not there when you arrive, just tell the landlady or servant that you're a friend of mine—& the room will be forthcoming. But I hope I *can* be at home—& I will be if you can let me know about what time to expect you. You can reach me until Thursday *c/o W. Paul Cook, 7 Hancock St., Boston, Mass.* if there's any eleventh-hour information to be delivered. But in any case I expect to be home again around the 8th. ¶ Now as to the way to get up here—in case you can't supply information which will enable me to reach your vehicle, be it train or motor-coach. You'll land either at the railway station or at one of the nearby 'bus terminals. Ask to have *Dorrance St.* (which in any case will be near at hand) pointed out to you, & walk along that (from the large square called EXCHANGE PLACE where it begins) toward the south. The first intersecting street (ask, if there's any doubt) is *Westminster St.*—the city's principal business thoroughfare. This is the corner where you wait for your car, which will come up Westminster from the east—or left hand side as you strike Westminster from Dorrance. Wait on the

northeast corner—in front of Pierce's Shoe Store or Gibson's soda &
candy place. Take any car with an oval or circular sign on the front
marked (T) or [TUNNEL] —the regular sign will say Hope St.,
Elmgrove Ave., Butler Ave., Rumford, or Phillipsdale. Ride through
the tunnel under the great hill, & get off at the first stop on the
other side—Thayer St. Pay as you leave the car—fare 8¢, or 7¢ if
you have 5 metal tokens for 35¢. Better buy the tokens, for you'll
probably have use for them during your visit. Ask, as you pay, for a
transfer to a *Brown St.* bus—which will be free, although other city
transfers cost 2¢. Wait for the 'bus where you get off the car—in
front of the Abbott Hall Coffee Shop. When you get the 'bus, ask
the driver to let you off at *Barnes St.* From this corner—Barnes &
Brown—walk along Barnes to the left (reckoned from the direction
in which you have been riding). #10 is the farther side of a large
brown double house—a fussy wooden affair in the worst taste of
the 1880's—about ¾ of a block from Brown, on the right hand side
of Barnes St. Keep this sheet of directions for reference—for all this
is too complicated to memorise. I'll certainly be delighted to see
you when you blow in! By the way—the house telephone is DExter
9617—in the name of the landlady—Miss Reynolds.[1]

   If for any reason you want to hunt up Brobst first, proceed to the
corner of Dorrance & Westminster as hereinbefore indicated, & take
a *Butler Ave.* car. In this case, you won't need to change to any 'bus—
just ride straight on beyond the tunnel for a considerable distance,
asking the operator to let you off at Butler Hospital—which as you
know is in Blackstone Boulevard. You'll recognise the great brick gate
when you alight. The hospital buildings are quite a distance within—
in the midst of extensive & beautiful grounds. Probably Brobst has
told you what building to inquire at—I don't know the right one.
N.B. Of course, you're not obliged to choose #10 as a stopping-place.
If you'd prefer to be downtown near restaurants, the Crown is an excellent place.

   I fancy you'll find enough hereabouts to keep all your available
days filled—& I wish you could spare a longer time. I greatly enjoy
showing off the scenic & antiquarian high spots of the town & its vi-
cinity, so you needn't feel that you're imposing on my time-schedule
in any way. Glad of the chance to air my accomplishments as a guide!
Hope you won't find my modest array of books disappointing. I don't

go in for rarities or first editions at all—contents alone determining my purchase of a book. It will be a pleasure to hear some of your new poems—though I'm afraid you'd find my newer tales (I've only written two in the last year) rather a poor recompense because of their great length & slow movement. By the way—if you like my article on Supernatural Horror in Literature I believe I can spare you a copy for permanent retention. I hope we can get down to Newport, & there are other quaint old Rhode Island towns that I wish you could see. It would be doubly pleasant if Donald Wandrei's visit could coincide with yours—but he can't be sure of dates as yet. I assume you have seen his work in Weird Tales.

Your recent reading programme is surely formidable enough. I read an excellent thing of Werfel's a few years ago—the play called "Goat-Song",[2] which was full of macabre tragedy. I thought you'd like the "Episodes of Vathek". The unfinished state of the third & final one is rather a tantalisation, & I am urging Clark Ashton Smith to use his great ingenuity & command of Oriental exoticism in preparing an appropriate ending. He could do it better than anyone else I know. Powys is undoubtedly an author of real importance, though I don't care much for him as a critic.[3] In Santayana I feel convinced that we have not only the *greatest* living philosopher, but perhaps the *only* living philosopher of the very first rank.[4] He cuts through fallacies which deceive & obscure almost everyone else.

By the way—I must give directions for the Crown Hotel in case you prefer to stop downtown near the restaurants. Go through Dorrance—or any parallel street such as Eddy, Union, or Mathewson—toward Westminster, & keep on *beyond* Westminster (past Middle St.) to *Weybosset Street*. The Crown is on the south (farther) side of Weybosset more than 2 blocks west of Dorrance—between Union & Mathewson. The following sketch of the downtown district may prove useful:

Well—now I'm off for Boston, the eclipse zone, Montreal, & Quebec! Send any last-moment news care of Cook, as previously stated. Hope to see you next week, & am sure that you, Brobst, & I will have some enjoyable sessions.

Best wishes—
Most cordially & sincerely—
H P L

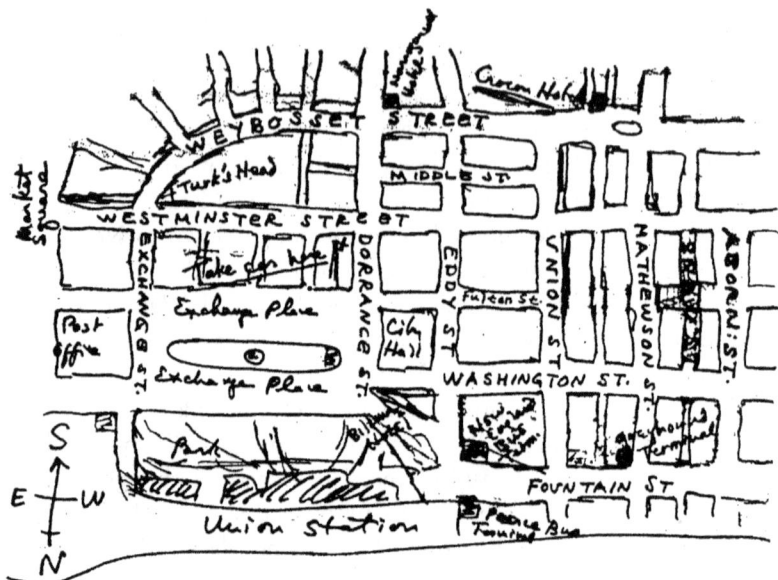

Notes

1. Florence F. Reynolds.

2. Franz Werfel (1890–1945), *Goat Song*, tr. Ruth Langner (Garden City, NY: Doubleday, Page & Co., 1926). A translation of *Bocksgesang* (1921).

3. John Cowper Powys (1872–1963), author of *Wolf Solent* (1929), a complex social novel set in Dorset. HPL owned his *One Hundred Best Books* (Haldeman-Julius, 1923).

4. George Santayana (1863–1950); cf. *SL* 5.312–15.

[13]   [ANS][1]

[Postmarked Boston,
1 September 1932]

Had a fine view of the total eclipse from Newburyport. We chose a high rural spot with a view, & saw the countryside bathed in spectral light. Then came darkness, the flaming corona, & the pale stars—& after an interval a weird, sinister dawning. Now for Montreal & Quebec—& home Septr. 7. Hope to see you on the 8th, & trust you received my letter of directions concerning Providence. Regards & best wishes

    H P L

I suppose you saw the eclipse as partial.

Notes

1. *Front:* Dr. Peter Toppan House, built 1697, Newburyport, Mass..

[14]   [ANS][1]

[Postmarked Montreal,
5 September 1932]

Greetings! Montreal is fascinating, though not as full of antiquarian material as Quebec. I start for Quebec tonight—& home Wednesday night. Hope to see you Thursday.
Regards
          —H P L

Notes

1. *Front:* Notre-Dame de Bonsecours Church, Montreal, Canada.

[15] [ANS][1]

[Postmark obliterated (probably Quebec),
c. 6–7 September 1932]

Here's the high spot at last! Utterly fascinating—I hate to go home! Hope to see you Thursday.
Regards—
          H P L

Notes

1. *Front:* St. Louis Gate, Quebec, Canada.

[16]   [ANS][1]

Saturday [17 September 1932]

My dear Strauch:—
                    Welcome home to Allentown! No doubt you received the joint card from Wandrei & me, in which my distinguished guest expressed regret at not meeting you. I've just been showing him the Harris Collection—where we dug up the work of two forgotten or semi-forgotten poets—Frederick Tuckerman (1813–71) & Park Barnitz[2]—the latter a vivid decadent of the fin de

siècle period who modelled his verse on Baudelaire & killed himself
soon after graduation from Harvard. Incidentally—here's a poetry
critique of mine,[3] issued by the Natl. Amateur Press Assn., which
may amuse you for a second. Keep it—I have many copies. Brobst
was to have been over last night, but didn't come. He was slightly
under the weather Thursday—a feverish touch—but I hope he's
better now. I've told him on a card of your impending letter—sorry
your finger is out of commission! ¶ Glad your Boston stay was so
enjoyable, but sorry you couldn't be in Providence longer. You must
get up this way again! ¶ We had a veritable flood here yesterday—
they are still pumping out the inundated cellars down town.

Best wishes—

H P L

Notes

1. *Front:* University Hall and Manning Hall, Brown University. The post-
card was neither stamped nor addressed, and thus must have been mailed
with the booklet mentioned below.

2. David Park Barnitz (1878–1901), author of *The Book of Jade* (New York:
Doxey's, At the Sign of the Lark [1901]). See *SL* 4.[66], 69. HPL had visited
the Harris Collection with Strauch during Strauch's visit in September,
where "perusal of *Mr. Muling* and *Suppose*" by HPL's revision client David
Van Bush "convuls'd both young Strauch and the librarian" (*SL* 4.69).

3. *Further Criticism of Poetry* (Louisville, KY: Printed on the Press of George
G. Fetter Co, 1932); ms. entitled "Notes on Verse Technique" (18 April
1932).

[17]   [ALS]

10 Barnes St.,
Providence, R.I.,
Novr. 3, 1932

My dear Strauch:—

I learn with the keenest interest of your progress
on the novel, & surely hope that the finished result may amply satisfy
your artistic sense. Deciding on the right proportioning must be a
gruelling task—but as you say, it helps to train your instinct in such
matters, so that each new effort will be at least slightly less exacting
than the preceding one. In course of time I hope to see your novel—

& I surely hope it may eventually land with a publisher, though this is
indubitably the worst publishing period in recent history.

Enclosed is Smith's "Vathek" ending[1]—together with the comment made by our friend Brobst upon it. I am inclined to think
Brobst is right in saying that Smith has not quite caught Beckford's
sweep of cosmic shadow—though the style & colouring are certainly reproduced with admirable fidelity. I hope that W.T. may accept this item—for printing, of course, in conjunction with the
earlier & Beckfordian part of the episode. So far Wright has not issued any decision. Read this at your leisure—& don't keep it to
yourself if you know of anyone else who would enjoy it. Smith likes
an appreciative audience, & often sends his MSS. on quite extensive
rounds. He would, incidentally, enjoy hearing from you if you like
the fragment. Address Box 385, Auburn, California.

Under separate cover I am sending—or will as soon as I can get
to the P.O.—a copy of The Recluse containing my article on Supernatural Horror in Literature. I have finally dug up three duplicates,
& if you find the thing of enduring interest I'd be pleased to have
you retain it for your personal library with my compliments. The
magazine was an amateur venture launched by W. Paul Cook—
whom you didn't get to see in Boston—& it never reached a second
issue. You'll find other items in it of interest—including verse &
prose by Wandrei, verse by Smith, &c. &c. My article was written 6
years ago, & today I see the need of revision in several respects. In
several minor matters I would be inclined to reproportion my opinions, & the style in general strikes me as excessively florid. Moreover, there are many weird things published since 1926 which I
would like to include.[2] As a treatise it doesn't amount to much, but
it at least forms a rudimentary catalogue of the high spots of weird
writing. In preparing it I did more steady reading than I have ever
done before or since!

As for current W.T.—I haven't seen the new issue myself, nor
have I read the preceding two. Pressure of revisory work has completely disorganised my programme this autumn. Also unread is the
new Strange Tales—the final issue,[3] since the house of Clayton has
decreed its discontinuance.

I'll remind Brobst of his epistolary delinquencies the next time
I'm in touch with him, but I imagine he is desperately busy. He

hasn't been over here for a month—& as you see, returned the "Vathek" ending by mail in the greatest of haste. Hope they're not overworking him, & that he'll have more leisure as the season advances. He had quite a touch of feverishness just after your visit— resulting from neglect of the athlete's foot trouble of which he then complained—but a little treatment & time off his feet cleared that up quite effectively in a very little while.

There has been a great deal of rain hereabouts, though sunny days have not been lacking. From what I have seen, the autumn foliage would appear to have been below par; but owing to my heavy work programme my opportunities for observation have been limited. Just now it is too cold for me to enjoy the outdoors—I merely dart from place to place when I have to. That trip to Salem & Marblehead which I think I wrote you about—Octr. 9—remains my last rural outing of the season. I even get down to the Waldorf less frequently than of yore—depending a good deal on cans & their contents for nourishment.

The other day I copied your sketches of anti-hex designs for barn gables in a letter to my friend Talman[4] of Spring Valley, N.Y., who is conducting quite a little research regarding some vaguely similar practices of his own Holland Dutch ancestors of the Hudson River region. In that region the so-called "witch ball" (also known in England & New England) was extensively used—this device being (as perhaps you know) a glass globe filled with vari-coloured threads & hung in the window. A witch, attempting to enter the house, would always pause & try to count the threads—& upon failing would grow discouraged & retreat. Or else she would be detained till dawn, in which case she would have to vanish anyhow. None of this superstition now survives, however.

Well—here's wishing you success with the novel. And I hope the long-awaited weird fiction article won't prove disappointing to you. Get around here when you can, & see if you can better your ice-cream record at Maxfield's![5]

Yr most obt & hble Servt—

H P L

Notes

1. "The Third Episode of Vathek," completed c. October 1932. *WT* did not

accept the story as HPL had hoped, and it was published by Robert H. Barlow in *Leaves* 1 (Summer 1937).

2. HPL kept a list entitled "Books to mention in new edition of weird article" in the notebook he called his *Commonplace Book*. Many items on the list were incorporated into HPL's revision of SHL for the *Fantasy Fan*.

3. January 1933. HPL owned all seven issues (*LL* #852).

4. Wilfred Blanche Talman (1904–1986), correspondent of HPL and late member of the Kalem Club.

5. Site (in Warren, RI) of HPL's famous ice-cream eating bout with James F. Morton and Donald Wandrei in July 1927 (*SL* 2.157), where presumably HPL took Strauch (probably with Harry Brobst) when Strauch visited in September Brobst recalls going there "several times" (*Lovecraft Studies* Nos. 22/23 [Fall 1990]: 25).

[18]   [ALS]

Tenbarnes—
Yuletide [25 December 1932].

My dear Strauch:—

Congratulations on the completion of the novel! I can imagine the feeling of pride & relief which must attend the sight of the typed pages. 288 sheets ought to mean a rather ample book, & I surely hope it may find a publisher without too many futile submissions. But of course this is the worst possible season for marketing anything, so you must not feel discouraged if the process proves long & difficult.

I have been too rushed to read any number of W.T. since August, but I did glance through "Alfred Kramer"[1] because Wandrei told me it represented a drastic revision of the MS. version I had previously seen. I thought it excellent—the climax is certainly devastating enough—though perhaps not as good as Wandrei's cosmic stories, such as "The Red Brain." Do you mean to say you haven't read the latter? Ædepol! That is a defect in your education which must be remedied! It is in the Dashiell Hammett anthology— "Creeps by Night"—which your local bibliotheca publica, even if not the bibliotheca universitatis, ought surely to contain. No— Wandrei isn't up to Derleth as a writer, although I think his best tales (so far all weird) excel A W's *weird* work. He is working very hard, however, & has lately experimented in non-weird prose— though I haven't yet seen the results of this experimentation. So far

Derleth has a startling lead on all the other members of "the gang". He has a genuine & communicable understanding of life as a whole which most of us seem to lack, & is building up a real standing in the world of midwestern letters. Last week a Chicago speaker conducting a radio broadcast on the younger authors of the midwest singled him out as the salient representative of prose, as George Dillon[2]—a Pulitzer Prize winner—is of poetry.

I haven't seen Summers' "Supernatural Omnibus",[3] though various correspondents have—all pronouncing it very mediocre. I must try to see a copy, if only for the sake of the introduction. Summers surely is a queer old cuss—a tremendously profound scholar in his way, but as naive & superstitious as any of your local "hex" believers. He believes literally in witches, ghosts, vampires, & the like, & is even subject to hallucinations in this direction—having flatly stated that he has *seen* a priest levitate himself several inches from the floor whilst performing some obscure sacerdotal rite. I'd like to get a set of his original works—studies in witchcraft, vampirism, &c. They would form marvellous source-books.

Glad you enjoyed Klarkash-Ton's continuation of "Vathek". I can see what you mean by the occasional let-downs, although I fancy these were not so much unconscious slips as unsuccessful attempts to capture a certain prosy hardness—a Gallic touch—inherent in Beckford's original French. He has read the original Histoire du Caliph Vathek—although he never saw the Episodes till I lent him my copy. As for the plot—as you say, one can't tell just what Beckford would have done with the story. One perhaps misses a sort of supernal terror which Beckford was usually able to infuse into his grotesque terrors—but at any rate the thing is better than any similar attempt of my own could possibly have been. Smith has certainly caught the essential psychological keynote of the suave 18th century eastern tale.

Trust you'll duly enjoy the holidays. Roman literature is surely a diversion worth following—& I'm confident that your choice of a graduate course is very well-advised. I myself have always been utterly fascinated by the civilisation of Rome—indeed, when I survey the ancient world, it is always from the standpoint of a Roman, as if the Imperium of the Tiber were naturally my country before the formation of a settled Anglo-Saxon world. In all historic events I have a sort of involuntary Roman patriotism—being emotionally on the side of Rome, right or wrong, & having an actual anger when people attack or belittle the land of Lucretius, Cicero, & Vergilius. I like to imagine, as a matter of fictitious genealogy, that I am descended through some obscure strain from the Roman invaders of Britain—some legatus in the army of C. Suetonius Paullinus or of Cn. Julius Agricola, or some civil functionary of later years at Eboracum, Isca Silurum, or Aquae Solis. If you choose to send some epistles in the ancient tongue I shall do my best to revive my earlier acquaintance with it—though you must not blame me if the forgetfulness of declining years gives to my replies a less than Ciceronian purity & idiomatic grace!

Sorry you found the last Friedell volume disappointing—but all authors tend to be one-sided. Writers of every different nation survey the field of human achievement from their own particular angle, & formulate lists of salient persons & events which seem grotesquely misproportioned except in the land of the writer himself. Thus in a Frenchman's list of the world's great men, books, & deeds we find dozens of entries which we scarcely recognise, & miss dozens of others whose right to a place we take for granted. And a Frenchman feels the same bewilderment when reading one of our lists. Actually, one is probably about as correct as the other. Only an historian of the year 3932—if there are any historians then, & if any trace of early human civilisations has survived—could have a perspective sufficiently detached to give a perfectly just appraisal of the subdivided fabric of Western civilisation ...... & even he might have his biasses, as I have in favour of Rome.

Some good public lectures at Brown Univ. this month. Heard J. B. S. Haldane on "Biology & Politics", & Walter G. Everett on Spinoza. This latter lecture was one of a monthly philosophic series like that which I attended last winter. Around these courses a new "R.I. Philos. Society" has grown up—which I may possibly join. ¶ With best wishes for the holidays & for 1933—

Yr most obt & hble Servt—

H P L

[On envelope:] Your yuletide card was greatly appreciated! ¶ And now, just as I mail this epistle, comes a quite unexpected hop to the decadent jungles of Manhattan! The parents of my friend Long have invited me down to surprise him with a week's sojourn—& since the 'bus fare is down to $2.00 again, I'm accepting. Thus I'll have two Christmas dinners—one with my aunt today, & another at the Longs' tomorrow—since they've chosen the Monday holiday for Yuletide festivities. If by any chance you should be able to get around to Manhattan during the coming week, look me up c/o Long, 230 W. 97th St.

Notes

1. "The Lives of Alfred Kramer" (*WT*, December 1932).

2. George Dillon (1906–1968), author of *Boy in the Wind* (1927) and *The Flowering Stone* (1931), the latter of which won the Pulitzer Prize for poetry. Dillon translated Baudelaire's *Fleurs du mal* with Edna St. Vincent Millay (1936).

3. Montague Summers (1880–1948), ed., *The Supernatural Omnibus* (London: Victor Gollancz, 1931; Garden City, NY: Doubleday, Doran & Co., 1932).

`[19]   [ALS]

230 W. 97th St.,
New York, N.Y.,
Dec. 31, 1932

My dear Strauch:—
        Delighted to hear from you! If by any chance I do stay over another week here, I'll certainly keep you posted & arrange to meet you—but I don't wish to presume on the hospitality of my hosts. It seems damnably tantalising to miss you by less than a week—& I'm missing James F. Morton (now out of town) by a *single day* unless I do decide to depart from my schedule. Whenever I am in the metropolis again I'll certainly let you know, & hope that such a season may coincide with some suitable excursion from Allentown. The coach fare from Providence to N.Y., by the way, is down to $2.00. Toward spring I hope you may be able to get to New England again—& I surely wish I did have the influence to secure you a joint headship of the Germanic & Latin departments at Brown! Sorry, by the way, that your last week-end was so gloomy as to call out all your reserves of Catonic & Senecan stoicism!

I mourn the mortality in your congenial piscine circle, & trust that all your suspicions against the squib may prove to be unfounded. It is perhaps well to remove the haunted castle, since such foci of Gothic mystery contain dark influences disquietingly beyond our computation.

About that musical business—there were two sonnets set to melody by Farnese; "Mirage" & "The Elder Pharos". Both appeared in Weird Tales,[1] but if you didn't see them I'll be glad to supply the text as soon as I'm back home. Farnese hasn't sent me the music yet—but I couldn't get it suitably played just now even if I had it.

Your own new sonnet is delightful, & I hope it may obtain publication in some medium worthy of it. Good luck with the "Epistle to the World". Heroics used to be my favourite measure, since I have always been a devotee of the 18th century. Congratulations on the bookplate—which certainly does sound interesting. If you have the main design you want, I'm sure my artistic friend (*Wilfred B. Talman, Scotland Post Road, Spring Valley, N.Y.*—the chap who knows the old Dutch legends I spoke of) could fix you up. Why not write him? I saw him yesterday in his office (Texas Co.) on the 18th floor of the Chrysler Bldg. Why don't you write him? It would surely do you no harm!

Have been making the rounds of the museums with Long & Wandrei—the latter of whom is still in town finishing his novel.[2] You ought to see him on your next visit—his address is 84 Horatio St., Apt. 4-B, in the northwest part of Greenwich Village not far from the Hudson waterfront. You ought to look up Long also—whether or not I'm still here.

The newly acquired Greek Apollo in the Metropolitan Museum is highly impressive. Today I intend to see Whistler's famous painting of his mother, now at the Museum of Modern Art. Weather so far has favoured me—temperatures being unusually high for this time of year. I shall see the old year out (good riddance to a depressing twelvemonth) at the home of my friend Samuel Loveman, whose long prose-poem "The Sphinx" is about to be published as a small book. I think I showed you his volume—"The Hermaphrodite"[3]—when you were in Providence.

Well—I hope some miracle *will* detain me in N.Y. till your visit!
I'll tell you if it does.

Best wishes—

Y^r most ob^t Servt
H P L

Notes

1. *WT*, February–March 1931.

2. *Invisible Sun* (ms., JHL; unpublished).

3. Samuel Loveman (1899–1976), *The Hermaphrodite: A Poem* (Athol,
Mass.: W. Paul Cook, 1926; *LL* #549).

[20]   [ALS]

Jany. 28, 1933.

My dear Strauch:—

The visit was surely enjoyable, though I was
sorry it could not coincide with your own brief Manhattan appearance. I've forgotten how much of it had occurred when I wrote
you—but may mention that I saw a fair number of the gang
(though Morton was out of town), did the museums, & indulged in
the usual endless arguments. Wandrei is still there, & I saw a good
deal of him. On Dec. 30 the group met at Belknap's, & I saw the old
year out at Samuel Loveman's new flat in Brooklyn—where for the
first time his museum treasures are adequately displayed. Loveman
gave me a prehistoric stone image from Mexico & a primitive African flint implement with engraved ivory handle for my own modest
collection. Regarding the museums—I saw among other new things
the archaic Greek Apollo at the Metropolitan, the two Dutch
rooms (Holland—circa 1650) at the Brooklyn, the modernistic horrors & shrieking attic frescoes at the Whitney, & the American
primitives (many of Penn. German origin) & Whistler portrait of his
mother (lent by the Louvre) at the now adequately housed Museum of Modern Art in W. 53d St. Also—not to neglect the phenomena of the mechanised present—I took my first ride (for
exploration—not because it was the best route to my destination!)
on the new 8th Ave. subway—which is the finest of the city's sys-
tems, though ill-patronised because of its lack of a really central

route downtown. I returned to Providence by night 'bus—as I came—thus having 8 full days in the metropolis. Since my return Long has had a sharp attack of influenza, & Talman (the Dutch antiquity enthusiast) has had a son & heir.

As for weather—this, like last, is certainly my kind of winter! No snow hereabouts, & one day this week the mercury was up to 60°! I fear it's too good to last—but meanwhile my complete hibernation continues to be postponed.

Glad you've had an interesting fight with Derleth, whose touch of ego makes him quite a piquant controversialist. His tastes are somewhat capricious, but seem in the main sound. I suppose he pitched into some of your 19th century predilections with his usual gusto. He has just sent me the carbon of his newly revised "Evening in Spring", which promises to be a remarkable piece of work before he is through with it.

As for Rascoe's "Titans of Literature"[1]—I haven't read it as yet, but have heard several opinions in both directions. Nobody seems to love Milton any more—but just the same, I'm not taking down the ancient bust of him which dominates the skyline of my room.[2] The majesty of some of his lines & images, & the sheer beauty of most of his shorter & lighter things, can scarcely be wiped out by an occasional adverse dictum. As for Dante—he is indubitably tedious as a whole, but there are imaginative conceptions & pictures in his stuff which can hardly be duplicated elsewhere. Of course, it is against these old fellows that they were saturated in conceptions & values now obsolete—but for all that they have enough poetic substance to float them irrespective of background.

It's hard to realise that Brobst's first hospital year is almost up. I believe that Boston will be his next post—the N.Y. arrangement having been abandoned by the arrangers of such matters.

I shall be interested to hear what you say concerning the dialect MS.—a highly valuable accession for your library, it would seem to me. My own modest library has had a few accessions lately—notably a 3-volume copy of the famous "Melmoth, the Wanderer", given me by W. Paul Cook.[3] I have wanted this book for ages, but had quite despaired of acquiring it. It is the reprint of 1892—since which (though it is long out of print) I believe no new edition has appeared. Another accession is the delectable phantasy "The Worm

Ouroboros", by E. R. Eddison,[4] which I picked up as a remainder for
79¢. Derleth has just swelled my catalogue by forwarding six weird
anthologies just discarded from his library.[5]

There have been several interesting lectures & poetry readings
hereabouts of late. Last Wednesday I heard Schopenhauer expatiated
upon, & tomorrow I shall hear Robert Hillyer read from his own poetry.

With best wishes—

Yrs most cordially & sincerely—
H P L

Notes

1. Burton Rascoe (1892–1957), *Titans of Literature from Homer to the Present* (New York: Putnam's, 1932). Also published as *The Story of the
World's Great Writers.*

2. Mentioned in "The Whisperer in Darkness" and seen in the photograph
of HPL's study at 66 College Street in *Marginalia* (facing p. 214).

3. Charles Robert Maturin (1782?–1824), *Melmoth the Wanderer* (1820;
London: Richard Bentley & Son, 1892; *LL* #599).

4. E. R. Eddison (1882–1945), *The Worm Ouroboros: A Romance*, illustrated
by Keith Henderson (New York: A. & C. Boni, 1926; *LL* #291).

5. Cf. *SL* 4.146–47, where only one—Bohun Lynch's *Best Ghost Stories*
(1924; *LL* #558)—is mentioned.

[21]   [ALS]

10 Barnes St.,
Providence, R.I.,
Feby. 11, 1933

My dear Strauch:—

Although I generally see very few modern prod-
ucts, I did happen to read "The Fountain"[1] a couple of months ago. I
liked it exceedingly, I believe it has the substance necessary for survival. In some ways it is perhaps heavy & overweighted with pure
philosophy—& its whole underlying attitude is one which exaggerates the importance of human emotions—but despite all objections it
has a sound vitality & abiding beauty which make it memorable. Derleth does not like it, but other correspondents of mine are almost incoherent with enthusiasm over it. Reviews—including comment by

the local literary columnist—seem uniformly favourable. I have not read "People Around the Corner."[2] As for your novel—you know best how much revision it needs. It would, indeed, be highly unusual if a first novel did not require some further polishing after the completion of the original draught. Long passages of poetic prose probably would be out of place—although of course prose-poetry is sometimes an asset when it contributes something essential to the central theme.

As for the Victorian period—I never could abide anything in it except its zeal for natural science. Faraday, Darwin, Huxley, Haeckel, Tyndall, Lubbock, Kelvin, Clerk Maxwell, Tylor, &c. &c.—those are its real ornaments. In architecture it was an insane nightmare. In painting it was tawdry & unimaginative. In poetry it was shallow & affected. In music—except for Wagner—it was saccharine & insipid. In fiction it was insincere, rambling, unlifelike, & unconvincing. In politics & sociology it was superficial & dependent upon false premises. Scientific progress is what redeems it. And yet I think the present age has many follies & shallownesses of its own, which to posterity will appear as absurd as those of the Victorian age do to us. I like the 18th century—in which I am more at home than in any other period. Like you, I detest the *attitude of revolt*, which seems to me to be antagonistic to the spirit of artistic creation. A civilisation may well eliminate, by gradual steps, elements which are either obviously untrue or obviously anti-social; but to discard or repudiate whole backgrounds of inherited moods & habits is culturally suicidal—for these backgrounds are all that give people the illusions of significance & direction in the cosmos, & all that make life worth plodding through for individuals of highly evolved mind & sensitiveness. To my mind there is nothing but destructiveness in the shrill, whining attitude of discontent held by aesthetes of the e. e. cummings, Waldo Frank, & John Dos Passos school—a school, alas, toward which more than one of my younger friends (including Long, whom I visited last month) seem to be inclined.

What you say of Charles More is interesting in the extreme—& the fact that he is still living adds zest to the matter. You really ought to look him up, for you might be instrumental in gaining for him a belated recognition both local & national. There is certainly a growing regard for regional folklore & literature in the United

States—an 11th hour reaction against standardisation—& amidst
such a movement the absolutely unique culture of the Pennsylvania
German area ought to fare very well indeed.

I read "The Golden Bough" years ago, & marvelled at the erudition of the venerable author.[3] He is a good example of the encyclopaedic & indefatigable scientific man of the Victorian age. This
work seems destined to remain as a permanent anthropological
landmark.

Your recent 'bus trip was undoubtedly more picturesque than
restful. Odd company is one of the penalties of cheap 'bus or excursion travel—but if one lacks cash & wants to get from place to
place, there is nothing to do but put up with it. My worst travel
experience—bar none—was the return trip of a cheap Quebec excursion in Sept. 1930. Most of the humble fellow-passengers had evidently sought the quaint old French fortress town for reasons less
antiquarian & more alcoholic than my own—& their plebeian revelry
& bottle-passing from Charny to the U.S. line was a memorable
study in coarseness. Thank heaven, most of the swine fell into a
drunken sleep in the stretches south of Newport, Vt. And yet, the
sight of Quebec was worth the penalty—so much so that I took an
equally cheap Montreal-Quebec excursion last summer, despite my
full expectation of a similar ordeal. Miraculously, I was spared such
an ordeal—for the denizens of the return train were comparatively
well-behaved. The clown of the journey (for every cheap excursion
seems to have its self-appointed buffoon)—a comical little Jew in
an American Legion uniform—was actually sober! ¶ Frightful cold
spell last week, but it broke Saturday. On the whole, the winter has
averaged very decent!

Best wishes—
                    Yr obt hble Servt—
                              H P L

Notes

1. Charles Morgan (1894–1958), *The Fountain* (New York: Knopf, 1932).
2. Thyra Samter Winslow, *People round the Corner* (New York: Knopf,
1927), a collection of short stories.
3. Sir James George Frazer (1854–1941), *The Golden Bough* (1890).

[22]   [ALS]

10 Barnes St.,
Providence, R.I.,
Feby. 24, 1933.

My dear Strauch:—

Thanks tremendously for the Muhlenburg views. The old Alma Mater surely does show up prepossessingly—& the scene of your bibliothecal labours stands out like a fragment of Dunsanian dream. I feel sure that the reality can't be *very* ugly! The landscaping seems to be extremely judicious—& I can well imagine the beauty of the grounds twenty years hence.

What you have added concerning Charles More interests me greatly, & I surely hope you may be able to bring him some of the recognition—both local & national—which he so amply deserves. I hope your library can arrange to get the hand-written MSS. typed before long, so that they may be ready for publication when some opportunity presents itself. Glad your article for the library journal[1] was accepted, & hope you can later plan something of the sort in one of the general magazines.

I read with extreme interest your remarks on the Victorian age, & certainly agree that your generation is more likely to view it with historical impartiality than that which was born during its own declining existence. At the same time I really don't think that my estimate is the product of hate & reaction; since I am not very prone to indignations, & am not at all animated by the hysterical anti-Puritan complex of the Dreisers, Andersons, & Waldo Franks. I think that in many ways the code of the 19th century involved more honour & good breeding than the code—if any—of the 20th. My own objections are quite abstract & impersonal, & based wholly on a love of truth for its own sake. I find the mood & institutions of the 19th century rather absurd & unsatisfying (rather than hateful) because they were so largely based on assumptions contrary to fact. The art of the period seems to me in so many instances curiously *irrelevant*—involving a whole system of values, emotions, & attributed motivations without any counterparts in the actual working fabric of society, & postulating a purposeful cosmos grotesquely at variance with what the eminent men of science were even then uncovering. There was a singular inability to appreciate the philosophic implications of the expanding conception of the universe & its phenomena. Mankind is just as stupid in one age as in another, but there are times when the discrepancy between its manifestations & reality is especially marked. It was not that the Victorian was *narrower* than the modern, but that the particular direction of his limited vision was (no doubt accidentally) farther from taste & reason than is the direction of the modern's equally limited vision. That is, the modern simply *happens* not to be quite so absurd (although he is in many ways absurd enough).

As for my inclusion of non-English culture-streams in an estimate of the middle 19th century—I cannot help thinking of all Western civilisation as to some extent a unit; though of course sharp local differences do occur, while some nations reach a given identical condition earlier or later than others. But there certainly was a vague homogeneity in the European world of 70 years ago—a common lack of decorative taste, a common background of sententious, romantic, & mediaevally-influenced bombast, & so on. Undeniably, however, the given characteristics appeared most emphatically in the Anglo-Saxon world.

I do not dissent when you point out the 19th century's *historical* importance as part of a modifying culture, or when you find interest in the picturesque figures which its naive individualism produced. I merely state that to me the aesthetic products of the period seem to have disconcertingly little vitality or convincingness. Plato & Emerson do not appeal to me, because I regard their feelings toward the cosmos as hopelessly coloured by conceptions of values & of existence whose whole source lies in myth & error. Matthew Arnold seems to me overrated except in rare poetic fragments like "Dover Beach". For Thackeray—in whom lingered much of the 18th century—I have some respect. Meredith, despite a grotesque moralism, seems at least sincere in his reaching for truth. Pater impresses me as accomplished but insignificant. Swinburne had real poetry at the start, but soon began merely repeating himself in diminishing echoes.

Probably most of the newer writers are inferior as artists to the greater Victorians, but their handicaps are so much lessened (except in the case of the slaves to chaotic theories) that they succeed in producing material much closer to life. They do not cripple their art at the outset by trying to conceal the purposeless, cosmically valueless, impersonal, largely deterministic, & man-dwarfing nature of the blind, automatic universe. Of course I exclude frivolous sur-face-skimmers like Arlen & van Vechten, & technical experiment-ers like Joyce & Cummings & Eliot, from the list of actually *producing* artists. Incidentally—I don't think that *any* defence of Victorian architecture, costume, & general decoration can be at-tempted seriously. The age was simply a lacuna—an hiatus. By the way—I heard a poetry reading by T. S. Eliot this week. Quite a boy—though I disagree with him in nearly all of his artistic theories. ¶ With all good wishes—& asking pardon for opinions which you will no doubt deem superficial—I remain

Yr most obt Servt—

H P L

Notes

1. Carl F. Strauch, "A Library Goes Regionalist," *Wilson Bulletin for Li-brarians* 8, No. 4 (December 1933): 213–15; see p. 114.

[23]   [ALS]

10 Barnes St.,

Providence, R.I.,

March 18, 1933

My dear Strauch:—

Your reading programme quite overawes me, insomuch as I cannot even begin to compete amidst the turmoil of tasks awaiting my attention. Last week I had to go to Hartford to assist on a job of research which a client was conducting at the li-brary there,[1] & meanwhile the accumulation of material here was appalling. Hartford, though an old city, has lost much of its antiqui-ties; hence is rather uninteresting as a whole—& especially in a raw, drizzling March rain. However, it has two ancient suburbs—Farmington & Wethersfield—which amply atone for its deficien-cies. Farmington—where I elected to stop in an ancient inn whose oldest portion dates back to 1638—is situate in a splendid rolling countryside & adorned with magnificent elms. A large proportion of its colonial houses still stand—including a finely preserved 1650 specimen with overhang—& the 1771 steepled church remains in perfect condition. Restrictions on real-estate have made for a great selectness of population & a refreshing preservation of the original quaint atmosphere. Wethersfield is also very quiet, select, & ancient, though of radically different aspect. It lies in level country, & the flat, elm-shaded village common is of singular breadth & spaciousness. The old houses are largely well-preserved 18th century mansions with the distinctive earmarks of Connecticut-Valley architecture, & one of them is duly tableted as the scene of the military conference (May 1781) at which Washington, Rochambeau, Knox, & Trumbull planned the future battle of Yorktown. The church—of brick, erected in 1764—was thought when built to be the finest in New England outside Boston. It has a fine steeple, but the windows have been ruined by Victorian alterations. When the French officers of Rochambeau passed through Wethersfield they remarked upon the magnificent view from the church belfry—a view which even now must be impressive, though I had no time to ascend & sample it. One of the great Wethersfield elms is today said to be the largest east of the Rocky Mountains.

Yes—the youthful Comte d'Erlette is correct in saying that another attempt of mine is to appear in W.T.[2] He, moreover, is wholly responsible for its appearance there. I had given up contributing in disgust, but had lent this tale to M. Auguste-Guillaume for copying purposes. By chance he mentioned it to Editor Wright, & the latter asked to see it. M. le Comte complied, & Satrap Pharnabazus decided that he wished to purchase it. I gave my consent, even though I'm not especially fond of the tale, since the $140 offer looked decidedly alluring to my impoverished purse. It will appear in the July issue—out June 1—& the $140 will probably come hither about a month later. No—there was no violation of confidence on M. d'Erlette's part. Indeed, that amiable & enterprising youth deserves my sincerest thanks for his part in the transaction!

Your prospectus for a magazine sounds highly alluring, & I shall have my prose-poems on the weather (including some of the most thunderous invective ever printed) in readiness as soon as the rest of the text is assembled. I look forward with particular pleasure to Mr. Whitaker's[3] enlightening article, having been delightfully familiar with his poetic perspective in the days when *Peg-ass'-us* (his own pronunciation, as revealed by prosodical employment!) was a member of the National Amateur Press Association. I presume that you will assign to Noah the task of creating new words in emulation of MM. Jolas et Joyce[4]—or possibly you'll divide that fascinating labour. I ought to succeed fairly well at that trade, in view of the scores of synthetic names I have invented for the mythical entities in my horror-tales. Am I not the sponsor of Cthulhu, Yog-Sothoth, Nug, Yeb, & dozens of other daemons? But even so, I run a poor second in that line to Clark Ashton Smith.

How unenterprising of the hexers to let a winter pass without a murder! Well—they still have 2 days in which to make good!

Best wishes—
            Yr most ob^t h^{ble} Servt—
            H P L

Notes

1. Cf. *SL* 4.159.

2. "The Dreams in the Witch House."

3. Noah F. Whitaker, editor of the amateur journal *Pegasus*, which in 1924 published some of HPL's poems.

4. Eugene Jolas (1894–1952), poet, critic, and editor of the avant-garde magazine *transition*, and James Joyce.

[24]   [ALS]

            note well—   66 College St.,
            I've got two 6's now!   Providence, R.I.,
                                          May 31, 1933

Dear Strauch:—
            Here's just a line to apprise you of my changed address. I think I told you that economic pressure was forcing me to double up with my surviving aunt in a low-rent flat—but I have yet to tell you of the marvellous bargain we found . . . . . a bargain which makes our move *down* look like a move *up*, & which at last—after 40 years—places me for the first time in a *real colonial house*.

You no doubt remember our visit to the marble John Hay Library with its Harris Collection of Poetry. At that time it is just possible that I pointed out to you a yellow colonial house behind the library—at the back of a rather quaint rustic court leading off from the steep slope of College St.—mentioning that a friend of my

aunt's lived in the lower half of it.[1] Well—I live in the upper half of
it now! My aunt's friend—a high-school teacher of German—had
long wanted her to move in above her if ever the flat should be vacant. On May 1st. it *did* become vacant, & my aunt was duly informed. We looked it over, found it would be ideal for both, & at
once clinched the bargain. You can imagine how I felt at the prospect of living in a real colonial home! Our respective quarters will
be wholly separate except for dining room &c—& yet the general
effect will be that of a complete & homogeneous home—my study
corresponding to the library & my aunt's living-room to the parlour.
She has not yet moved in, although I am wholly settled. The place
looks ineffably homelike with my belongings, & since I have 2
rooms of my own I don't have to crowd the furniture as I did at 10
Barnes. Arranging my books & files was a hellish job—I had to get 4
new cases & a cabinet for pamphlets—but it is done at last. Tomorrow my aunt moves in & completes the family circle.

   The house is a square wooden
edifice of the 1800 period—as
you may possibly remember. The
fine colonial doorway is like my
bookplate come to life, though of
a slightly later period with side
lights & fan carving instead of a
fanlight. In the rear is a picturesque, village-like garden at a
higher level than the front of the
house. The upper flat we have
taken contains 5 rooms besides

bath & kitchenette nook on the main (2nd) floor, plus 2 attic store-
rooms—one of which is so attractive that I wish I could have it for
an extra den! My quarters—a large study & a small adjoining bed-
room—are on the south side, with my working desk under a west
window affording a splendid view of the lower town's outspread
roofs & of the mystical sunsets that flame behind them. The interior
is as fascinating as the exterior—with colonial fireplaces, mantels, &
chimney cupboards, curving Georgian staircase, wide floor-boards,
old-fashioned latches, small-paned windows, six-panel doors, rear
wing with floor at a different level (3 steps down), quaint attic
stairs, &c.—just like the old houses open as museums. After admir-

ing such all my life, I find something magical & dreamlike in the experience of actually *living in one* . . . . . I keep half-expecting a museum guard to come around & kick me out at 5 o'clock closing time! And yet the whole thing costs only what I've been paying for one room & alcove at 10 Barnes. The house is owned by the university, & steam heat & hot water are piped in from the adjacent John Hay Library. Little did I think, when we were there last summer, that from that classic building would come my daily supply of caloric! Since I now have so much space, I have picked up a camp cot to enable me to accomodate an occasional guest. Thus the next time you're here—which I hope will be during the present summer—you need not worry about hotel bills. What lodging could be more appropriate for you than one next the Harris Collection of American Poetry? Brobst has seen the place twice—once before the moving & once since I've been settled. He agrees that it's a pretty homelike dump. Incidentally, he wants to know why he hasn't heard from you lately.

Derleth says that you may be heading for Sauk City before long. Hope you aren't going back on the historic east! A trip to Wisconsin, though, would certainly be delightful—I shall take one myself some day, since I have an unusual number of friends & correspondents in that state . . . . at least five that I'd want to call on.

Did I tell you that Clark Ashton Smith is issuing six of his unpublished stories as a booklet[2] at the modest price of 25¢? That will be an item worth getting—it can be obtained from him at Box 385, Auburn, California. And incidentally, my own "Shunned House" is about to appear at last as a small book. Cook found the unbound edition in good shape, & Walter J. Coates—the *Driftwind* editor—is going to bind & try to market it.[3] I wish him luck! By the way—did I mention in my last that my story "The Dreams in the Witch House" will appear in the *Weird Tales* out July 1st? Hope all goes well with your novel.

I shall not, I fear, be able to take any long Southern trip this year; but may get to New York early in July for the convention of the Natl. Am. Press Association. This moving has kept me from getting out to the country & enjoying the spring weather!

Best wishes—

Yr ob^t Servt—

H P L

[On envelope:] Pardon the envelope. Nobody's dead, but I found some of these in looking over my things & want to get rid of 'em!

Notes

1. The Samuel Mumford House (c. 1825), now standing at 65 Prospect. The downstairs tenant was Alice Sheppard.

2. *The Double Shadow and Other Fantasies* ([Auburn, CA]: The Auburn Journal, 1933; *LL* #810).

3. He never did so. See S. T. Joshi, "R. H. Barlow and the Recognition of H. P. Lovecraft," *Crypt of Cthulhu* No. 60 (Hallowmass 1988): 47.

[25]   [ALS]

Out in the Sunlit Woods—
June 5, 1933.

My dear Strauch:—

Et tu, Brute! Migration seems to be an epidemic, for you are the second person to respond to the news with a report of kindred activities. Congratulations on the quarters into which economy has precipitated you! The place sounds delightful— especially the garden glimpses & the arrangement of your lettered lair—& I trust you can hang on to it as long as possible. I enjoyed your chart very much, & will endeavour to reciprocate with two of my own —Plate A shewing the general plan of the flat, & Plate B illustrating my own individual 2-room layout.

Here is Plate A—the main or second floor. The attic has 2 rooms with low, sloping ceilings & flat windows high up. From each of these rooms little low doors open into a pitch-black, sinister space running around the eaves—just the kind of crypt to hide a nameless body or something of the sort. The small garden around the house is really delightful, & my aunt plans to train ivy up the front facade—she has a slip down from the original

ivy of Genl. Washington at Mt. Vernon. The more I see of the place the fonder I become of it. My aunt moved in last Tuesday, & by Saturday night her living-room was fairly settled. In many ways it eclipses my own rooms, since she has a more tasteful fireplace, & also many old family possessions (furniture, paintings, statuary) from the old home that excel my reliques. But I don't envy her, since the things I have are the things I need. But here is Plate B, shewing the arrangement of my personal quarters: (rotten proportioning—I ought to have had the rooms shorter from N. to S.)

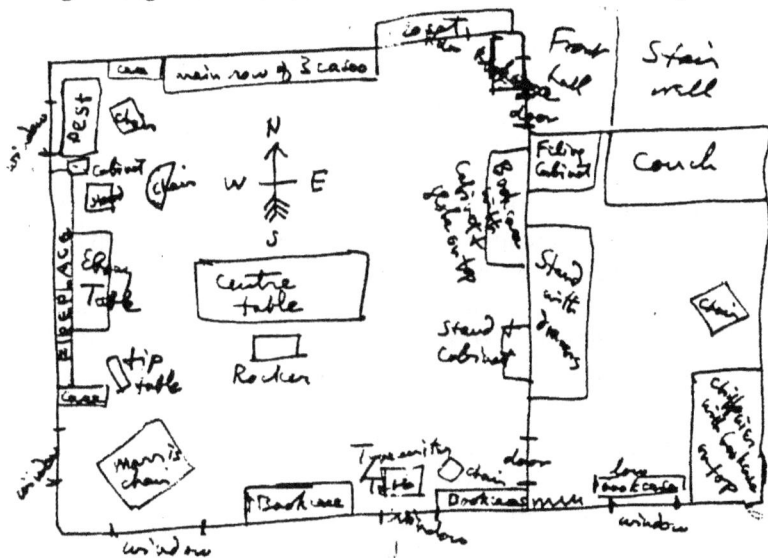

I have plenty of old candles, pictures, &c—you know the stuff at 10 Barnes—& they shew to much better advantage at #66. I have had two oil paintings framed, & they fit finely into the scheme. I certainly hope you can get around here next September—or whatever is the best time. Let me know ahead, & I'll be on hand! You'll find the place delectable, I'm sure . . . . even though my collection does not contain any gems comparable to those on your impressive list. The best items I have are a Greek version of the Necronomicon, a copy of the Book of Eibon bound in the tanned skin of an Atlantean emperor, & a copy of the original Düsseldorf edition of von Junzt's hideous *Unaussprechlichen Kulten*—unexpurgated, but with one page missing . . . . probably torn out by some horrified reader.[1] But of course there are many other interesting trifles—& you can also see the collection of my next-door neighbour John Hay!

I am certainly sorry that your job has gone glimmering, & hope
that something else will turn up before prospects get desperate. But
the enforced leisure really will be a boon for you literarily. Hawthorne owes the unhurried writing of "The Scarlet Letter" to the
fact that he lost his job at the Salem Custom House. Glad to hear
that the novel is coming along, & hope to see a specimen of it in the
course of time. Bring it along when you come hither.

Your local art theatre seems to be a genuine civic asset, & I am
glad that it is getting around to the recognition of regional folklore.
All over the country—from Vermont to Texas & California—there
seems to be a growing interest in local historic backgrounds which
gratifies me immensely. Hope your Charles More article will appear
soon, & that it will help in the movement to reëstablish dialect literature.

I wish I could accompany you on your Ephrata explorations. One
of the buildings there has always been known to me through descriptions & illustrations in works on colonial architecture, & I can well
imagine that a vast amount of bygone atmosphere must remain. The
whole Pennsylvania-German scene deserves more popular exploitation than it has yet received. It was an important & distinctive culture, & yet it is not commonly known to any such extent as that to
which the New-Netherland Dutch, Louisiana French, & Southwest-
ern Spanish cultures are known. Perhaps a new wave of interest is
about to dawn—I noticed last January that Pa. German work figured
largely in the folk-art exhibit at the N.Y. Museum of Modern Art.

Glad you've had a poem accepted .... & too bad *Wings* is
adopting such a flimsy standard. No—Parker hasn't discontinued
L'Alouette, but its issuance has always been highly irregular. Which
reminds me that I must tell P. of my new address—he has an adver-
tisement of my revisory service for his coming issue.[2]

You won't be disappointed in Klarkash-Ton's booklet. I'll later
get you a copy of my own "Shunned House", which is likely to be
bound & issued at last. Early in July Cook, Parker, & I may all attend
the N.Y. convention of the National Amateur Press Association—
seeing Long, Loveman, Wandrei, &c. I'll remember you to Brobst
when I see him—& trust you'll drop him a line. He will not go to
Boston till October.

¶ It's getting a bit cold & windy to write outdoors, so I guess I'll

move on & enjoy the scenery .... the sun being still goldenly radi-
ant. Fortunately I have a vest in my inevitable black bag. You must
see more of the Rhode Island countryside when you get here.

I've just been reading Derleth's two new novelettes "Nine Strands
in a Web" & "Place of Hawks".[3] Damn good stuff, although in the last-
named he introduces a disconcerting number of *coincidences*. He has
a rather chimerical theory about *coincidence* in life & art which is
likely to form a substantial literary handicap (though his work is
powerful enough to float in spite of it) if he doesn't get rid of it before long.

Fear I can't take any really long trips this year. This is the first
spring I have spent in the north since 1928, & I am reminded afresh
of the irritating tardiness of the season in these subarctic latitudes.

Well—best wishes, drop a line when you can, & try to get here
during the summer.

Yr oblig'd ob[t] Serv[t]—

H P L

Notes

1. The *Necronomicon* was, of course, a book of HPL's invention; the *Book of
Eibon* was created by Clark Ashton Smith and *Unaussprechlichen Kulten*
by Robert E. Howard. Here HPL pretends they are real, but in many letters he explained apologetically to inquirers they were not.

2. In the September 1924 issue of *L'Alouette* (ed. Charles A. A. Parker), published a joint ad by HPL and James F. Morton for revisory services; see *CE*
5.283. No doubt the ad referred to here is some amended version of this, as
HPL was no longer collaborating with Morton in such services.

3. The novelettes were published in Derleth's *Place of Hawks* (New York:
Loring & Mussey, 1935; *LL* #235).

[26]   [ALS]

66 College St.,

Providence, R.I.,

June 27, 1933

My dear Strauch:—

        I envy you your trip through rural Pennsyl-
vania, & hope that I can explore that region some day. While I don't
care for fishing, I certainly am an ardent devotee of landscapes & local colour—hence imagine that the Pocono region would prove a

rich field for me. Do you find many old-fashioned stone farm-houses? That solitary grave must indeed have been pathetic, & I hope to see your poem on it. No doubt you could unearth whole cycles of spectral folklore if diligent enough in listening to the hearthside grandams.

66 College St. has a chronicle of disaster to record. On June 14 my aunt broke her right ankle while descending the stairs in answer to the doorbell during my absence. Doctor . . . specialist . . . ambu-lance to R.I. Hospital . . . . X-ray . . . . setting in a plaster cast under ether . . . . room in Ward K . . . . . prospect of confinement to bed for six weeks & crutches for several more . . . . & a financial drain of cataclysmic & ruinous proportions! Naturally I have been kept dev-astatingly busy—completing the settlement of the house & visiting the hospital each day—& all my plans for travel have perforce been called off. Next week my aunt will probably be brought home—with a trained nurse in constant attendance. It certainly is, so to speak, a hell of a housewarming!

But my spring & summer have not been devoid of modest out-ings. On warm & pleasant days I have taken some of my typical long walks—among other things exploring a rural region which, despite comparative nearness to town, I had never seen before. It is north of the city & west of my favourite Lincoln Woods region—with at-mosphere & scenery of the most fascinating sort. Hills, woods, old stone walls, lakes, farmhouses, & several especially fine vistas. On other days I have walked southward—to Roger Williams Park, to old Fort Independence on the bay (with its striking view up & down the harbour), & to the quaint old fishing village of Pawtuxet. The average distance I cover in any one walk is about 12 miles.

You'll be sorry to hear that good old Mrs. Maxfield—proprietor of the Warren ice-cream emporium—died last month. However, the place is incorporated, & will carry on as usual. This reminds me—I'll bet you couldn't guess what I had for dinner last night! The answer is, an *entire* blueberry pie plus half a pint of ice cream. No more, no less! There is a new cheap pastry shop in a part of the town through which my southward walks take me, & the *10¢* pies in the window have for some time excited my curiosity. Last night I thought I'd try one—so got the ice cream to round the dinner out. Nor was I at all disappointed. Of course the pie was not large, nor did I expect first

quality. But it was genuinely palatable, & to all appearances whole-
some (no cramps or colic thus far). Good value for the money—I
think I'll patronise this joint again. That part of town—seedy & humble—has some good bargains in many lines if one knows where to
look for them.

Haven't seen Brobst lately—he must be uncommonly busy. He'll
certainly welcome your record-breaking epistle, & before summer is
over we must all sample the frigid produce of the Maxfield estate together. I expect W. Paul Cook here Saturday—on his way to the N.Y.
convention which I had expected to attend. E. Hoffmann Price (the
W.T. author whom I met in New Orleans last year) is also due here
soon.

Glad Comte d'Erlette sent you a photograph. Why can't you reciprocate with a good-looking portrait? Nature did her part, & cameras aren't hard to get. Incidentally, I wouldn't mind a shot of you
for my private Rogues' Gallery!

Enclosed is a circular of Smith's new brochure—a bargain I can
recommend. Great stuff!

Best wishes—

Yr most ob^t hble Servt—
H P L

[27]   [ALS]

66 College St.,
Providence, R.I.,
July 8, 1933

My dear Strauch:—

Knowing of the recent accident, you will be
prepared to pardon any laxity on my part as regards promptness,
critical comment, & the like. My aunt returned home last Wednesday with a trained nurse, & the arrangement is such as to keep me
tied up more than ever. I have to be on duty every afternoon while
the nurse is out, & on such occasions can do very little uninter-
rupted writing. However, the change is an advantageous one, for the
patient feels vastly better than at the hospital. She must remain in
bed 3 weeks or so more, & then can get about on crutches—
complete recovery not being expected till October. Thus you will
probably see her during the crutch period.

Hope your N Y trip proved pleasant—though you must have envied the friend so lately revelling beneath classic Grecian skies! As I feared, I couldn't get to the N.A.P.A. convention—but a highly congenial assemblage right here proved ample compensation. E. Hoffmann Price arrived on June 30 in his archaic Ford Juggernaut, & kept things enlivened for the better part of four days. Saturday afternoon W. Paul Cook stopped a few hours on his way to the N Y convention, though I could not persuade him to stay overnight. Brobst was over twice—partaking of the exotic East Indian curry which Price, in his infinite Oriental wisdom, ceremoniously prepared. On one occasion the three of us stayed up all night discussing literature & philosophy—& making a trip to the hidden hillside churchyard (which you doubtless remember) at 3 a.m.[1]

On Sunday Price brought the Juggernaut into the service of antiquarian exploration—taking me to a Rhode-Island region which, despite my lifelong residence less than 30 miles away from it, & my $1/3$ ancestral connexion with its ancient families, I had never (through lack of public transportation facilities) seen before. This was the historic "South County" or "Narragansett County" west of the bay, where before the Revolution there existed a system of large plantations & black slaves comparable to that of the South. The scenery of this territory is ineffably beautiful, as I had long known from reading, though some of the finest areas can be glimpsed from the main trunk highways. On this occasion we began with the marvellously unspoiled colonial seaport of Wickford, & worked southward through the magical land of yesterday. We saw the rambling old snuff-mill where Gilbert Stuart was born in 1755, & the vast Rowland Robinson mansion (1705) amidst its gigantic, centuried willows. The lone & deserted Ferry Church on a windswept headland claimed our notice, nor did we ignore the abandoned "Glebe" or rectory of the Rev[d] James MacSpadden (1727), now spectrally overgrown with a lush profusion of vines & briars. We climbed a hill to the well-known "Hannah Robinson's Rock" (around which revolves a pathetic story) & enjoyed what is probably the finest view in Rhode Island, if not in all New England—winding blue river, rich green meadows & woodlands, white headland church in the distance, & the far-off shimmer of the half-glimpsed sea. Great stuff! But the climax was the wholly unspoiled colonial village of Kingston—ancient county-seat of King's County, & virtually unchanged since men in knee-breeches & periwigs congregated there for the assizes. The well-kept, centuried houses, the gigantic shade-trees, the venerable court building, & the quaint 1746 inn all remain as of yore to fascinate the beholder. And to think I had never seen this gem of antiquity before! On our way back Price got a typical R.I. Shore Dinner at the ancient fishing village of Pawtuxet (6 m. S. of Prov.)—whilst I (whose loathing for sea-food you know) got something fit to eat at a Waldorf when we hit town.[2]

Wright turned down "Feigman's Beard"[3]—the Derleth tale based on Brobst's account. He would! And by the way—if you read any thing in the current W T, be on your guard against 2 bad & misleading misprints—"magical *love*" (should be LORE) on p. 92, & "*human* element" (should be KNOWN) on p. 107.[4]

Now about your story. It arrived during the "near-convention" here, & I brought it up toward the close of a spirited triangular session with both Price & Brobst on hand. Price read the text aloud, & critics were urged to interrupt with comments. I acted as secretary & set down all the opinions expressed. Most of the opinions came from Price himself—as you may see, since I am enclosing my secretarial records with the MS. Hope you can interpret the hastily jotted comment. The session had to break up before we could cover more than 9 or 10 pages (for every point raised brought with it numerous time-consuming side-issues), but in finishing the MS. alone I continued a series of comments which I will append. I hope you won't find the criticisms excessively drastic. Price is quite a carper, & brought up all sorts of minute matters (as you will see) which would never have occurred to me at all. However, I agree with many of his observations. Of course, he realised that this is a *first story*, hence did not mean his pointers to be taken as actual derogation.

As for a general personal estimate of my own—I think that there is damned good stuff in this story, & that with a few changes it ought to have a chance with Wright. The chief fault, perhaps, is a sort of *diffuseness* & excessive length, coupled with a jaunty, 1890-ish style of unmistakable artificiality. I know that this style has been used for weird stuff—Wilde's "Dorian Gray", some of Machen's things, &c.—but really think it is a handicap rather than an asset for this purpose.

It does not afford the dark *tenseness* necessary for a macabre theme. If I were you, I would first try to reduce the length of the whole tale by cutting down descriptions, reflections, conversations, whimsical character-touches, & suggestions of scholarship. Abandon the leisurely, conversational, clubroom tone, & let the tempo be feverish, brooding, & rapid. Better take Price's & Brobst's advice & make Hopkins less of a "pretty boy"—that kind of thing savours of Yellow-Book affectation. Also—be less minute in describing the seven old-time philosophers—except, of course, von Hohenloe. Purely as a concession to professional taboos, you'll have to soft-pedal all references to bestiality or anything suggesting abnormal eroticism. Cheap editors draw a rigid deadline against anything of the kind. Also—go over the phraseology closely, & delete anything peculiarly savouring of naiveté. Price & I have pointed out certain passages apparently needing attention. Also—as implied above—kill the touches of "smartness", paradox, & other incongruous elements suggesting the Wilde tradition. Be more *direct* & *simple*.

Analysing more closely—*compression & simplicity* are the things wanted. Make less of Meininglake unless you change the plot & use him as a sort of agent of the long-dead sorcerer. Toward the end be very careful about incidents & climax. The intrusion of Hohenloe's personality & body (oddly enough, a theme I've used in a tale never exhibited or even typed) must be managed with the most extreme care. I wouldn't have actual German over the telephone—be more subtle. When the major climax occurs—the transformation of the newly-shot body—there ought to be a greater impressiveness & intensity of style to register the stark, cataclysmic horror of the spectators—who are witnessing a violation of the basic laws of Nature as they know it.

Cut the post-climactic *explanations* as short as you can, for every word after the main punch tends to have a weakening effect. Try to make everything knit together with the utmost naturalness, closeness, & sense of inevitability. That is, let the motivation of everything seem so plausible as to admit of no question & cause no hesitation or perplexity on the reader's part. As it is, some of the threads seem a little loose or vague at the end. The matter of Meininglake's body & its return somehow carries a faint air of farfetchedness.

But don't take all this as a "panning." It's a good story—extremely good for a *first* one—& all it needs is a bit of simplification & tightening up. The style shews great power & gracefulness despite the possible inappropriateness of the tone. It is mature, cultivated work, & bespeaks a mastery of your medium which will work to the highest advantage when the problem of tone-choosing is thoroughly worked out. Why not send the text to Derleth (either as it is, or after revision) & let him pull it to pieces? He will probably be as savage in his candour (judging from the way he lit on young J. Vernon Shea's work), but will beyond doubt have many helpful suggestions to offer. You have all the makings of success in the story field if you'll stick to it, exercise care, profit by experience, & refuse to be daunted by the critical observations of competent & unprejudiced readers.

Thanks very much for the privilege of reading the MS. I honestly enjoyed it, & hope that it may achieve ultimate publication—either in its present form or after a suitable course of condensation, simplification, & general strengthening.

Yesterday & today have been delightfully warm—94° yesterday afternoon—but prior to that there was a cold spell which nearly froze me. However, I have got my oil heater repaired, & am now prepared to combat the leering frost-daemon. Work—interrupted by my aunt's illness & by the festivities incidental to Price's visit—is piling up at an alarming rate—but none of it promises any appreciable profit. If I can ever dispose of current obligations I hope to get at some stories of my own—but the date of that disposition seems constantly to recede. Latterly (on warm & pleasant days) I've been doing my writing on Prospect Terrace—that place I showed you (off Congdon St.) where there is a wide westward view of the lower town & of the bordering hills beyond.

Your bookbuying self-denial is surely commendable. Recently I found a bookshop with certain items priced at 2 *for 5¢*. For a single thin dime I procured 2 American histories, a copy of Bulwer-Lytton's "Coming Race",[5] & an edition of Smith's "Student's Gibbon"[6]—all in very fair condition! My new shelves will soon be sadly overtaxed!

Best wishes, & hope you'll find the enclosed critical remarks helpful—

Yr most ob^t h^ble Servt—

H P L

Notes

1. See E. Hoffmann Price, "The Man Who Was Lovecraft," in *Lovecraft Remembered*, ed. Peter Cannon (Sauk City, WI: Arkham House, 1998), 292–93.

2. Ibid., p. 284.

3. *WT*, November 1934.

4. HPL refers to errors in "The Dreams in the Witch House" (*WT*, July 1934).

5. Baron Edward George Earle Lytton (1803–1873), *The Coming Race; or, The New Utopia* (1871; *LL* #132).

6. Edward Gibbon (1738–1794), *The Student's Gibbon: The History of the Decline and Fall of the Roman Empire*. Abridged, incorporating the researches of recent commentators, by William Smith (New York: Harper & Brothers, 1864; *LL* #352).

[28]   [ALS]

66 College St.,
Providence, R.I.,
July 13, 1933

My dear Strauch:—

Glad the returned MS. & critical notes safely reached you—& that the ruthless carping of the Terrible Three did not seem too savage & sadistic after due digestion. I strongly advise you to let Comte d'Erlette see the MS.—although his type of comment may make you see red for a while. As I possibly mentioned—his critical candour seems to have scared off one youth who received a sample of it!

I shall be interested in seeing any later forms which the story may take. The locale is really of rather minor interest—that is, it does not matter much where the setting is, since the real punch is all in the *events* & antique background. However, if you had it in the Pa.-German region you ought to introduce some thread of continuity between the old philosophers & the present scene—some family legend from Germany handed down through successive generations. In later tales, of course, it would be a good idea to use Pa. folklore as a main theme & background. It seems to me that you have made a splendid beginning in fiction, & I have no doubt but that after a few experiments you will produce notable results. In the course of time—after you have applied all the finishing touches of revision that you wish—I hope to see your novel.

Glad the material from Klarkash-Ton duly arrived. "The Willow Landscape" surely is a delightful prose-poem. My own favourites in the brochure seem to be "The Maze of the Enchanter", "A Night in Malneant", & "The Double Shadow." I was interested in your reaction to Smith's very early "Star-Treader"[1]—which coincides with that of many readers. There certainly is a somewhat noticeable emphasis on the rhetorical element, & a devotion to long & bizarre words which mars the directness & simplicity necessary for utmost poignancy. If Smith has any conscious poetic model it is probably George Sterling, whose friend & protege he was. Sterling's "Wine of Wizardry" mood & manner really form the keynote of the poetic Klarkash-Ton. In our group, opinions on C A S's poetry differ amusingly. Wandrei exalts it to an almost amusing degree,[2] & Long is not far behind. Others have almost no use for it. I value it highly, though conceding certain obvious limitations. C A S would be delighted to see any poems of yours—as would I. I shall be awaiting that group including the "Epistle to the World."

No—I haven't seen the Frost magazine, though I have heard many glowingly favourable references to it. I'd certainly be grateful for a glimpse of the July number. These sheets vary greatly in their standards. I don't pretend to keep track of them, but the best I've seen lately is *The Carillon*. I'm sure that Parker couldn't possibly be offended by your comment. He is a rotten correspondent—indeed, I don't think I've heard from him since my visit nearly a year ago! Cook, though, carries news & greetings betwixt us. Parker tries to maintain a fairly decent standard of poetry, though not one of supreme rigorousness. His own taste has improved spectacularly since he first launched the magazine a decade ago.

Brobst was over the other day while I was out—I regretted missing him. I'll give him your greetings when I see him. Last week he was all agog for that record-breaking letter you promised! My aunt sat up yesterday for the first time, & will repeat the process each day. The cast, though, can't come off for a fortnight.

Hope the "Witch-House" won't disappoint you. In the same issue, "The Horror in the Museum"[3] is largely of my workmanship. Glad that others around your way like my stuff. Don't know when I can produce anything more, for my whole programme is shot to hell just now.

Cold weather lately—but my repaired oil stove helps matters. Long & his parents may stop here in a week or so on their way to Onset, Mass. And we shall be looking for you in September.

Regards—

                              H P L

Notes

1. *The Star-Treader and Other Poems* (San Francisco: A. M. Robertson, 1912; *LL* #814).

2. Donald Wandrei, "The Emperor of Dreams," *Overland Monthly* (December 1926); rpt. *Klarkash-Ton: The Journal of Smith Studies* No. 1 (1988): 3–8, 25.

3. By Hazel Heald.

[29]   [ANS][1]

                              [Postmarked Providence, R.I.,
                                        15 August 1933]

Glad to hear that all is well in the Lehigh Valley—as, indeed, a recent traveller thither has just reported. Too bad the good old Saint (in whom, I understand, the Great Powers of Muhlenburg implicitly believe) has been dragged into the black void by the emissaries of Tsathoggua! ¶ Glad you liked the W T stuff—has Contemplation been egging you on to the creation of similar material? ¶ Last week I had a letter from the Knopf outfit asking to see some of my stuff with a view to possible book publication. *Possible* is good! I shot along a few items[2]—though previous disillusionments have taught me how little such requests really mean. ¶ Hope to see you around these Plantations before autumn sets in. Have seen Brobst twice since his return. ¶ Blessings of Yog-Sothoth—H P L

Notes

1. *Front:* Betsy Williams Cottage, Roger Williams Park, Providence, R.I.

2. HPL submitted "The Picture in the House," "The Music of Erich Zann," "The Rats in the Walls," "The Strange High House in the Mist," "Pickman's Model," "The Colour out of Space," and "The Dunwich Horror" in his letter to Allan G. Ullman of Knopf dated 3 August 1933. With a subsequent letter (16 August) HPL submitted another eighteen stories.

Appendix: A Library Goes Regionalist[*]

Regionalism seems to be the order of the day. In its cruder political manifestations it is reduced to an absurdity: the Poles throw off Russian oppression, and the Ruthenians revolt against the Polish political and racial tyrannies. In the arts, however, it has in the past been responsible for much great work, and it is today a vital creative principle for many writers who feel that they need something closer, something warmer, something more real than a hollow megalopolitanism and an empty universality, which, by forfeiting a county for the world, loses the whole earth. Jean Sibelius, who had been writing music for over a quarter century without much embarrassing acclaim, has within the last two years received favorable notices here and abroad. His work has been identified with his Finnish background even more closely than Stravinsky's and Prokofieff's with their Russian sources. For critics have discovered in the Finn a true regionalist, an idiosyncratic, an artist who feels his land and his people. But Stravinsky and Prokofieff, by the infusion of a modernistic and sophisticated element in their works, have sacrificed the integrity of their music. In literature, regionalism has had its European exponents; Thomas Hardy, René Bazin, Gustav Frennsen, and hundreds of other writers, many of whom will never achieve even national fame, because they so closely identified themselves with their regions by writing in the patois.

In the United States regionalism as a conscious literary movement that possesses national significance has flourished only in the last decade. The Boston and the Concord groups were not regionalists; and whatever sectional literature we have had has either been the creation of isolated writers (Bret Harte in California and James W. Riley in Indiana), or has lacked greatness to make it of national importance. Today, however, young men and women do not flock

---

[*]By Carl F. Strauch, Formerly Assistant Librarian, Muhlenberg College, Allentown, Pa.

to New York so eagerly and in such numbers as they did in the lusty dayspring of Eugene O'Neill and Edna Millay; they stay at home and set up literary shop around the corner from the old cracker-barrel or the hitching post. Ernest Hemingway and Glenway Wescott, expatriates, were regionalists in their early work. Elizabeth Madox Roberts and Maristan Chapman are famous regionalists. Caroline Gordon has recently produced a fine regionalist novel, *Penhally;* and the group of Tennessee poets, of whom her husband, Allen Tate, is the most prominent, is a good example of that conscious literary movement we call Regionalism.

All this is by way of introduction to a tale of how one small college library has, by reason of its favorable location, come into a rich store of regional-dialect literature. Obviously, a college library that opens its portals on the clamor and the distraction of a great metropolis will in the first place have no incentive to make such collections and little occasion in the second.

The Pennsylvania-German Dialect

But regionalism is in the air; and Mulhenberg College is situated in a region, one of the really unique sections of these United States. The Pennsylvania-German countries of southeastern Pennsylvania have stubbornly resisted the Anglo-American influences which have elsewhere absorbed less tenacious cultures; and Allentown, the seat of Muhlenberg College, is near the very heart to these rich agricultural countries. Eastward lies Bethlehem, with its Moravian traditions and memories of the almost apocryphal Count Zinzendorf; southward lie Lancaster, York, and the famous cloisters of Ephrata; and southeast, on the main road to Philadelphia, dreams the beautiful suburb of Germantown. These Pennsylvania-German counties have kept the old cultural faiths. They are true to the old superstitions, charms and hexeree, the doctrinal vagaries and quiddities of the sects, Dunkards, Mennonites, Schwenkfelders, the Amish; and to this day Pennsylvania-German dialect holds its own with English in the larger towns and cities, and in the more remote agricultural sections is the preferred speech.

Naturally there has been a vast dialect literature in prose and verse over a whole century; and its historians have had a unique field of research and study. Among these has been Dr. Harry H. Reichard, whose *Pennsylvania-German Dialect Writings and their Writers* is an interesting and valuable study of more than thirty authors, of whom Charles C. More is a distinguished example. Dr. More, who has honored Mulhenberg College Library by making it the permanent depository of twenty-one manuscripts of his dialect writings, is an author whose works are distinguished by a conscious artistic purpose.

Charles C. More

Mr. More was born in Allentown in 1851. At the age of seventeen he went to Europe and studied in Berlin and taught German and French in Switzerland. In 1876 he returned to America, but the same year went back to Germany and was appointed clerk of the American legation at Berlin, then under Bayard Taylor. He remained ten years and became familiar with the dialect writings of Klaus Groth, Hermann Nadler, and Berthold Auerbach, whom he knew. More was inspired to use his own dialect as these authors had theirs; and it was with this inspiration that he returned to Allentown and wrote some remarkable dialect stories and verse. Some of them have been published here, a few in Stuttgart; and Dr. More has been honored for his literary labors by the Munich Academy of Arts and Sciences and received the attention of scholars here and abroad. "More has said," writes Dr. Reichard in a graceful peroration to his story of this dialect writer, "that dialect stories can be written which hold the mirror up to nature, and we need not stoop to vulgarisms to attract attention, for the dialect combines that much vaunted Irish wit with the good old homely German humor; we need only be imbued with an honest pride in our ancestry and their language, and then the dialect will live by its own momentum. More has done more than an ordinary man's share to make it live."

Only three of the twenty-one manuscripts which Dr. More has given to Mulhenberg are typewritten copies. The remaining eighteen are first, second, third, and sometimes fourth drafts and fair copies of his stories. They are all products of his best creative period, the first ten years of the century, altho only three are dated.

Because the Pennsylvania-German dialect is little known and almost never heard outside Pennsylvania I was at first persuaded, against my desire, to omit any specimen of More's dialect-writing. The temptation, however, is too great, for his stories, poems, and aphorisms are worthy of critical attention. Here is a three-stanza poem, which appears on page 176 of the typewritten ms. of "Die Lein Fens," one of his best long stories. It is a good sample of More's work, spontaneous and simple, and of the Pennsylvania-German dialect, which students of German will find an interesting variation:

> Wann die Gnospe widder schpriessen
> Un die Halme widder schiessen,
> Wann die Vejjel widder singe in de Beem,
> Wann die Blume widder bliehen
> Un die Droschel nardwaerts ziehen
> Nort is der Friehling widder do bei uns deheem.
>
> Wie frein sich dann de Leit!
> Deer un Fenschter schpaerre weit,
> Zum Willkomm far der Bot' vumm Himmels Zelt.
> "Griess Got du Blumme-Ritter!
> Mach's gut un komm ball widder!
> Uns bischt der liebschte Gascht in daere Welt!"
>
> Doch kommscht, oh Mensch, du haer,
> Du finnscht ken uff'ni Deer,
> Dir winkt ken freindlich Willkomm vum der Schwell--
> Die Sunn geht juscht so nidder--
> Du gescht un kommscht net widder,
> Oh, heemetloser Wandrer, faerriwell!

The aberrations from the classic German are quite obvious: "Gnospe" for "Knospe," "Vejjel" for "Vögel," "Beem" for "Bäume," "widder" for "wieder," "schpaerre" for "sperren," "liebschte Gascht" for "liebste Gast," and others. The last word in the poem, "faerriwell," is to be regarded as the Pennsylvania-German adoption of the English "farewell" rather than a dialect form of the high German "fahre wohl." One is tempted by the singing quality of the verses to try one's hand at translation; but the special loveliness of this poetry cannot be transmitted from language to language. Its fresh simplicity would become an embarrassing awkwardness and the poem itself seem naked of any beauty.

Of course, none of More's dialect writings has as yet contributed influence or color to our national literature. Like the ballads of the hill country of Kentucky and Tennessee, like the Indian chants of our great Southwest, like the cowboy songs of the vast plains, these writings have been distinguished by their intense preoccupation with the local scene--in this case Lehigh County, its simple and superstitious folk, the humor and the tenderness, the natural poetry.

Our library has in these writings valuable source-material for the writer who wants to saturate himself in the peculiar atmosphere of this Pennsylvania-German region. There are, of course, other such writers and collections of writings; but the Muhlenberg College Library collection of the Dr. Charles More mss. is unique, we believe, and will be of great interest to scholars and creative writers. It is besides the rare beginning of what should with the years become an important collection of the dialect literature of the region in which the college is situated.

Briefly Noted

The Intersection of Fantasy and Native America: From H. P. Lovecraft to Leslie Marmon Silko, edited by Amy H. Sturgis and David D. Oberhelman (Altadena, CA: Mythopoeic Press, 2009), contains a substantial article on Lovecraft by Marc A. Beherec, a former contributor to *Lovecraft Studies* and the *Lovecraft Annual*. The article, "The Racist and La Raza: H. P. Lovecraft's Aztec Mythos" (pp. 25–37), discusses Adolphe de Castro's "The Electric Executioner" and the Zealia Bishop stories for their treatment of Aztec myth, Hispanics, and related subjects.

The Construction of Race in the Early Poetry of H. P. Lovecraft

Phillip A. Ellis

I will not apologise for H. P. Lovecraft. He was, as many were and still are, a racist. Nor will I condemn him for being a racist. I accept it as part of his being, part that I abhor and oppose. Yet I am aware that Lovecraft uses his fiction and poetry to develop both images of race and his racism, and it is instructive to see how he does so. We can also learn from him the ways that he communicates those same images. In doing so, we can begin to understand that his methods, while not unique, are illustrative of those used by other racists. He is an example of how a racist thinks, how they create their mental image of race. And, as a result, this essay will look at how Lovecraft constructs race in his poetry, particularly his political poetry of the First World War. It will look at some of the strategies used to convey the poetry's messages about race, and it will look in greater detail at the language used to create patterns of reference to race. That there are clear patterns will be demonstrated. Also, some remarks derived from these will attempt to show how they can be used to observe how others wrote about race. We can learn from Lovecraft how to identify a potentially racist statement. In doing so, I will not act as an apologist for Lovecraft or his racism, but as one party interested in what I can derive from a neglected area of study in his oeuvre. To begin with, though, it is useful to examine briefly some of the strategies employed to construct Lovecraft's image of race.

Lovecraft uses various ways to create an image of race in his poetry. All of these are literary and linguistic: the choice of poetry as the medium determines the means employed. For the most part, these strategies are those commonly employed to denigrate and attack in print. Ridicule, satire, and other common strategies are employed. Some, though, are worthy of especial mention, such as Lovecraft's use of projection, invective, and sarcasm. Lovecraft clearly employs projection early in his poetic career. This is seen most clearly in the "Northern bigot" of *"De Triumpho Naturae"* (*AT* 13, l. 1). Though it is true that this is not a reference to race, it is associated with race. It is the bigot, that is, who frees the black slaves, thereby "condemning" them to their death. Another, later example, occurs in "Germania—1918," where Lovecraft complains of a German prince being "As rich in arrogance as poor in wits" (*AT* 418, l. 24), where his paucity of intelligent argument is matched equally by his arrogance at his own superiority of judgment.

A second strategy employed is the use of invective, common in the political poems. As one example, I need only refer back to that preceding "chinless Princeling [who] sits, / As rich in arrogance as poor in wits" ("Germania—1918," *AT* 418, ll. 23–24). This strategy seeks to use extremes of language to convey the particular construction of race that Lovecraft proposes to us. They use broad strokes, eschewing strict veracity and subtlety to construct what is, essentially, a caricature. These are figures seen not as individuals but types.

The third and final examined strategy that Lovecraft employs is sarcasm. Here, I need only quote an extended passage to help convey the means whereby he achieves this. Again from "Germania—1918," the passage runs:

> How can I sing, without Ovidian skill,
> The metamorphos'd Goth in time of ill?
> That sov'reign, who for nations lately sigh'd,
> Whines for his stricken land, and chokes his pride;
> No more he flings his challenge to the air,
> But begs th' indignant foe his race to spare;
> The injur'd peaceful monarch fain would know
> Why the cold world dislikes his people so! (*AT* 420, ll. 91–98)

I have particularly used this poem because it is an almost perfect example of the strategies used by Lovecraft to construct an image of a race, in this case the German one. He uses these three strategies, which have been briefly discussed, as well as others. Yet these strategies are not unique to the poems that construct race. They are present, in varying degrees, in other poems. What really determines the way that race is constructed is the language employed, and this, then, is where our attention shall be directed.

Lovecraft uses language in certain patterns to create the references that construct his poetic vision of race. There are a number of these, primarily references to certain concepts or ideals, that are usually loaded with a significant amount of emotion. He need not believe in these in order to employ them, as can be seen from the first such pattern of references. The ones initially examined here will invoke, in turn, God, law, and justice, civilisation, reason, honour, and nature. Others examined will deal with dehumanisation of other races, the concept of racial impurity, the inversion of the natural order, binary oppositions, especially that of elevation and debasement, colour, dialect and language, and other, miscellaneous rhetoric. By looking at the language we see most clearly how Lovecraft constructs race: he needs language, as the act of poetry is a linguistic act and art, reliant upon language to convey its meanings to us. That Lovecraft dealt hollowly with the sentiments thus conveyed is apparent from his invocation of God and holiness.

Although we know that, by the time that the bulk of the mature poetry had been written, Lovecraft was an atheist, this did not stop him from invoking God in his poetry, especially in relation to the construction of race. In doing so, he seeks to demonstrate that his positions regarding race are legitimate by an appeal to divinity. Anything, that is, that he does not approve is "Against God's will," as it were, to quote from one of his lines. The problem, here, is not that Lovecraft is an atheist, and, therefore his appeals are those to a perceived majority, but, rather, that these appeals are in regard to ethical and moral positions that are human, rather than known to be divine. It is easy to claim divine favour for a secular position, and, in this way, too often have evils been done under a "moral" banner. The first and most obvious example of Lovecraft's appeals to God is in the early *"De Triumpho Naturae."* Here, in line 10, he calls the Civil War "impious" (*AT* 14), and, later in the same poem, he remarks how "Against God's will the Yankee freed the slave" (*AT* 14, l. 23).

However, the bulk of the references to God are found in the later political poems. Here, the race in question is the German one, and the hollowness of Lovecraft's sentiments becomes almost glar-ingly obvious. For instance, Germany works "wonted evil" (*AT* 399, l. 4) in "The Crime of Crimes," invoking the concepts of good and evil that underpin Christian morality; not for nothing are the Ger-man armed forces referred to as "infernal hordes" (*AT* 400, l. 44). In this poem, the implicit equation of the Germans with devilish, "in-fernal" forces opposed to God is made. There is also, surprisingly, the equation of Germany with the serpent from Garden of Eden ("The Crime of Crimes," *AT* 400, ll. 47–60); what Lovecraft hoped to achieve with this is beyond my comprehension, save only the possibility that we are meant to "bruise" the German's head with our heel. We see also a further mention in relation to Germany, when we read of its "wild profanation" (*AT* 414, l. 19) in "Ad Bri-tannos—1918."

These citations show that the bulk of the invocations to the con-cept of God or holiness are negative examples. The race or races are considered evil, infernal, akin to demons or devils. There are more positive invocations to God, however. Yet these are as racist as the negative ones: they boost, that is, British racial supremacy. We read, for instance, that "thou, Britannia, art by heav'n endow'd / To spare the humble, and subdue the proud" ("1914," *AT* 397, ll. 27–28), which leads us to ask by whom is Britain thus endowed. The an-swer lies clearly elsewhere: "Heav'n's own pow'r is close ally'd / To Virtue's and Britannia's side" ("Britannia Victura," *AT* 406, l. 30). It is God, Heaven, that will ensure a British victory, won with Ameri-can aid (after all, one of Lovecraft's consistent concerns in this po-etry is the stimulus of American might to ally itself with London). In these ways, Lovecraft invokes the conceptions of God and holi-ness in his construction of race.

Related to that is the invocation of law and justice, as similar con-cepts that help define certain races in his poetry. The invocation of these elements in relation to race shows some interesting features. Like the invocation of God, there are both negative and positive ex-amples. One such negative example is the early couplet where Love-craft intones about how "The halls where Southern justice once had reign'd / He now with horrid negro rites profan'd" (*"De Triumpho Naturae,"* *AT* 14, ll. 13–14). This is a reference to the fact that, after receiving the vote following the Fourteenth Amendment to the U.S.

Constitution, the slaves elected black politicians to many of the state legislatures of the Southern states, and that, shortly afterwards, blacks were essentially barred from voting or holding office through "Jim Crow" laws.

Likewise, another negative example is in "Ye Ballade of Patrick von Flynn." Here, the Irish speaker states: "we've no use fer sober laws, but all fer fraydom shtand!" (*AT* 206, l. 12). This is negative, as it serves to define the Irish as lawbreakers, criminals in their association with the Germans. Another example, this time in "1914," is where Lovecraft speaks of the Germans in relation to the British that their "naked, murd'rous sword / Defies thy edict, and ignores thy word" (*AT* 397, ll. 5–6). What he assumes is that British law and authority have no place outside of British dominions. Again, he writes of the Germans that they, "like ancient vandals, seek / To wrong the guiltless and despoil the weak" ("1914," *AT* 397, ll. 11–12). Again there is a strong connotation of lawlessness, and disregard of the legal rights of others, in the construction of the German race. Elsewhere, Lovecraft asks "what laws can curb or sway / The Prussian wolf" ("The Crime of Crimes," *AT* 399, ll. 13–14), and Germany is also called a tyrant ("Ad Britannos—1918," *AT* 414, l. 41), and "unjust" ("1914," *AT* 397, l. 10). That these references all uniformly describe the relevant race in negative terms is clearly evident.

Yet, like the references to England, which we saw in the paragraph on the invocation of God, Lovecraft uses positive references for his most highly esteemed people. Great Britain, for example, has "true justice to dispense" ("1914," *AT* 398, l. 59). He also invokes the concept of "England's judgment as the final court" ("1914," *AT* 398, l. 66), and, more mythologically, notes that Justice "hail'd Britannia's reign" ("Britannia Victura," *AT* 405, l. 6). Indeed, he argues that Britain "was fashion'd for pow'r and dominion" ("Ad Britannos—1918," *AT* 414, l. 47), and that, as a result, he believes that other nations, such as Germany, must follow its lead. In these ways does Lovecraft invoke the conceptions of law and justice, in his construction of race.

Related to these two terms is a third one of importance, civilisation. Like the two earlier patterns of reference, to God and holiness, and to law and justice, most of the invocations of civilisation in the construction of race are negative. One common term is "savage." Lovecraft speaks of "The savage black" (*AT* 14, l. 19) in *"De Triumpho*

Naturae." He calls the Germans "savage" ("1914," *AT* 397, l. 10; "Ad Britannos—1918," *AT* 414, l. 39; "Germania—1918," *AT* 418, l. 11), and he speaks of "savage hordes in lands unknown" ("Britannia Victura," *AT* 405, l. 14). This language is especially rich when considering the Germans. He calls them by the names of barbarian tribes: "Goth" ("1914," *AT* 397–98, ll. 5, 36, 41; "To Greece, 1917," *AT* 409, l. 20; "Germania—1918," *AT* 419–20, ll. 47, 67, 92; "To Maj.-Gen. Omar Bundy, U.S.A.," *AT* 425, l. 51), "mad Goth" ("Germania—1918," *AT* 418, l. 3), "Hun" ("To Greece, 1917," *AT* 410, l. 37; "Ad Britannos—1918," *AT* 413, l. 17), "Teuton" ("To Greece, 1917," *AT* 410, l. 31), and "Vandal" ("Iterum Conjunctae," *AT* 406, l. 13; "To Greece, 1917," *AT* 409, l. 28). He says that the Germans "[play] the fuming brute" ("1914," *AT* 397, l. 7), and that they are "bold barbarians" ("1914," *AT* 397, l. 19). He even invokes the same word in relation to "barbarian Wilhelm" (*AT* 409, l. 12), in "To Greece, 1917."

Again, the positive references all point to the British. We read of them this grudging acceptance by the speaker of "Ye Ballade of Patrick von Flynn": "Sure all they iver done fer us was civilise our land" (*AT* 206, l. 11). And in another poem we read how the Greek, Roman, and Germanic races "in *one* race their virtues wrote" ("Britannia Victura," *AT* 405, l. 10; my emphasis)—that this race is British need not be made explicit.

Lovecraft also invokes reason and sanity. Unlike the preceding references, he here uses negative examples alone to construct race. There are only two references proper to reason, when we read "Oi'll slanther England all Oi dare, an' rayson niver hear" ("Ye Ballade of Patrick von Flynn," *AT* 207, l. 58), and "Insensate German! Blindly to oppose / A conqu'ring race that naught but vict'ry knows" ("1914," *AT* 398, ll. 47–48). But it is linked to questions of sanity, which, in the negative examples, could be considered a lack of reason itself. We read of "madden'd hordes" ("1914," *AT* 397, l. 11), and the "mad Goth" ("Germania—1918," *AT* 418, l. 3), for example. Likewise, we read of the "raging Prussian" ("1914," *AT* 398, l. 40). The German is also "Craz'd with the Belgian blood so lately shed" ("The Crime of Crimes," *AT* 398, l. 1), and this is linked to the phrase "Prussian madness" ("The Crime of Crimes," *AT* 400, l. 45). Finally, there is the interesting phrase with its consonance of the letter b, in "beserker and blind" ("Ad Britannos—1918," *AT* 414, l. 32). In all these instances of a

reference to sanity or, rather, the lack of it, Lovecraft specifically creates a uniformly negative image of race.

Lovecraft also does similarly by invoking the concept of honour.
He does so through both negative and positive references. Negatively, he uses the following in "Ye Ballade of Patrick von Flynn":
"At jooty's call we tache our sons sedition in the schools" (*AT* 206, l.
22). More famously, he speaks of how the gods "Fill'd it with vice"
("On the Creation of Niggers," *AT* 393, l. 8) when they created
blacks, and this poem, and reference, are arguably the nadir of
Lovecraft's poetic oeuvre. Germany, too, is called a "wretched cow-
ard" (*AT* 399, l. 3), in "The Crime of Crimes." In positive terms,
however, we read how the British "fight for Justice and Mankind"
("Britannia Victura," *AT* 405, l. 24), as opposed to the Germans, and,
presumably, the German allies. These constitute the bulk of the
references to honour; by invoking this abstract concept, Lovecraft
continues the invocation of civilisation, by referring to a prime
quality of civilised life, as well as to God and holiness, by looking at
a specific religious virtue.

What follows is the final pattern invoked, nature, which is related
through alterity to the concept of civilisation. This invocation tellingly occurs in *"De Triumpho Naturae,"* and it occurs in relation to
the invocation of God. Lovecraft, that is, combines both with his line
"deaf to Nature, and to God's decree" (*AT* 14, l. 11), which suggests
that the two, if not identical, are certainly in close concord with the
other. Indeed, Lovecraft later invokes this "will of Nature" (*AT* 14, l.
18): it is nothing less than the death of all blacks outside slavery. For
Lovecraft, who was to believe in a purposeless, aimless cosmos, such
an invocation to nature must read as among the hollowest of sentiments he was to produce in his poetry. It is, in short, ugly.

This brings us to one major strategy of Lovecraft's rhetoric about
race: the dehumanisation of his fellows. By dehumanisation I mean
something both more and akin to demonisation. Indeed, we have
seen that demonisation in the invocation of God and holiness, in the
mention of "infernal hordes." By dehumanisation, a more general
method is employed that equates the human and natural with the
animal and unnatural. This occurs early on: in "On the Creation of
Niggers" we read how "A beast they [the gods] wrought" (*AT* 393, l.
7). This reminds us of the later "rav'ning beast" (*AT* 418, l. 6) and

"gen'rous beast" (*AT* 420, l. 103) of "Germania—1918." We read, too, of how Germany is called a "snake that spreads his writhing, pois'nous coils" ("The Crime of Crimes," *AT* 400, l. 49). A more common reference is "wolf," in "The Prussian wolf, with manhood cast away" ("The Crime of Crimes," *AT* 399, l. 14), and "German wolf" ("Germania—1918," *AT* 418, l. 19); there are also the more general "wolf" ("Germania—1918," *AT* 421, l. 129) and "rabid wolves" ("The Crime of Crimes," *AT* 399, l. 41). That reference to "Prussian wolf," by the way, is a telling one for the concept of dehumanisation of certain races. Related to the "wolf" imagery is the following line, again telling: "Like slinking cur, he bites" ("The Crime of Crimes," *AT* 399, l. 5).

Another form of animal that is a favourite with Lovecraft is the monkey or ape. He speaks of "the ape-resembling beast" (*AT* 14, l. 19) in *"De Triumpho Naturae,"* and of the "Afric ape" ("The Isaacsonio-Mortoniad," *AT* 209, l. 41), in particular. He also mentions, of miscellaneous foreigners, how they "Live their low lives, themselves in filth degrade / As monkeys haunt a palace long decay'd" ("New-England Fallen," *AT* 391, ll. 105–6). In more general terms, the word "bestial" is commonly used. We read the following phrases, for example: "bestial Prussian" ("The Crime of Crimes," *AT* 398, l. 2), "bestial presence" ("Germania—1918," *AT* 419, l. 31), and of Germany's "bestial cohorts" ("To Greece, 1917," *AT* 410, l. 37). Related is a single reference to the German "brutish horde" ("Germania—1918," *AT* 420, l. 68), which invokes both reason, as earlier, and the image of the Germans as dumb animals.

These are not the only forms of dehumanisation. When we read that the gods "call'd the thing a NIGGER" (*AT* 393, l. 8) in "On the Creation of Niggers," we find that their creation is a "thing," and not a person. Likewise we find a cognate reference in "New-England Fallen": "A vicious crew, that mock the name of 'man'" (*AT* 392, l. 119). Again, they become other than human in this reference. The other major form of dehumanisation, though, other than the equation of race with the animal, is with the monstrous. This reminds us of the earlier invocation with God; indeed, the reference to both "fiend" ("Ad Britannos—1918," *AT* 414, l. 39) and "fiends" ("Germania—1918," *AT* 419, l. 34) can be read as a form of that demonisation as well. Lovecraft speaks of the "monstrous menace of the Vandal

curse" ("To Greece, 1917," *AT* 409, l. 28), and of German "monsters"
("Ad Britannos—1918," *AT* 414, l. 37). He also invokes, tellingly, the
image of "the crawling Hydra of the North" (*AT* 410, l. 68), in "To
Greece, 1917." Overall, this pattern of references to a dehumanised
race helps create a sense of race as the other—other, that is, to the
human and the Anglo-Saxon of Lovecraft's imagination.

Related, in a way, to this dehumanisation is the concept of racial
impurity, to which we now turn. Racial impurity, and the dangers
of racial impurity, are not uncommon themes in Lovecraft's work
and letters. Racial impurity itself is associated with the construction
of race in the poetry, in particular. We find that the phrase "sink the
white man in a mongrel line" ("The Isaacsonio-Mortoniad," *AT* 209,
l. 42) brings forward the use of language; here, "mongrel" associates
the mixed races with curs, dogs of impure breeding. The word is
used elsewhere. We read of "mongrel Villa" ("To General Villa," *AT*
394, l. 12), and of "mongrel slaves" ("An American to Mother England," *AT* 400, l. 17) in other poems, for example. There is another,
curious reference to racial impurity. With the phrase "negro Bravas"
("Providence in 2000 A.D.," *AT* 191, l. 20), we have an association of
blacks specifically with mixed races. It is as if the latter drag themselves down to the former's level by virtue of their "innate" impurity and degeneration. This reading is reinforced by the superlatively
negative connotations of the infamous "You're three-quarters Injun,
and tainted with nigger" ("To General Villa," *AT* 394, l. 6). This reminds us that there is a principle of alterity in the treatment of race
by Lovecraft, one with an associated binary construction: pure
whites and impure others.

This leads us to consider other forms of binary construction, especially those of elevation and debasement. Usually, with Lovecraft,
we only see one aspect of the binary oppositions that he creates in
relation to the construction of race. His "My name is Smith, I'm an
American!" (*AT* 192, l. 70) in "Providence in 2000 A.D." leads us to
consider the other, non-Anglophonic races as, by extension, non-
American, "foreign." His phrase "freaks of alien blood" ("New-
England Fallen," *AT* 390, l. 70) allows us to see that he regarded
white Anglo-Saxon Americans and British as the norm, and as "natural." We read also in the phrase "alien serfs" ("On a New-England
Village Seen by Moonlight," *AT* 393, l. 9) another complex of binary

constructions; by contrast, the whites are "native" yeomen, stolid middle-class farmers rather than dubious peasants. This leads into a consideration of the binary opposition of elevation and debasement: yeomen, after all, are higher socially than mere "serfs." We read, then, of "base foreign boors" ("New-England Fallen," *AT* 391, l. 103), with its denigration of the non-English to the lower strata of society, both economically and intellectually. We read, likewise, the phrases "rabble" (*AT* 393, l. 4) and "sordid crew" (*AT* 394, l. 19) in "On a New-England Village Seen by Moonlight." The lines "mongrel slaves crawl hither to partake / Of Saxon liberty they could not make" (*AT* 400, ll. 16–17) of "An American to Mother England" may be hard to digest, but they testify to Lovecraft's belief that liberty is only commensurate with Anglo-Saxon values. The position of England, for example, is amply illustrated by a single reference to it as "Queen of Nations" (*AT* 397, l. 9) in "1914."

These serve as examples of how Lovecraft uses the binary oppositions while constructing race in his poetry. One other way he does so is his references to colour, particularly to blacks. There are two main ways that Lovecraft refers to a race's colour, and each is illustrated by a couple of clear examples. First, he uses what are now the denigrative words "negro" or "nigger." We have already seen the reference to "negro Bravas" ("Providence in 2000 A.D.," *AT* 191, l. 20). We also read of "negro lore" (*AT* 209, l. 45) in "The Isaacsonio-Mortoniad." The other term he uses is "swarthy." He talks of "swarthy men" ("Providence in 2000 A.D.," *AT* 192, l. 44) and of "swarthy sailors" ("New-England Fallen," *AT* 390, l. 70) in a couple of his poems, and this term is employed only for foreigners, non-whites. He has referred to "whites" in the line "sink the white man in a mongrel line" that we read earlier, but the main and telling references are to the non-whites.

This leads us to consider the role of dialect and language in the poetry. Language and dialect, in the construction of race, appears in the poetry of H. P. Lovecraft. The most obvious example is "Ye Ballade of Patrick von Flynn" (*AT* 206–7), which is written in a stereotypical Irish dialect. Part of its humour is derived from the intermingling of Irish and Germans, to the point that the languages become confused. There is another reference to language. Where we read of "a city fill'd with foreign cries" ("Providence in 2000

A.D.," *AT* 191, l. 14), we can only realise that the "cries" are foreign to both the speaker and to the city itself. This reminds us of the "ribald foreign cries" (*AT* 392, l. 117) of "New-England Fallen," which ties together the foreignness as expressed in the language, and the lack of proper morals. Importantly, it must be remembered that language itself is the medium of the poems themselves. In a sense, by reverting to an archaic and dead diction for his poetry, Lovecraft is denying the degree to which non-English elements had been assimilated into, and had changed, the English language of his contemporary world. That he failed, in essence, should be no surprise. Lovecraft was a creature of his times, and incapable of living that imaginative revolt against time and his circumstances that he was attempting with his archaic verse.

This leads us to consider some final, miscellaneous considerations, before attempting a summation about the construction of race in Lovecraft's poetry. There are other examples of Lovecraft's rhetoric, in constructing race in his poetry. Most examples of his language that fall outside of the various patterns already discussed are negative. When we read of the "grinning Aethiop" (*"De Triumpho Naturae,"* *AT* 14, l. 16), we are made, and meant, to feel distaste at the image. This is not the sober Anglo-Saxon that Lovecraft admired. We also read into these reinforcements of negativity. Clearly, the phrase "some foul alien's sty" ("New-England Fallen," *AT* 392, l. 132) does so with cumulative impact of that "foul" and "sty" in conjunction with the "some . . . alien's." Germans are a particular favourite. They are "insatiate" ("1914," *AT* 397, l. 5), and we read of "Vainglorious Prussia" ("1914," *AT* 397, l. 23). They are not alone, though. We read likewise of the "fickle Russian" ("Germania—1918," *AT* 419, l. 53), reminding us that, for the purposes solely of the moment, the Germans are Lovecraft's favoured whipping-boys. Interestingly, the telling "his Saturnalian feast" (*"De Triumpho Naturae,"* *AT* 14, l. 20) relates to the patterns of elevation and denigration studied earlier, but in the form of the inversion of a natural order. The blacks are briefly king, but Lovecraft sees this as temporary, and an aberration. In this poem, he argues that the natural order will be restored: white Anglo-Saxons will dominate, the blacks and base foreigners will be relegated to the lower orders, if not die out.

Lovecraft certainly was no saint. His racism is proof enough, but this does not make him a devil. Each of us has degrees of good and bad within ourselves. Lovecraft's Jungian shadow happened to be racism. Yet the point of this essay has not been to judge Lovecraft, nor has it been to condemn him. It has been to try to understand the ways that Lovecraft helps to construct race, particularly non-white races, in his poetry. It is important to do so because, if we see where and how this is done here, we can apply what we have learned to other writers. If we allow Lovecraft's racism to affect our appraisal of him, then being able to read the racism in, say, T. S. Eliot, we should modify our reactions accordingly. Most of all, I find the racism of Lovecraft an indelible stain against his good name. It is the one major blot that he failed to compensate for, and, although it lessens my estimation of him as a man, it reminds myself that I am no saint either. I have a like tendency toward racism, which I find hard to combat, but I try. If I will learn anything from this study, from this discussion of the construction of race in Lovecraft's po-etry, it will be how to detect incipient racism in myself and others. This knowledge and self-knowledge is integral to our modern lives, if we are to become the best people that we are.

Briefly Noted

Llewellyn Worldwide, an occultist publisher in Minnesota, is about to issue a volume called *The 13 Gates of the Necronomicon*, by Donald Tyson, described in a press release as "a workable system of magic from the stories of H. P. Lovecraft." We shall be interested to see how "workable" the book is—for of course few of us would wish the fabric of the universe to be endangered while we are still on this earth. Tyson, who has written the splendid historical novel *Alhazred* (2006) as well as a number of other books about the *Necronomicon*, is also the author of *The Dream World of H. P. Lovecraft: His Life, His Demons, His Universe*, due out from Llewellyn in the fall of 2010. It is on the whole a relatively orthodox biocritical account, but with an emphasis on Lovecraft's dreams and his possible ties to occultism. Mercifully, Tyson explodes the Internet-generated myth that Love-craft or Sonia Greene were acquainted with Aleister Crowley.

The Ecstasies of "The Thing on the Doorstep," "Medusa's Coil," and Other Erotic Studies

Robert H. Waugh

> This is the very ecstasy of love,
> Whose violent property fordoes itself
> And leads the will to desperate undertakings
> As oft as any passion under heaven.
> * * *
> That unmatched form and feature of blown youth
> Blasted with ecstasy.
> —Shakespeare, *Hamlet* 2.1.102–5, 3.1.160–61

"The Thing on the Doorstep" is a remarkably unsatisfying yet compelling story. When we read it with any attention the questions it raises, lacking any convincing answer, seem without end, caught as they are in the flickering light of countless gender transformations. With some dismay we face their increasingly perverse implications and call out with Macbeth as the phantom descendants of Banquo parade before him, "What, will the line stretch out to th' crack of doom?" (*Macbeth* 4.1.133). In this story the line is a matter of ancestors. It stretches out until we realize that both Edward Derby and Asenath Waite are dead, and it is with a great finality that her name, in the possessive form, is the last word in the story.

With some hesitation, then, I wish to offer another reading, one that may seem highly unlikely, examining it as though it were Lovecraft's study of erotic love. True, Edward Derby seems a pallid figure to imagine as an erotic lover. I think, however, that in this story we meet in some distortion and repression a work that deals with Eros, with erotic love and erotic obsession, as Plato and the theolo-

136

gian Josef Pieper understood it. Yes, we can learn something about the hermit of Providence from Platonism and Neo-Aquinian thought. In part we are involved in another palinodia, very like the one that Plato and Pieper describe; we confess to Helen of Troy that we have insulted her, that she, the goddess, if she was a goddess, was never the cause of that endless war that caused the deaths of so many men. No, she, the handmaid of Eros, was always guiltless; and like her Asenath and Marceline were also guiltless; not only guiltless, they were spiritual lights that led the men who fell in love with them into a higher realm of being (Pieper 78–80).

So we cannot read "The Thing on the Doorstep" in this light without reading "Medusa's Coil" in this light also. A great difference seems to exist between the narrators; in the first story the narrator is a friend of the tragic lover, in the second story the central narrator is the father of the lover and the peripheral narrator a traveler who knows none of the main actors. Their levels of concern, responsibility, and personal engagement are quite different, as is the mere difference in the generations. Granted these differences, we shall see that several of their details are comparable and that the parabola of love, its dream of ascent and its destruction, a destruction that neither Plato nor Pieper envisage, follows a roughly similar trajectory. Having determined the different stages of this trajectory, we shall find that it is also possible to read "The Dreams in the Witch House" and "The Whisperer in the Darkness" in the light of their erotic ecstasis.

I

> Set me as a seal upon thine heart, as a seal upon thine arm: for love is strong as death; jealousy is cruel as the grave: the coals thereof are coals of fire, which have a most vehement flame. (Song of Solomon 8:6)

In a few superficial ways "The Thing on the Doorstep" and "Medusa's Coil" are not that incomparable. Different as the narrators are, they certainly seem to be narrators on the margin of the story, not at its center, so that the true subject of the plot remains impenetrable. These two stories seem to be the only ones in which the overt concern of the plot is the erotic connection between a man and a woman; though Lovecraft may seem uncomfortable with such a subject, it is remarkable that given such a discomfort he does deal with the subject twice. At the center of the horror in both stories lies the body buried in the cellar that will not stay dead; and that body represents a connection between this world and an archaic world that lies beyond our accepted histories and our accepted dimensions. In both stories a rather weak young man consummates a marriage with a daemonic figure that leads him beyond the world we know; and in both stories the narration insists that an old, honorable family, represented in both stories by a father, is destroyed; we might recall that this is the final point of Romeo and Juliet. Finally, almost as an afterthought, the narrator assures the reader that the true horror lies in an act of miscegenation, in the first story with a fishlike creature, in the second story with a black; which of these acts from our contemporary perspective is less horrific or less embarrassing we must leave to our individual sensibilities, but surely something is imbalanced in such narratives.

These comparisons, however, must yield to the theme of erotic, ecstatic love, as Plato outlines it in his description of Eros in the *Phaedrus*. First, he places it within the context of a divine mania, a characteristic it shares with prophecy, healing, and poetry (244a–245a). Properly understood, these are gifts from the gods; they do not depend upon the intellectual, technical skill of the prophet, doctor, or poet. Before Socrates proceeds to Eros, however, he finds it necessary to establish the immortality of the soul (a consistently important tenet of the Platonic system). In this dialogue the immortality is established by the argument that the soul depends upon a first principle that, as it were, exists as the basis of the soul by which, through the soul's own nature, it moves of itself (245c–246a); the activity of the soul is its first principle. It is at this point that Socrates compares the soul to a charioteer who must control two very different sorts of horses. Founded upon its autokinesis, the soul does not perish because it does not come into existence.

Consider this principle within the context of "The Thing on the Doorstep" in which the reader is persuaded to believe that Asenath is controlled by her father's soul, which itself is controlled by an entity that has nothing to do with humanity; this "it" is the true basis of the soul, to speak as Derby and Upton speak, that animates Asenath and

that strikes Derby out of himself. In "Medusa's Coil" Marceline, whatever the details of her biography, whether she did or did not come from
Martinique, actually incarnates something older than anything that can
be located within human prehistory; the Great Zimbabwe is as true and
mythological a place as the Marse Clooloo to which Sophonisba appeals, presumptively Cthulhu as we turn the name. Soul meets soul
outside of time. Thus the erotic event begins in an ecstasis in which the
soul stands outside itself, an ecstasis caused by the sudden recognition of
a very concrete, physical beauty. In this ecstasis one feels winged, ready
to take part in the procession and banquet of the gods, overcome by a
memory of one's origin and a promise of return (246d–247b, 249d–e).

Because of this memory and its promise of a return to an authentic self, Socrates insists that erotic mania is superior to the three
other divine manias he has passed over so swiftly, though Pieper
claims that those three—the prophetic, the cathartic, and the creative—are in some fashion summed up by the erotic. Love is prophetic, cathartic, and poetic. To consider it as a catharsis is
especially interesting, since Pieper argues that Plato does not have in
mind here the diseases of the body but the diseases of the soul: call
them fate, call them the anger of the gods, call them a family curse
"from the third and fourth generation of them that hate me; and
shewing mercy unto thousands of them that love me, and keep my
commandments" (Ex. 20:5–6). Doubtless the main thrust of this
commandment offers mercy, but that was not how the Puritans
read it, and it renders tersely the sense of such Greek works as the
Oresteia. From depth psychology we are dreadfully aware of the
inertia of our flaws within the family. Suicide, addiction, abuse, and
incest—their effects are carried out through the innocents who
thereby inherit and act out guilt. We must be healed, but that can
only happen at a severe psychic price. Whether this price shall be in
the hands of divine powers or in the hands of the unconscious is
difficult to say; the *theia mania* always feels external, like a gift, not
something that the self has accomplished (Pieper, *Begeisterung* 98–
105). The structure of Eros, then, implies that the god must make a
person mad, stricken outside of the self, in order to heal the self.
The personality must be destroyed before it can be reconstructed
on a higher plane of existence.

How can that be so? Pieper's commentary upon divine mania,

especially the divine mania of the erotic, offers us a number of details that will enrich our description of Lovecraft's story. First, let us note that the prophet suffers a raptus or an ecstasis; the words are roughly equivalent, but a raptus implies that the self is stolen, whereas as the ecstasis implies simply that the self, for whatever reason, is stricken outside the self. Aquinas uses the word raptus for the suffering of the prophet that he describes as *contra naturam*. It is a spiritual act, but it is also an act that the prophet suffers. (*Ver.* 13, 1 obj. 1 and *Sum. Theol.* 2, 2. 171 prolog.; cited in Pieper, *Begeisterung* 96–97); and in the same manner the lover suffers his ecstasis, his being put outside of himself. He does not, however, merely stand outside himself as the word ecstasis suggests. In fact, the state is described in two ways. Either the person is possessed (245a), so that it seems as though someone or something else were speaking through him; or he is violently torn away from himself, no longer living the daily life to which we are all accustomed—too accustomed, Plato insists—but living elsewhere, transposed to the life of the gods as they circle the universe. It is no surprise then that Edward Derby suffers his encounter with Asenath or that Denis de Russy suffers his encounter with Marceline. Pieper emphasizes that the comparison of the soul to a winged chariot pulled by horses with contrary goals in mind is simply that, a comparison that because it treats of such things as soul and god is insufficient; but no comparison can exhaust such subjects or reduce them to objects of the pure understanding: "Es ist uns nicht gegeben, von Gegenständen wie Seele, Geist, Gottheit mit dem Anspruch der direkten Kennzeichnung zu redden" [It is not granted us to speak of such objects as soul, spirit, divinity with the pretension of direct signs] (*Begeisterung*127). In a similar way, I do not think it was granted Lovecraft to speak in such a manner; instead he employs narrative, one narrative after another, none of them sufficient to the subject at hand, the terrors and elations of the spirit.

This problem of language is one reason that Plato is so often driven to a variety of different myths that outline his basic doctrines; thus, for instance, he develops two different myths of the afterlife, one at the conclusion of the Republic and another at the conclusion of the Phaedo. So we find in the Symposium a variety of different speeches in praise of Eros, some of them quite interesting and others clearly wide of the mark; only the last speech, reported by Socrates as the words of the priestess, seems to be valid. In this speech she reveals that love is a spirit, neither mortal nor immortal but between the divine and the human. It is like all the other spirits,

> the envoys and interpreters that ply between heaven and earth, flying upward with our worship and our prayers, and descending with the heavenly answers and commandments, and since they are between the two estates they weld both sides together and merge them into one great whole. They form the medium of the prophetic arts, of the priestly rites of sacrifice, initiation, and incantation, of divination and of sorcery, for the divine will not mingle directly with the human, and it is only through the mediation of the spirit world that man can have any intercourse, whether waking or sleeping, with the gods. [. . .] There are many spirits , and many kinds of spirits [δαίμονες], too, and Love is one of them. (202e–203a)

In this passage we see that Eros is an important messenger and translator between the divine and the human; he fulfills something of the role that is so often given to Hermes, whose name is embedded in the hermetic art; but we also see that Eros, a messenger of the gods, is not a god himself but a daemon. In the Platonic world this is not unimportant, for he makes much of the daemon that shaped Socrates' life.

This passage had a great deal of influence over Goethe, who habitually referred to the daemonic in human affairs. It was for him incommensurable, active in the political world, in poetry, and in love. In all these matters the irrational was at play, compelling unaccountable actions as though it were a personality: "Das Dämonische [. . .] ist dasjenige, was durch Verstand und Vernunft nicht aufzulösen ist. In meiner Natur liegt es nicht, aber ich bin ihm unterworfen" [The daemonic . . . is that which cannot be resolved by the reason or understanding. It does not lie in my nature, but I am subject to it] (Eckermann 438). We already noted this point in Pieper's commentary; it is not possible to reduce love to a rational account. To continue in this mythic mode, it is not simply a matter of the lover and the beloved: "Und dann, was nicht zu vergessen, kommt als ein mächtiges Drittes noch das Dämonisches hinzu, das jede Leidenschaft zu begleiten pflegt und das in der Liebe sein eigentliches Element findet" [And then we must not forget that the daemonic appears as a mighty third that is accustomed to accompany every passion and that finds in love its very own element] (Eckermann 671). Doubtless Goethe is speaking in a mythic fashion, a mode that may not have much to do with facts but very much to do with truth. Something happens in this ecstatic relation that seems to introduce an alien power that overcomes it, taking the lovers into a new space that neither had expected.

The transformation of the personality through love, which as we have seen must feel like a sickness, feels at last like a sickness unto death; but it also feels beyond all hope like a sickness that shall transcend death. St. Paul asserts very clearly that the individual that truly loves Christ must be buried in Christ to share his resurrection (Rom. 6:4). Edward Derby is resurrected after he is buried in the decaying body of his wife, and the resurrection does bring him to his triumphant last meeting with his friend and to a revenge on the other side of the grave upon the woman and the spirit behind her that has taken him outside himself. For love is suffering.

To step back for a moment, we need to ask what is erotic about Asenath, what in her awakens desire in Derby, who is something of a cold fish? We only have the words of the narrator Daniel Upton, which might or might not reflect Derby's words, as well as the various words, hers included, that describe Sonia Greene. Lovecraft himself was very careful to refrain from such language. Let us then consider Daniel Upton's words. She "was dark, smallish, and very good looking" (*DH* 280), words that might account for Derby's attraction. With some distaste Upton calls her eyes "overprotuberant" (280), adverting then to her background in Innsmouth and recounting as rumor and legend the story that Lovecraft's readers might well remember from the earlier novella "The Shadow over Innsmouth"; but some might call her eyes spiritual or sensitive, for we are accustomed to say that the soul looks out of the eyes. In some accounts the hypnotist works through the eyes, and Upton grudgingly allows that she is "a genuine hypnotist" (281), so her blazing eyes, which Upton suggests are actually the eyes of her father, become a recurrent and compelling phrase in the story.

This beauty, perhaps because of its unconventional nature, has an apparently immediate effect upon Derby; "wildly taken with her appearance," he suffers an upheaval from merely looking at her (*DH* 281). To Upton this is a mere infatuation. This word, however, may be understood in other ways than Upton means it. Though Dr. Johnson glosses it pejoratively, "to strike with folly; to deprive of understanding" ("Infatuate"), the root of the Latin word "fatuus," foolish, is "fatigo," to make weary or to exhaust (Tucker). An infatuated man is rendered quite other than he is; and in the crisis of his infatuation Derby vacillates between a great vigor and a severe exhaustion. What is happening to him is not what happens to a teenager, despite Upton's opinion that Derby is a "perennial child" (*DH* 282); this is not a hormonal but a spiritual eruption.

This judgment that Daniel gives upon Derby's love may be the reason for the immense insult Derby presents when he appears on the doorstep and the smell of his body, the body that is actually Asenath's that he has with great pain clawed out of the grave in which he had thrust it, rocks Daniel back on his heels. That "insufferably foetid wind" that "almost flung [him] prostrate" (*DH* 301) represents an act of aggression that I think we can only account for if we realize how belittling Upton's language is. He really cannot sympathize with the ecstatic aspect of Derby's love. How can he? Though he is married, he says almost nothing of his own wife, who must have taken some kind of part in the drama that is now unfolding; but since he says nothing about her we must assume that his own marriage is not in any way excited by the ecstasis that Derby experiences. But there is more to this aggression than simply Upton's sheer misunderstanding.

II

> One cannot maintain that the world was very grateful to psychoanalytic research for its discovery of the Oedipus-complex. (Freud, *General Introduction* 174)

A further comment Upton makes upon the affair as he understands it brings us into another region: "The perennial child had transferred his dependence from the parental image to a new and stronger image, and nothing could be done about it" (*DH* 282). From this point of view the marriage may not be such a bad thing, he believes, for

"the *change* of dependence" might at last lead "to responsible independence" (*DH* 283). This language that Lovecraft is using rather
loosely he learned from Freud, whom he had begun to read by 1921,
though he said at that time he preferred Adler's thinking (*SL* 1.134);
despite this preference, however, he refers to Freud three times as
often in the *Selected Letters* as he refers to Adler. Thereafter he refers to Freud most often in conjunction with other thinkers, but it
is difficult to establish what he has actually read; rather, his knowledge of Freud seems to be at second or third hand. Nevertheless, he
had time in which to learn the basic Freudian concepts. In *The Interpretation of Dreams*, which first appeared in English translation in
1913, Freud had discussed infant sexuality and treated the myth of
Oedipus at length as a model of infantile male desires and fears
(294–97). Perhaps more useful for Lovecraft was Freud's *General
Introduction to Psychoanalysis*, which lays out the basic concepts of
Freudian theory at that time: the theory of the unconscious as revealed in slips of the tongue; the doctrines of the manifest and la-
tent structure of dreams and of the operation of the wish-
fulfillment in dreams; and the doctrine of the polymorphous perverse in children that gives rise to normal sexuality and abnormal,
perverse sexuality. Most interesting is Freud's insistence to his audience of the original lectures that "the trouble is that you believe in
the illusion of psychic freedom and will not give it up" (31); or, as
he puts it later in the book, "In each one of you there is a deep-
rooted belief in psychic freedom and volition, a belief which is absolutely unscientific, and which must capitulate before the claims
of a determinism that controls even the psychic life" (84). This is
the claim that Lovecraft cannot accept.

Or rather, better put, he does accept it intellectually but he cannot accept it artistically—and what artist truly could? I have little
doubt that Lovecraft could have accepted the theory of infantile
sexuality if only Freud had not expressed it in so deterministic a
fashion. This is one of the points at which Adler becomes more
sympathique to Lovecraft because the unconscious for Adler, the
seat of the self, is not deterministically formed; it is not the past
that matters for it, but the future that it imagines for itself. The self
is creative, aimed toward a goal that Adler expresses in a variety of
fashions but is nevertheless a viable fiction that shapes the self at

the same moment that the self creates it.[1] The unconscious for Freud is as mechanistic as it was for Locke, for both of them insist upon the associative process, which in Freud becomes the associative technique employed in the psychoanalytic treatment. What Lovecraft did not realize, fortunately so as far as his creative process was concerned, was the ease a reader has in reading his fictions as though the unconscious were indeed operative. Charles Dexter Ward, for instance, so heavily dependent upon his family, becomes so fascinated by the figure of his powerful ancestor Joseph Curwen that he at last acts as though he were that figure; the story plays out the wish-fulfillment of a dream.

The central problem about Freud for Lovecraft is the theory of dreams in which the theory of the unconscious is realized. In March, 1926 he wrote to his aunt Lillian, "I don't believe you'll find much sound science in Freud's 'Dream Psychology', since his theory of dreams is perhaps the weakest link in his whole chain. Many of his hypotheses can be punctured quite readily by careful evidence, & it is one of Mortonius' many ambitions to refute Freud in a ponderous treatise on dreams" (ms., John Hay Library). Lovecraft is content to leave the scut work to his friend James F. Morton. The point here is that the dream is radically important to Lovecraft as an emblem of his own creative power and his own authentic privacy. The dream belongs to him and he belongs to the dream; it happens outside his ken, but it is his dream and no other's. The various Freudian interpretations, especially any that proceed out of the darkness of childhood, have no power upon it.

How, then, if Freud and Adler were presented with the Platonic myth of the winged chariot as though it were a dream, would each man interpret it? For Freud the answer is simple: every dream of flying is a sexual dream, a means of sublimating the desire for orgasm and preventing a wet dream (*General Introduction* 127). For Adler the answer is more difficult, since he insists that the psychic life of every individual is peculiar to the individual and not to be interpreted by a normative scheme like Freud's collection of symbolic equivalences.

---

1. Heinz and Rowena Ansbacher point out how strongly Adler was influenced by the *Als-ob* philosophy of Hans Vaihinger (76–87), which makes much of the Zweckmäßigkeit, expediency of purposiveness, of the useful fictions that form the core of his thought (cf. 1–13, 135–36, 174).

"We need to warn ourselves," Adler insists, "that we cannot explain a dream without knowing its relationship to the other parts of the personality. Neither can we lay down any fixed and rigid rules of dream interpretation" (362). He would certainly argue that the dream is aimed into a future that it imagines as a feast of the gods and a parade around the universe; the individual imagines a coherent, social future through the creation of a work within the cultural sphere. Perhaps, then, neither psychoanalyst is as distant from Plato as we might imagine; Freud emphasizes the erotic significance of the dream, Adler the preparative and prophetic.

One aspect of Plato's description of the erotic ecstasis, the flight through the universe that the lover experiences, would seem to be lacking in Lovecraft's description. Though the Lovecraftian weird tale aims at the breakthrough of natural law, its basic mode is naturalistic; the breakthrough will not be convincing if natural law is not well established throughout most of the narrative. So it is simply not possible for Derby to sprout wings and ascend into the stratosphere. Instead, when Derby is in his ecstatic state he climbs into Asenath's "powerful Packard" and drives it with a dash that he had never exhibited before, "handling it like a master, and meeting traffic entanglements with a skill and determination utterly alien to his accustomed nature" (*DH* 284). He is like the charioteer in Socrates' account, driving a winged chariot by which he confronts every nook and cranny of the universe. Derby drives to northern Maine, where he descends the secret steps and finds his way outside the universe as we know it. This detail is all the more impressive when we consider how seldom cars play a major role in Lovecraft's stories, which are more often peripatetic than motorized.

In its flight through the universe the soul participates in the parade of the gods, though one goddess does not take part, Hestia, who "abides alone in the gods' dwelling place" (247a). Plato may be playing here on a pun, for the word ʽεστια means the banquet that is associated with the hearth, the center of the house. While the gods and the soul circle the universe the banquet that is the intimate identity of the self remains at the center. This imagery is akin to the medieval statement that god is the center that is everywhere upon the circumference; in Plato's language the lover who pursues the track of the gods there feasts upon true being (247e). For Lovecraft this feast takes place in the Walpurgis Night that takes place outside the world we know; but if we keep in mind the Platonic pun, that extra-physical banquet has an identity in the ecstatic lover.

In his extreme state Derby battles against his attraction to Asenath, talking about the need to save his identity (*DH* 284); but that is specifically what the lover ought not to do. The identity needs to be sacrificed in the name of the larger world that the lover enters. The great moment of the love is expressed in the words, "I'll kill that entity . . . her, him, it . . . I'll kill it!" (*DH* 287). At this point the life of the self, the self that the person thought was authentic but was not, is in a life-and-death struggle for itself; and in this struggle it utters the great secret as it admits the shape-changing it experiences. "Her, him, it." Eros is transsexual and impersonal, erasing the categories by which we are accustomed to identify ourselves. This is the point at which Eros and Thanatos exchange identities, the point at which they melt into each other.

In this extreme state Derby exhibits strange objects to his friend, "elusively coloured and bafflingly textured objects like nothing ever heard of on earth, whose insane curves and surfaces answered no conceivable purpose and followed no conceivable geometry. These things, he said, came 'from outside'; and his wife knew how to get them" (*DH* 286). If we think of them, however, as his own works and of him as the Platonic artist who does not know the meaning of his own work, we understand once more that the divine mania is at work. It is a favorite theme for Plato that none of the Homeric rhapsodes can account for their work. It is a favorite and thoroughly understandable theme in Lovecraft that strange objects, as in "The Shadow over Innsmouth," need to be explained away as objects from elsewhere, never from the hands of a mere mortal; the exception to this pattern of denial is Henry Anthony Wilcox, who admits that he woke up to find himself working on the bas-relief that is the first premonition of the rise of Cthulhu (*DH* 128–29).

The story concludes in the identification of the thing on the doorstep as Asenath, her dental work and her crushed skull. Before this moment, however, the reader of the story performs an act of recollection and regression in attempting to sort out what has happened in the soul of the story. Derby is possessed by Asenath, who is actually Ephraim, who had years earlier possessed his daughter;

but Ephraim is actually an alien being, "some monstrous intrusion" (*DH* 290) that is unimaginably in excess of humanity. So in erotic ecstasis the male and female being is fused into the macrocosmic hermaphrodite from which all human appearances have descended; this hermaphroditic nature appears both in Aristophanes' comic fable in the *Symposium* (189d–e), which was taken so seriously in the Renaissance, and in the Kaballistic doctrine of the Sephiroth, whether in terms of the triads that emanate from the Ên Sôph or in terms of the human soul that is male and female before creation ("Kaballah"). We have long argued over the status of this being in Lovecraft's story, but I think it is best that we finally accept that whatever it is it is at least two or that as two or as something else it transcends the divisions of human gender.

In turning to "Medusa's Coil," the question again arises about the nature of the attraction that Marceline exerts. A part of that answer again lies in her eyes, "large and very dark" like the eyes of Asenath (*HM* 172), but the title suggests more profoundly that it is the coil of hair, "that dense, exotic, overnourished growth of black inkiness" (*HM* 173). The word "coil" of course is very striking. According to Johnson the verb is defined as "to gather into a narrow compass; as to coil a rope, to wind in a ring" ("Coil"), and this meaning suggests the way that she binds men to her; but the word has a secondary meaning as noun that is now more archaic than in Johnson's day, "tumult; turmoil; bustle; stir; hurry; confusion"; and his three citations from Shakespeare are arresting. There is "this mortal coil" that Hamlet contemplates shuffling off (3.1.66); but there is also Prospero's question to Ariel, his own daemon, about the magical storm the spirit has created, "Who was so firm, so constant, that this coil / Would not infect his reason?" (1.2.208–9), as well as Hermia's accusation of Helena, "You, mistress, all this coil is 'long of you" (3.2.340). Her words suggest the irrational sexuality that gives rise to a coil out of which a man cannot escape, very pertinent to this story.

The coil of hair of course is the snake, several of them, braid by braid, or the one within which all the other hairs exist. This description is justified by the myth of Medusa that the story alludes to and meditates upon, which I do not mean to say much about, except later when we consider how the face and hair of the goddess turns people to stone. There is another myth, however, that the story lightly alludes to, the dance of the virgin and the snake, most thoroughly realized in Flaubert's novel *Salammbô*, in which the Carthagenian priestess of Tanit has a most remarkable relationship to her black python: "Sa démarche rappelait les ondulations des fleuves, sa température les antiques ténèbres visqueuses pleines de fécondité, et l'orbe qu'il décrit en se mordant la queu l'ensemble des planètes, l'intelligence d'Eschmoûn" [Its motion recalled the waves of rivers, its temperature the antique darkness, viscous and full of fecundity, and the circle it formed in biting its tail the order of the planets, the intelligence of Eschmoun] (187; ch. 10). The serpent symbolizes (though not to the weary eye of the author) the totality of the world, the water, the fecund, primitive heat, and the circle of the world. One detail in this description is not present in the De Russy plantation as the narrator encounters it; it is no longer wet or fecund, but dry and sterile, waiting for the apocalypse that any stray flame shall bring it.

As a result of a good classical education the grandfather suggests a further understanding of the hair when he alludes to "the later Ptolemaic myth of Berenice, who offered up her hair to save her husband/brother, and had it set in the sky as the constellation Coma Berenices" (*HM* 170). Our immediate familiarity with this story comes from Catullus' translation of a Greek original. Once more we owe so much to Catullus, just as we owe the story of Atys to him that appears in "The Rats in the Walls." So we should not ignore this short allusion here. It is possible that Denis has not gone to France to find his other in Marceline but his sister, confirmed as she is in the last paragraph of the story that reveals that he has married the black woman with whom, as such things go, he was raised. I have in mind here, I must confess, such novels of incest and miscegenation as Faulkner's *Absolom, Absolom!* Lovecraft, the innocent Northener, would like nothing better than to believe the best of the South, but instead he stumbles in horror upon its most comfortable secret. Marceline is a black, just as Asenath is a fish.

I suggested earlier that the car of the narrator stands in the place of the flight, but much more interesting in this regard is the painting that Frank Marsh creates. Despite the time that he spends with her he emphatically denies that he loves Marceline or could ever be in love with her, but then admits something more subtle: "The case simply is, that one phase of her half hypnotizes me in a certain way—a very strange, fantastic, and dimly terrible way—just as another phase half hypnotises you in a much more normal way. I can see something in her—or to be psychologically exact, something through her or beyond her—that you don't see at all" (*HM* 178). In the language of the Renaissance his love is heroic[2]; uninterested in physical attractions, with a certain unconscious snobbery at Denis's merely physical love, it passes through appearances to the Platonic idea. De Russy is rather skeptical, but finally agrees that Marsh's claim must be true.

The remarkable aspect of the painting is the sense of a complex space that it creates within which all seems possible. This is, if you will, a virtual flight in which the poetic mania, led by the erotic, has constructed a representation of "the ultimate fountainhead of all horror" that is R'lyeh. Marsh has created much better than he knows. Besides the nude, inviting portrait of Marceline a Witches' Sabbat is taking place in which she is the high-priestess, accompanied by "the black shaggy entities that are not quite goats—the crocodile-headed beast with three legs and a dorsal row of tentacles—and the flat-nosed aegipans dancing in a pattern that Egypt's priests know and called accursed!" (*HM* 193). This is not the banquet of the gods as Plato understood in his myth, but it is a banquet that celebrates its own understanding of the world.

Having come this far, let us consider what follows if we extend this discussion by considering the breakthroughs experienced in "The Whisperer in the Darkness" and "Dreams in the Witch House," arguing that those stories are also erotic in their underpinnings. This extension seems possible because both Henry Akeley and Walter Gilman suffer an ecstasis, being taken out of themselves, and a raptus, a flight through the universe. More difficult for us to understand is the nature of the erotic encounters that they suffer, for the only encounter that Gilman seems to have is with the hateful crone Keziah, and Akeley is a widower.

In "The Dreams in the Witch House" the beloved is a demonic version of the beloved, for she is Keziah (a perfectly fine Biblical word that means cassia, one of the daughters of Job after his great

---

2. Cf. Marvell's poem "The Definition of Love" and Bruno's poems in *Gli eroici furori*.

afflictions [Job 42:14]). There is nothing spicy, though, about the witch. From the beginning of the story Gilman desires her, for he took his apartment for no other reason than the fact that she had lived there more than two hundred years earlier and offered him the possibilities of "lines and curves," a repeated phrase, through which he could "delve deeper" than anyone had before; the sexual aspect of the language is patent. His study in geometry at Miskatonic University has another aspect that would have interested both Freud and Adler. She fascinates him with hypnotic eyes, an "unmotivated stare" (*MM* 268) that almost makes him shiver, and through her he enjoys and suffers a series of rapt ecstasies across the universe. The dream becomes the means of joining the procession of the gods. Before the narrator can exposit the dreams, however, he has to describe this room in great precision, one of the first moments in the story where a geometrical language is required; and though the narrator does not say so, I think that with some confidence we can say that it is the same shape as the object in "The Haunter of the Dark"—it is a trapezohedron. Only an asymmetrical, irrational shape can be the proper springboard into a non-Euclidean universe.

This outline of his situation is of course troubled by her age and by the presence of Brown Jenkin. We cannot but suspect that the actual beloved is the mother and that Brown Jenkin is a double of Gilman, since it "was nursed on the witch's blood" (*MM* 266). The difficulty with this analysis is the creature's beard. Gilman is young, but the ratlike creature is old, so it is possible that it represents the father. We suspect this all the more because of his ratlike appearance, for we have here a similar imagery to that of the vermin army pouring downward. When Gilman hears the sounds of rats in the ceiling he braces himself "as if expecting some horror which only bided its time before descending to engulf him utterly" (*MM* 266). At the conclusion of the story one of these rats, presumably Brown Jenkin, kills Gilman by eating through his heart after the young man kills Keziah. In the Oedipal conflict the father almost always wins, even if the son kills him.

The title of this story, "The Dreams in the Witch House," implies that the important thing as far as the plot is concerned is not Keziah or Brown Jenkin but the dreams that the narrator describes in great detail. The first paragraph devoted to the dreams says that although Gilman "plunges through limitless abysses" it is difficult to employ a physical language for his experience, since "he did not walk or climb, fly or swim, crawl or wriggle" (*MM* 267). Though the language is negative, properly so, it resembles the language that Milton employs to describe the journey of Satan through the uncreated world to the throne of Chaos:

> So eagerly the fiend
> O'er bog or steep, through strait, rough, dense, or rare,
> With head, hands, wings, or feet pursues his way,
> And swims or sinks, or wades, or creeps, or flies.
>
> (*Par. Lost* 2.947–50)

Like Love, Satan is always, not matter what he does, an αγγελος and daemon, fallen and reduced, but thereby a messenger between the spirit world and the human world; he is, however, Love's opposite, the spirit of hatred and fear and opposition, not the spirit of connection, though the one may be mistaken for the other. Gilman hates Keziah fiercely, but we should suspect the roots of that hatred; and he fears that in the middle of the raptures that constitute his dreams he shall be carried to the throne of Azathoth, Lovecraft's central incarnation of the principle of chaos.

In order to render Gilman's experience the narrator turns to geometric terminology, a language that Lovecraft uses often in his last stories as a part of his program to move the stories into the mode of science fiction. This terminology has other purposes, however. First, it is a language that distances the narrator and the reader from the language of the suffering subject and his somatic condition. It is enlightening that immediately after the passage we have just examined of Gilman's progress through the higher dimensions "of his own condition he could not well judge, for sight of his arms, legs, and torso seemed always cut off by some odd disarrangement of perspective" (*MM* 267). At the beginning of these dreams the body vanishes, perhaps because of a bodily *pudeur*.

The dreams are of two kinds as far as Gilman is concerned, though the reader soon understands more about them than he does. There are the dreams that recount raptures through space and time, perhaps to a state where time does not exist (*MM* 285), and the dreams that often encapsulate those raptures, dreams characterized by a violet light and by the presence of Keziah, Brown Jerkin, and the imposing figure of the tall black man. The former dreams take place within a state of multiple dimensions or upon alien worlds, so the language of these dreams is necessarily metaphoric. The latter dreams take place within the witch house and within the environs of Arkham; they are real, immediate, and inescapable until Gilman at last takes his fate into his own hands and attacks the figures of the phantasmagoria.

Gilman has many dreams, dreams beyond count, but only six are recorded in the story. I think it is useful to read them backwards, beginning with the last and moving toward the first, to unpack the meaning and the emotion that they contain. I do this for two reasons: first, I have in mind Gadamer's suggestion that this procedure may be enlightening in certain poetic cases; and second, I have in mind Freud's suggestion in *The Interpretation of Dreams* that dreams can be read backwards. I confess, thereby, that I mean to read these dreams precisely as Lovecraft would not have wished them to be read, in a manner consistent with Freudian thought. We find Lovecraft here in some difficulty. As Burleson has shown, Lovecraft liked to write as though "the world of deep dream may be as real as, or more real than, the waking world" ("On Lovecraft's Themes" 136), rather in the same way as Tolkien liked to speak in his letters as though Elves really existed. Both write and speak in this way because they assert something rather important by such language. In Lovecraft's case, he asserts the way that dreams seem to come from sources quite other than our personal daytime concerns and that they give us insights that would otherwise be quite impossible. He has to deny the reductionism that he found in Freud's theory of dreams. With such a caveat then, reading these dreams with the admission that they certainly mean more than a Freudian reading, let us proceed crabwise.

In the last dream Keziah tries to force Gilman to take part in the Sabbat and kill the child that she has kidnapped. This is a matter of course. Arkham knows that at the time of the Sabbat children will be kidnapped and killed; it does not approve but it seems incapable of preventing the murders despite the threat. It is perhaps to that extent complicitous in the murders; no matter what polite Arkham believes, the university and the common people know what hap-

pens at the Sabbat. Gilman, however, refuses to agree and kills
Keziah. His last words, rendered in indirect discourse, are ecstatic:
"Iä! Shub-Niggurath! The Goat with a Thousand Young. . . ." (*MM*
293). His last words are ejaculations toward the gods of fertility,
words we should keep in mind in our further reading. Though he
himself is rendered deaf, cast out from any immediate human
communication, he has conquered; the woman who has plagued
him and attempted to seduce him is dead. Yet Brown Jenkin, her
simulacrum, lives to drill through Gilman's breast and eat "his heart
out" (*MM* 295). His heart is at the root of the matter. He has conquered, but he has not because he is too concerned in these matters.
For "each man kills the thing he loves" (Wilde 726). Though Lovecraft has transcended his decadent period it still exerts its own peculiar power. Though this dream is victorious, it is also fearful.

Not only are the dreams fearful, they are increasingly infantile.
In the fifth dream the next morning after the one in which Keziah
attempts to drag him through a deep mud to the tall black man, he
finds "that his feet and pajama-bottoms were brown with caked
mud" (*MM* 287). The dream continues as she drags him into "a dark
open doorway," up "evil-smelling staircases" (*MM* 286) and presents
him with a baby that she thrusts into his arms. In shock "he plunged
recklessly down the noisome staircase and into the mud outside"
(*MM* 287). This repetition of the word "mud" is significant. No
doubt the word "pajama-bottoms" refers to the cuffs of the pants,
but one cannot but hear the pun that suggests he has shat in his
pants out of fear. Despite the geometric terminology, the somatic
pathos of the story grows as it approaches its climax.

The wide-awake world the next day explains the dream. "The
two-year-old child of a clod-like laundry worker" has been kidnapped (*MM* 288). The ugly word "clod-like" begs the question of
what this woman does. She has no husband that is ever mentioned,
"and her friend Pete Stowacki would not help because he wanted
the child out of the way anyhow" (*MM* 288–89). I believe this is the
closest that Lovecraft ever comes to suggesting that one of his characters is a prostitute, and the actions of Keziah during that night
seem in retrospect the actions of a madam, first trying to bring
Gilman into the seductive allure of the violet light and then breaking off to rid the brothel of an unwanted child.

The fourth dream is relatively short, but in it the "tall, lean man of dead black colouration but without the slightest sign of negroid features" first appears (*MM* 281). The denial of negroid features attempts to place Nyarlathotep outside of American prejudices at the same time as it touches on those prejudices; from his first appearance in Lovecraft's imagination, Nyarlathotep came from Egypt with a dark complexion. In *The Dream-Quest of Unknown Kadath* he is swart, so this description "dead black" places him in a thoroughly different condition, but Lovecraft here asserts the negritude of the god and denies it. The newspapers of Arkham have no difficulty in identifying the figure as negroid, and we need to admit this appearance as one more to the various transformations that Nyarlathotep assumes in the stories in which he takes part. But if we ask why this description is made, I think the answer lies in the miscegenation of "Medusa's Coil." It seems that the beloved must have something that is strongly other.

But something significant happens in this dream. Keziah thrusts into Gilman's right hand "a huge grey quill" with which to sign his name to the devil's book and to provide the necessary blood Brown Jenkin races across his body, up to his shoulders and down his right arm, to bite him in the wrist, causing a "spurt" of blood at which Gilman faints (*DH* 281). The next morning "his cuff was brown with dried blood" (281). The stories of the devil's book are, let us admit, rather unimaginative, but they conceal a masturbatory fantasy that seems actually at work here. Gilman faints away because he cannot accept the wet dream. More generally, like the mud the blood dirties him, but that is another part of the attraction Keziah exerts.

The third dream begins with the approach of Keziah and Brown Jenkin, but Gilman escapes them, "glad to sink into the vaguely roaring twilight abysses," though he finds the pursuit of their shapes projected into the geometries of an "iridescent bubble-congeries" and a "kaleidoscopic little polyhedron" rather "irritating" (*MM* 276). If it were not for the distancing effect of the geometric language and the brilliance of the words "iridescent" and "kaleidoscopic," the word "irritating" would seem understated. He then finds himself on a sunset terrace looking out giddily across an enormous city two thousand feet below him. Peter Cannon has analyzed this image, which appears throughout Lovecraft's work, magnifying his favorite view of

Providence; both parts of the dream admit that they come from Gilman's own concerns. The end of the dream, however, denies this, for when he wakes up he finds in his hand an alien object that testifies to the reality of the dream, an object of "exotic delicacy" that his right hand falling upon had steadied him until he broke it off (*MM* 278). At that crisis Keziah and Brown Jenkin appear once more, in the company of three aliens so terrifying that he wakes. Once more the masturbatory imagery and his anxiety are patent.

The second dream begins with Keziah now much more clear than she was in the first, for it is as though she and her familiar are in fact materializing slowly out of his own consciousness; he wishes to see her and she slowly responds to that wish. In this moment "the expression on her face was one of hideous malevolence and exultation" (*MM* 272). The exultation is understandable; because of his interest in her she is gaining more substance. The malevolence, however, is hard to understand; either she is simply evil, bearing an evil will when she lived in Arkham and bearing that evil will with her when she unaccountably escaped from prison, or she has reason to hate him and he will have to discover that reason in himself. She does, however, promise to introduce him to the Black Man and to Azathoth. As we have seen, though, such a promise is not necessarily fearful, for he is being invited to the center of the universe and the center of its meaning. He escapes into the deeper abyss, where flight is wonderful, but suddenly the next night, in a dream that seems a continuation of that previous flight, finds himself in an alien landscape from which Keziah and Brown Jenkin show him the way back. He owes them more than he seems to admit.

There is no first dream. The narrative simply speaks of the dreams that he begins to have in the witch house, so often at first simply the dreams of flight through geometries of "prisms, labyrinths, clusters of cubes and planes, and Cyclopean buildings" (*MM* 267). The dreams begin in the vaguest abstractions and only gradually concretize into the visions of Keziah and Brown Jenkin; the clearest language we have already noted, the way that the language compares him to Satan as he flies through "intricate Arabesques roused into a kind of ophidian animation" (*MM* 267). The dreams begin in the turmoil of an unspecified desire that must rehearse itself through the many dreams before it begins to find its object in Keziah, whom he must kill. Something, however, is shocking in that conclusion when we consider her in the light of Fritz Leiber's suggestion that she represents the hag aspect of the triple goddess (192),

This unsatisfying beginning is mirrored by an unsatisfying conclusion. I do not have in mind here the death of the protagonist; it is a given that in Lovecraft's fiction the protagonist shall die, and this death seems particularly suitable given our analysis. What disturbs me is that no banquet of the gods is available. The Walpurgis Night occurs as expected, but it is a relatively minor affair in which Gilman does not take part, except in attempting futilely to save the child whose life is offered up in the traditional parody of the eucharist.

"The Whisperer in Darkness" may appear as one of the more aseptic of Lovecraft's stories. Here is a widower bereft of his head. This plot would seem to be as distant from erotic matters as one could imagine. Still, like Gilman he is offered an extreme raptus, and certain other details suggest that the erotic may be at work in the story. Let us at least assume that as a possibility and see how far it takes us in our reading.

The most striking aspect about the story from the beginning is the landscape, those "wild domed hills" and "endless trickles of brooks" that we are told upon the first page Henry Akeley "mortally feared" for no immediately evident reason (DH 208). Only later does the narrator, referring to Akeley's second letter, speak of "the pits of primal life, and of the streams that trickled down therefrom" (DH 223), responding to the question that is left hanging earlier of "the streams [that] trickle from unknown sources" (DH 210). Through the next pages the narration refers often to the hills and the brooks, the "crowded green precipices and muttering forest streams" (DH 215), as though they had something to say that remains impossible to utter. Much later when Wilmarth is trying to sleep in Akeley's house after his conversation with the whisperer, the only exception to the great silence is "the sinister trickle of distant unseen waters" (DH 262). Probably these trickling streams, so fearful and yet so difficult to understand, are the correlative in the landscape of the whispering that becomes fearful; this significance, however, lies within the context of the total landscape. Once we are sensitized to this imagery, it begins to assume a meaning that lies beyond the merely topographical; it feels like the imagery of a dream before one has begun to dream that dream, and we realize how sexual this language is. The sexuality of

the language is all the more evident when the narration begins to describe the floods that bring down "swollen, organic shapes" (*DH* 209)
that bear "superficial resemblances" to the human (*DH* 210), "pinkish
things" (*DH* 210), a phrase that is varied as "monstrous pinkish forms"
(*DH* 223). This language does not make sense unless either the narrator
or Henry Akeley, with whom the narrator comes to sympathize profoundly, have problems in facing the female body that, as a misogynist
would put it, bears only a superficial resemblance to the human, i.e.
male, body. The story, then, is sexualized from its earliest pages.

   After much periphrasis and indirect description the story comes
to the imperfect transcript, recalled only in memory, that Akeley
has sent the narrator Wilmarth. The striking aspect of this transcript, after we have pondered "The Dreams in the Witch House,"
is that we find once more the names of Shub-Niggurath, the figure
of fertility, and of Nyarlathotep, designated here a Mighty Messenger and a Great Messenger (*DH* 226).

   For several pages after this transcript Wilmarth copies the various letters he receives from Akeley, and little here is of interest to
our reading except the sense that though Akeley is truly terrified he
expresses a good deal of ambivalence about leaving his farm, so long
in his family, to join his son in California. For a New Englander that
might as well be across the universe. Twice Wilmarth says that
Akeley is a recluse "with very little worldly sophistication" (*DH*
215), "a man of much simplicity [. . .] with little worldly experience"
(*DH* 249). Despite being a widower, he rather resembles the young
Derby. Then a remarkable letter arrives that records an utter transformation in him; anxiety and repulsion are suddenly transformed
to desire. He casually announces that he shall now be the inter-
preter of the aliens upon earth and that though he will not be called
upon to undertake "any trip *outside* just yet" he seems confident
that he "shall probably *wish* to do so later on" (*DH* 239). If we had
read this letter within any other context would we not have said
that the speaker had fallen in love? Before these words Akeley had
realized that the creatures, whatever they might be, possess "un-
doubted telepathic and hypnotic powers" (*DH* 231), powers such as
we saw Asenath and Marceline possessed, and thus it seems clear
that they as an aggregate are the beloved. As it turns out, these
words about the journey, the great journey outside, are not Akeley's

words at all, or probably not, for he has quite literally lost his head. The words of the lover, in the state of ecstasis, are not his words but those provided by the daemon Eros. But if this were Akeley what a bumptious, confident Akeley he is: "With such an exchange of knowledge all perils will pass, and a satisfactory *modus vivendi* be established. The very idea of any attempt to *enslave* or *degrade* mankind is ridiculous" (*DH* 239). These words remind us of the easy optimism of a newlywed who ignores all the emotions that lie in the past of every couple, not so easily dealt with through a superficial rationalism, and who ignores all of the possibilities of a patriarchal society versed in ancient feelings of sadomasochism.

Wilmarth reacts to the letter with complex feelings but finally comes to an erotic agreement with the Akeley that he thinks has written the letter. What that man had loved he shall love, "the same old passion for infinity" (*DH* 242): "to shake off the maddening and wearying limitations of time and space and natural law—to be linked with the vast *outside*—to come close to the nighted and abysmal secrets of the infinite and the ultimate" (*DH* 243). This desire for knowledge is thoroughly tinged with an erotic imagery that we are familiar with from the Romantic period. Wilmarth's reaction is to leave for Akeley's home in Vermont, though he takes care not to arrive at night; and leaving when he does he realizes on the train that he "was entering an altogether older-fashioned, ancestral New England without the foreigners and factory-smoke, billboards and concrete roads" (*DH* 244). What a relief! He is regressing to a prior state and remembering things that had not bothered him for many years. As the mysterious Noyes drives him to Akeley's farm Wilmarth comments on "the hypnotic landscape" in which "time had lost itself"; and after comparing the landscape to the backgrounds of paintings by Leonardo da Vinci he concludes: "we were now burrowing bodily through the midst of the picture, and I seemed to find in its necromancy a thing I had innately known or inherited, and for which I had always been vainly searching" (*DH* 248). This ecstatic experience stands in the place of the raptus we had expected when either he or Akeley were escorted through the universe by the Outer Ones. The closest we approach that ecstasis in the narrative comes in a paragraph in which a series of variations on the phrase "I was told" bears the reader along in a rhetorical increase in the tempo of the whisperer's words (*DH* 256).

The following page declares the conditions of such an ecstasis, the "harmless" extraction of the brain and immersion in the metal cylinder. The whisperer insists that the brain would enjoy "a full sensory and articulate life—albeit a bodiless and mechanical one," though there is some contradiction between that "full sensory [. . .] life" and that "bodiless" life; the process was "as simple as carrying a phonographic record about" (*DH* 257). For this ecstasis one need only lose one's head. To Wilmarth, however, the details come down to a mere "mechanical mummery" (*DH* 259), an experience that has nothing to do with the strenuous philosophic path outlined in the *Phaedrus*. When Wilmarth fully realizes this in his confrontation with the wax mask and hands, he escapes in Akeley's old Ford—the man clearly has no need of it again.

This Ford was mentioned at the beginning of the story when he referred to it as "a commandeered motor" (*DH* 208), and Akeley offhandedly referred to it in his account of his daily life (*DH* 229) and later suggested that someone would meet Wilmarth with his car (*DH* 241). Sensitized as we are to this imagery in "The Thing on the Doorstep," we must wonder whether once more it represents the Platonic chariot; but in fact the old Ford is good for nothing but escape. Much more significant a vehicle is the new model that Mr. Noyes drives, "bearing Massachusetts licence plates with the amusing 'sacred codfish' device of the year" (*DH* 246). There is nothing amusing, however, about this drive through the landscape that is the actual ecstasis of the story.

In this story, however, neither Akeley nor Wilmarth ascends to the parade of the gods nor to their banquet. If Akeley ever does ascend to the realm of Yuggoth and the worlds beyond, he does so probably without his consent. We are fairly certain, despite the language he uses in that remarkable conversion letter, that he is now at the conclusion of the story either dead, a dead letter, or merely a head in a metal cylinder. He leads now only a mechanized life that has been made possible through a symbolic castration. This story, then, is the bleakest of Lovecraft's accounts of the erotic life.

My description so far of the erotic in these stories may be accurate, but we must confess that it still misses something basic to the whole tenor of the stories. Nothing is pretty here, and nothing saves us; but the erotic mania as Plato and Aquinas understood it offers at least an insight into the construction of the world and sets the manic lover into the center of that world at the banquet of Hestia; erotic love reconstitutes the Ptolemaic universe. This kind of moment allows us to see that Lovecraft searches for other moments in his worldview than the destruction implicit in materialism; but there is no doubt that for Lovecraft this divine mania is demonic. Given the very existence of these stories as weird tales, we have either not addressed or only glancingly so their demonic nature. "The Thing on the Doorstep," "Medusa's Coil," "The Whisperer in Darkness," and "The Dreams in the Witch House" demonize the erotic narrative into tales of murder, suicide, castration, and mutilation. I do not, however, see this as a great problem. In the *Symposium* Socrates had argued that Eros is not a god, certainly not one of the major gods, but a daemon, a rather eerie and untrustworthy being that moves as a messenger between the gods and humanity. Eros is a being that communicates our need and lack and purveys mere opinions that may or may not be true. He is rather similar to the muses that meet the poet Hesiod and announce that often they tell falsehoods and also, if they wish, sometimes gossip the truth (*Theogony* 25–27); and they are goddesses! As Socrates had argued, the poets may tell the truth, but they may not know when they do; as humans, however, because we have little else than opinion, we deeply need poetry and even more Eros.

Now I do not mean to argue that the relation of the words daemon and demon is definitive or convincing. However, as far as humans in their daily lives are concerned, the daemon Eros stands as a judgment and accusation: we do not live as we ought, we do not pay heed to what we ought, and we do not prize beauty, truth, or goodness as we ought. Since we do none of these things, unless we are lovers or philosophers, that is to say unless we seem to others demented, since we have no experience to bring to bear from our daily lives, we are clumsy and inept; we seem to ourselves erratic, and lost in that error as though we were lost in a labyrinth we stagger through the corridors of our lives until we meet the Minotaur. *Quel dommage.*

Works Cited

Adler, Alfred. The Individual Psychology of Alfred Adler: A Systematic Presentation in Selections from His Writings. Ed. Heinz L. Ansbacher and Rowena R. Ansbacher. New York: Harper & Row, 1964.

Bruno, Giordano. *Gli eroici furori*. Ed. Nicoletta Tirinnanzi. Milan: Rizzoli, 1999.

Eckermann, Johann Peter. *Gespräche mit Goethe*. Ed. Fritz Bergemann. Baden-Baden: Insel, 1981.

The Encyclopaedia Britannica. 11th ed. Edinburgh: A. & C. Black, 1875–98.

Flaubert, Gustave. *Salammbô*. Paris: Éditions de Cluny, 1937.

Freud, Sigmund. *A General Introduction to Psychoanalysis*. Trans. G. Stanley Hall. New York: Boni & Liveright, 1920.

———. *The Interpretation of Dreams*. Trans. James Strachey. New York: Avon Books, 1965.

Hesiod. *Theogonia, Opera et Dies, Scutum*. Ed. Friedrich Solmsen. *Fragmenta Selecta*. Ed. R. Merkelbach and M. L. West. Oxford: Oxford University Press, 1970

Johnson, Samuel. *A Dictionary of the English Language*. 4th ed. London: W. Strahan, 1773. 2 vols.

"Kaballah." *Encyclopaedia Britannica*.

Leiber, Fritz. *The Second Book of Fritz Leiber*. New York: DAW, 1975.

Marvell, Andrew. *The Complete Poems*. Ed. Elizabeth Story Donno. New York: Penguin, 1985.

Milton, John. *Complete Poems and Major Prose*. Ed. Merritt Y. Hughes. New York: Odyssey, 1957.

Pieper, Josef. *Begeisterung und Göttlicher Wahnsinn*. Munich: Kösel-Verlag, 1962.

Plato. *The Collected Dialogues Including the Letters*. Ed. Edith Hamilton and Huntington Cairns. Princeton: Princeton University Press, 1963.

———. *Opera*. 5 vols. Ed. John Burnet. Oxford: Clarendon Press, 1900.

Shakespeare, William. *The Norton Shakespeare*. Ed. Stephen Greenblatt. New York: W. W. Norton, 1997.

Tucker, T. G. *Etymological Dictionary of Latin*. Chicago: Ares, 1985.

Vaihinger, Hans. *Die Philosophie des Als Ob*. 10th ed. Leipzig: Felix Meiner, 1927.

Wilde, Oscar. *Works*. London: Spring Books, 1963.

Notes on a Nonentity

H. P. Lovecraft

[The following is Lovecraft's 900-word version of the essay "Some Notes on a Nonentity," written in November 1933 for William L. Crawford's *Unusual Stories* but not published there. The manuscript of this item was thought to have been lost, but it recently resurfaced and has been made available to the *Lovecraft Annual*.—ED.]

I was born in Providence, R.I.—where I have ever since lived—on August 20, 1890, of old Yankee-English stock. The interests which have led me to fantastic fiction were very early in appearing, for nothing has ever seemed to fascinate me so much as the thought of some curious interruption in the prosaic laws of nature, or some monstrous intrusion on our familiar world by unknown things from the limitless abysses outside.

When I was three or less I listened avidly to the usual juvenile fairy lore, and Grimm's Tales were among the first things I ever read, at the age of four. When I was five the Arabian Nights claimed me, and I spent hours in playing Arab—calling myself "Abdul Alhazred", which someone had mentioned as a typical Saracen name.

But for me books and legends held no monopoly of fantasy. In the ancient hill streets of my native town, with their fanlighted colonial doorways, small-paned windows, graceful Georgian steeples, and mystical sunset vistas, I felt a magic then and now hard to explain. Before I knew it the eighteenth century had captured me utterly, so that I used to consume long days in the attic, exploring the 'long-s'd' books banished from the library downstairs, and unconsciously absorbing the style of Pope and Dr. Johnson. One effect of this was to make me think of *time* as a mysterious, portentous entity in which all sorts of unexpected wonders might be discovered.

Nature, too, keenly touched my sense of the fantastic. My home was near what was then the edge of the settled residence district, so that I was just as used to the rolling fields, stone walls, giant elms, squat farmhouses, deep woods, and sinister hollows of rural New England as to the archaic urban scene. This brooding, primitive landscape seemed to me to hold some vast but unknown significance.

When I was six I encountered the mythology of Greece and Rome through sundry popular juvenile media, and was profoundly influenced by it. I became a veritable Roman, and for a time actually thought I glimpsed fauns and dryads in certain centuried groves. About this period the bizarre illustrations of Gustave Doré affected me powerfully. For the first time I attempted writing—the earliest piece I can recall being a tale of a hideous cave, perpetrated at the age of seven and entitled "The Noble Eavesdropper".

Around the age of eight I acquired a strong interest in the sciences—chemistry, geography, and finally astronomy. When sixteen I broke into print with astronomical matter; contributing monthly articles on current phenomena to a local daily, and flooding the weekly rural press with more expansive miscellany.

It was while in high-school that I first produced weird stories of any coherence and seriousness. They were largely trash, and I destroyed the bulk of them when eighteen. At this stage most of my interests were scientific. Reason had removed my belief in the supernatural, and I am still a mechanistic materialist in philosophy. As for reading—I mixed science, history, general literature, weird literature, and absolute rubbish with complete unconventionality.

Ill health prevented college attendance, but informal studies at home helped to save me from total illiteracy. Around 1910 I veered from science to literature, specialising in the classics and in the products of my favourite eighteenth century. My writings were mostly verse and essays—uniformly worthless and now mercifully vanished.

In 1914 I joined an amateur press association whose influence caused me—in 1917—to resume weird fiction-writing after an hiatus of nine years. About 1919 discovery of Lord Dunsany gave me a vast impetus, and in 1922 my fiction was first professionally published—a series called "Herbert West—Reanimator" appearing in *Home Brew*. The founding of *Weird Tales* in 1923 opened up an outlet of considerable steadiness.

Meanwhile improving health enabled me to be more active than before. Always an antiquarian, I now adopted travel as an avenue into the past; seeking traditional architecture and scenery in various historic towns from Quebec to Key West and New Orleans. This has become my almost sole non-literary recreation. But my native New England and its elder lore remain deepest in my imagination, and appear frequently in what I write. I dwell at present in a house 130 years old on the crest of Providence's ancient hill.

I now realise that any actual literary merit I may have is confined to tales of dream-life, strange shadow, and cosmic "outside-ness", notwithstanding keen outside interests and a professional practice of general revision. I do not hope to equal my chosen weird authors—Poe, Machen, Dunsany, Blackwood, and M. R. James—literary sincerity being the only virtue I claim. I never write except to express a mood already existing, and shun the cheap standards of popular magazines. Many tales of mine involve actual dreams. My speed and manner of writing vary widely, but I always work best at night. Of my products, I prefer "The Colour Out of Space" and "The Music of Erich Zann". Despite some anthological reprintings and citations in annuals, I have no published collection.

I believe that fantastic writing constitutes a serious—though of course very limited—literary field. Spectral fiction should be realistic and atmospheric, seeking lifelikeness except for the one central marvel, and eschewing emphasis on plot or character. Phenomena, not people, are the protagonists of the true weird tale.

Briefly Noted

Massimo Berruti has written a substantial treatise, *Dim-Remembered Stories: A Critical Study of R. H. Barlow*, due out later this year from Hippocampus Press. It features detailed analyses of Barlow's major fiction and poetry, with a special concentration on such tales as "A Dim-Remembered Story," "The Night Ocean," and "Origin Undetermined." Lovecraft's assistance to Barlow is addressed throughout the treatise, although Berruti properly recognises that such tales as "The Night Ocean" and even "'Till A' the Seas'" are substantially Barlow's in conception and execution. Such themes in Barlow's work as Dunsanianism, cosmicism, time, nature, and irony are discussed in detail, and Barlow's poetry is subjected to particularly careful analysis.

In Memoriam:
Dr. Harry K. Brobst (1909–2010)

Christopher M. O'Brien

Harry Kern Brobst was born at 10 P.M. on Thursday, February 11, 1909, at 843 Tatnall Street in Wilmington, Delaware. His parents were Harry Walter Brobst (May 10, 1874–June 10, 1932) and Cora Alice/Annie Kern Brobst (April 15, 1873–March 1979). A sister, Lucille (July 1, 1907–December 22, 1907) predeceased him as an infant.

Young Harry remembered his parents speaking German around the household much of the time and recalled the day in 1917 when his father burst in the door with the news that the United States had entered World War I. Harry could recall hand cranked cars and meeting Civil War veterans as a youth. He once saw Thomas Edison (1847–1931), with whom he shared a birthday, in a small town parade.

During the 1918 Spanish flu epidemic, his family cared for a sick neighbor and he recalled vividly arriving with food one day only to find the man's corpse.

The family moved to Allentown, Pennsylvania, in 1921, where he recalled tales of the "hexerei" among the locals. Harry's father had a great interest in spectacle and never missed an opportunity to witness something unusual. Thus young Brobst saw Harry Houdini (1874–1926) perform an outdoor stunt and heard a talk by Madame Curie (1867–1934).

Brobst was a reader of Hugo Gernsback's magazine *Science and Invention*, which contained many early science fiction works before the genre was given the name, and recalled with fondness the serial "The Man from the Atom" by G. Peyton Wertenbaker in the August 1923 issue, later reprinted in the premiere issue of *Amazing Stories*.

Graduating high school in 1927, Harry attended Muhlenberg College in Allentown for a year (*Letters to Robert Bloch* 24), but found employment scarce.

Brobst initiated a correspondence with H. P. Lovecraft and shortly thereafter entered a psychiatric nursing program through Butler Hospital in Providence, followed by "a medical-surgical affiliation at Boston City Hospital" (Murray 30) begun in October 1933 (*Mysteries of Time and Spirit* 331) and concluding in 1935. Brobst arrived in the city in February 1932, and Lovecraft treated him to tours of various sites and meals at Maxfield's, and noted their activities in his correspondence. Brobst occasionally enclosed notes to Lovecraft's correspondents such as Wandrei, Derleth, and Smith.

In September 1932 Brobst's friend Carl F. Strauch (1908–1989), whose volume *Twenty-Nine Poems* was already in print, came to visit (*Mysteries of Time and Spirit* 310–11). While he had an appreciation for the supernatural as a reader, Harry Brobst was not of a literary bent, nor the type to engage in amateur weird writing. However, his friend Carl Strauch was, and evidently Strauch bristled at Lovecraft's criticism of the writing sample he'd shown him.

During the 1930s, Brobst also journeyed abroad and saw Adolf Hitler give a speech at a rally in Munich. Though he wished to pursue studies at Cambridge, he was dissuaded by wartime conditions.

On July 4, 1933, fellow *Weird Tales* writer E. Hoffmann Price (1898–1988) was in town and Lovecraft invited Harry to join them (Price 49–51). Price continued to visit Brobst during his cross-country jaunts into the 1980s. Others of Lovecraft's associates whom Brobst met were R. H. Barlow (1918–1951), Donald Wandrei (1908–1987), and James F. Morton (1870–1941).

Brobst subsequently entered Brown as a psychology student, where he met his wife, Judith Sylvia Heideman (1906–1988), whom he married in 1935. After Brobst obtained a B.A. from Brown, the couple settled into 73 Brown Street (*Mysteries of Time and Spirit* 369), and Harry worked as a night supervisor at the Charles V. Chapin Psychiatric Clinic. Lovecraft enjoyed hearing the details of Brobst's work; for his part, Brobst expressed his doubts as to the sanity of Lovecraft's correspondent William Lumley (1880–1960) (*Means to Freedom* 1.288).

When asked what he felt was Lovecraft's best work, Brobst replied: "One story of his that I felt represented a high level of achievement was 'The Strange High House in the Mist.' I think it was probably the most poetic creation of his."

Regarding Lovecraft's reticence he once told me, "I got a strong feeling that there were certain things he didn't want to talk about and I respected that. He was in many ways a very guarded person."

I recall Brobst vehemently objected when I advanced the theory that the circumstances behind the deaths of Lovecraft's parents may have instilled in him a fear of hospitals, which prevented him from seeking medical treatment at the end of his own life.

During this time Lovecraft's political perspective was also affected by the political writings of Emanuel Haldeman-Julius (1889–1951), to which Brobst introduced him.

Harry and Judith visited Lovecraft during his final days at Jane Brown Memorial Hospital and attended Lovecraft's funeral on March 18, 1937. Harry wrote to some of Lovecraft's correspondents such as Clark Ashton Smith, R. H. Barlow, and the artist Virgil Finlay (1914–1971) to inform them of Lovecraft's passing. Smith noted Brobst's contention that "HPL's philosophic convictions, his atheism and disbelief in immortality, should be made plain in anything written about him and his work" (*Selected Letters of Clark Ashton Smith* 291), a stance that has been borne out in most modern Lovecraft scholarship.

Brobst was a doctoral student at the University of Pennsylvania (Philadelphia) when ENIAC, the Electronic Numerical Integrator And Computer, was built by John W. Mauchly (1907–1980) and J. Presper Eckert, Jr. (1919–1995), and he saw an early demonstration of it at the University's Moore School of Electrical Engineering. Brobst taught at the school from 1942 to 1944.

After earning his Ph.D. around 1946, Brobst entered the psychology department of Oklahoma A&M College (now Oklahoma State University), retiring in 1974. He was active in the Unitarian Universalist Church of Stillwater and a local humanist group.

Describing his travels abroad during the 1970s, particularly in Tunisia, Brobst foresaw many social problems on the horizon.

Judith passed away on February 24, 1988, and Harry remained in the small home a few blocks from the OSU campus, which he had purchased in 1963. Having long since lost or given away his letters from Lovecraft and anything else he had that was Lovecraft-related, Harry lived as a minimalist as his sparsely furnished home attested.

As interest in Lovecraft grew, Brobst was contacted by research- ers and consulted by L. Sprague de Camp for his biography. In May 1990 he was interviewed by Will Murray, the results of which ap- peared in *Lovecraft Studies* No. 22/23. Although he would have liked to attend the Lovecraft Centennial Conference held in Provi- dence that August, he begged off due to the emotional associations with the area.

I first came into contact with him in March of 1999 and visited him later that year, finding him well, although suffering from increas- ing macular degeneration and poor hearing in spite of two hearing aids. He then had a serious operation on his vertebrae in December 1999 that he didn't expect to survive, but from which he fully recov- ered.

Brobst allowed me to videotape an interview with him in the summer of 2000.

On November 4, 2000, Brobst was hospitalized for four months with a perforated esophagus and hiatal hernia. After dying on the operating table, being revived, and being tube-fed for months, his was a slow recovery and he spent the next two months in a Stillwa- ter assisted living facility, which he hated, before returning to his home in April 2001. Despite his ailments, he forged ever onward.

During my visit in spring 2001, I took a few additional minutes of video, this time asking Brobst to elaborate on his "remember the philosophers of old" comment to Lovecraft on his deathbed, and his discovery of *Weird Tales*.

Brobst once asked me about a story called "The Lip" that he re- membered from *Weird Tales*. I had assumed he had meant the story by Arthur Styron from *Weird Tales* of July 1925. I admitted to never having read it, but promised to find it and managed to secure a photo- copy from a collector. Brobst was delighted I was able to find the thing, but it no longer impressed him as it had in his youth. It struck me as a "Tell-Tale Heart" rip-off, and in hindsight he agreed. I now realize that he may have been talking about another story entirely, Henry S. Whitehead's "The Lips," from the September 1929 *Weird Tales*.

Dr. Brobst was a delight to talk to, and although his health was not the best, I was amazed that he was able to recall events of more than seventy years ago with crystal clarity. He was still very much aware of developments in the news, and was always surprised at the amount of information I was able to dig up online.

In 2005 relatives transferred Brobst to an assisted living facility in Joplin, Missouri, where he died on January 13, 2010. He joins Woodburn Harris in being a centenarian amongst the Lovecraft Circle.

Works Cited

Lovecraft, H. P. *Letters to Robert Bloch*. Edited by David E. Schultz and S. T. Joshi. West Warwick, RI: Necronomicon Press, 1993.

Lovecraft, H. P., and Donald Wandrei. *Mysteries of Time and Spirit: The Letters of H. P. Lovecraft and Donald Wandrei*. Edited by S. T. Joshi and David E. Schultz. San Francisco: Night Shade Books, 2002.

Murray, Will. "An Interview with Harry Brobst." *Lovecraft Studies* Nos. 22/23 (Fall 1990): 24–42, 21.

Price, E. Hoffmann. *Book of the Dead: Friends of Yesteryear—Fictioneers and Others*. Sauk City, WI: Arkham House, 2001.

Briefly Noted

Stanza Press, a division of PS Publishing (Hornsea, UK), has announced the publication of Lovecraft's *Hallowe'en in a Suburb and Others*, a collection of the Lovecraft poems that appeared in *Weird Tales*, which are evidently in the public domain. The volume has been announced for early 2010, but it has not yet been seen. It will sell for £12.00 ($19.20) hardcover. A volume of the poetry of Clark Ashton Smith from *Weird Tales*, titled *Song of the Necromancer and Others*, and of Robert E. Howard, *The Singer in the Mist and Others*, is also announced for early 2010.

Time, Space, and Natural Law: Science and Pseudo-Science in Lovecraft

S. T. Joshi

I. A Tripartite Nature

In 1920 H. P. Lovecraft made the following analysis of his own temperament:

> I should describe mine own nature as tripartite, my interests consisting of three parallel and dissociated groups—(a) Love of the strange and the fantastic. (b) Love of the abstract truth and of scientific logick. (c) Love of the ancient and the permanent. Sundry combinations of these three strains will probably account for all my odd tastes and eccentricities. (*SL* 1.110)

This is a remarkably perspicacious and prescient remark, and it is exactly those "sundry combinations" that not only clarify many of the "eccentricities" of his personality (his simultaneous adoration of the past—ranging from ancient Rome to the colonial remains of his native Providence, Rhode Island—and his enthusiasm for the most recent findings in the sciences, from Einstein's theory of relativity to the exploration of the Antarctic) but also help to illuminate the most distinctive features of his literary work. In a literary career that spanned less than two decades and comprised no more than sixty works of fiction (all of them short stories with the exception of three short novels and several novellas), Lovecraft performed a critical function in the development of supernatural fiction; Fritz Leiber, a late colleague and perhaps his most distinguished disciple, put it best when he wrote that Lovecraft "shifted the focus of supernatural dread from man and his little world and his gods, to the stars and the black and unplumbed gulfs of intergalactic space"

(Leiber 455). In effect, Leiber is maintaining that Lovecraft fashioned a unique hybrid, mingling those elements of the traditional supernatural tale that still remained scientifically and aesthetically viable with the emerging genre of science fiction, at whose birth Lovecraft could be said to have been a bemused eyewitness.

In order to effect this union, Lovecraft required not only a thorough grounding in the history of supernatural literature (a history he himself ably charted in his monograph, "Supernatural Horror in Literature" [1927]) but an awareness of the many sciences—physics, biology, chemistry, astronomy, geology, paleontology—that could conceivably be drawn upon for the new kind of horror tale he was writing. To be sure, Lovecraft did not set out with such a goal in mind; rather, that "triparite" nature he noted in 1920 led inexorably to this result, so that by around 1930 Lovecraft was quite aware that he himself was fashioning something new in the realm of fantastic literature.

All three aspects of Lovecraft's tripartite nature were remarkably early in manifesting themselves. His enthusiasm for such works as Grimm's fairy tales, Coleridge's *Rime of the Ancient Mariner*, and the tales of Poe—all absorbed by the age of eight—instilled in him a lifelong love of the "strange and the fantastic." His birth in an ancient colonial town, with tangible landmarks dating back two centuries, and his early absorption of the myths of classical Greece and Rome (initially through Bulfinch's *Age of Fable* and later through translations of classical texts and then first-hand knowledge of those texts after he learned Latin), did much to foster his taste for the "ancient and the permanent." But where did his taste for "abstract truth and . . . scientifick logic" originate? It is, of course, impossible to specify with precision, but Lovecraft himself provides an engaging account of one of his earliest encounters with science:

> The science of chemistry . . . first captivated me in the Year of Our Lord 1898—in a rather peculiar way. With the insatiable curiosity of early childhood, I used to spend hours poring over the pictures in the back of Webster's *Unabridged Dictionary*—absorbing a miscellaneous variety of ideas. After familiarising myself with antiquities, mediaeval dress and armour, birds, animals, reptiles, fishes, flags of all nations, heraldry, etc., etc., I lit upon the section devoted to "Philoso-

phical and Scientific Instruments". I was veritably hypnotised with it. Chemical apparatus especially attracted me, and I resolved (before knowing a thing about the science!) to have a laboratory. . . . By 1901 or thereabouts I had a fair knowledge of the principles of chemistry and the details of the inorganic part—about the equivalent of a high-school course, and not including analysis of any kind. Then my fickle fancy turned away to the intensive study of geography, geology, anthropology, and above all *astronomy* . . . (SL 1.74)

There are a number of interesting features in this account, to which I shall return shortly. But first, let us now read of his discovery of astronomy in 1902, which Lovecraft himself admitted did more to shape his entire world-view than any other single event:

I began to study astronomy in 1902—age 12. My interest came through two sources—discovery of an old book of my grandmother's in the attic, and a previous interest in physical geography. Within a year I was thinking of virtually nothing but astronomy, yet my keenest interest did not lie outside the solar system. I think I really ignored the abysses of space in my interest in the habitability of the various planets of the solar system. My observations (for I purchased a telescope early in 1903) were confined mostly to the moon and the planet Venus. You will ask, why the latter, since its markings are doubtful even in the largest instruments? I answer— this very MYSTERY was what attracted me. (SL 1.69)

Several things now become clear, chiefly the fact that Lovecraft was already combining his "love of the strange and the fantastic" with his burgeoning interest in science: it was exactly because the world revealed by science was, potentially, a world of mystery and even terror that he became enraptured with the sciences. Science was, certainly, a way of penetrating those mysteries, but there would always be further mysteries to be explored, and perhaps many that could never be fully explicated. Lovecraft speaks of writing many stories at this time—not only horror tales in the old-time Gothic mode but tales inspired by Jules Verne and by W. Frank Russell's histrionic tale of Antarctic adventure, *The Frozen Pirate* (1887). Many of these tales, if they survived, would certainly be considered proto-science fiction, dim antecedents of such later works as *At the Mountains of Madness* and "The Shadow out of Time."

At this point it is hardly necessary to examine in detail the pro-
digious amount of scientific writing in which Lovecraft engaged between 1899 and 1908. This material, still largely unpublished,
includes such things as two long-running papers, *The Scientific Gazette* (which began as a *daily* on March 4, 1899, later lapsing into a
weekly and maintained at least until 1905 or 1906; its focus was
chiefly on chemistry) and *The Rhode Island Journal of Astronomy*
(begun on August 2, 1903 as a weekly and continued until at least
1907), numerous small booklets on special subjects (e.g., *A Good
Anaesthetic*), and even such things as (apparently daily) weather
forecasts, a result of Lovecraft's new-found interest in meteorology.
Lovecraft had, of course, abundant leisure to engage in this literary
work, since he attended grade school only in the years 1898–99 and
1902–03 and high school in 1904–05 and 1906–08, leaving abruptly
without a diploma. His first appearances in print were astronomy
columns written for local papers—the *Pawtuxet Valley Gleaner*
(1906) and the Providence *Tribune* (1906–08). Fiction and poetry
were also being written during this period, but Lovecraft later admits that he destroyed all but two stories written between 1903 and
1908: "The Beast in the Cave" (1905) and "The Alchemist" (1908).

The importance of all this scientific work for the course of his
fiction writing would become apparent only after the passage of a
decade or more; but Lovecraft was aware of a more immediate result—the formation of a scientific world-view. He prefaces the
above account of his discovery of astronomy with the words: "To
trace, then, my philosophical views." And in the seminal essay "A
Confession of Unfaith" (1922) he states unequivocally:

> The most poignant sensations of my existence are those of 1896,
> when I discovered the Hellenic world, and of 1902, when I discov-
> ered the myriad suns and worlds of infinite space. Sometimes I
> think the latter event the greater, for the grandeur of that growing
> conception of the universe still excites a thrill hardly to be dupli-
> cated. . . . By my thirteenth birthday I was thoroughly impressed
> with man's impermanence and insignificance, and by my seven-
> teenth, about which time I did some particularly detailed writing
> on the subject, I had formed in all essential particulars my present
> pessimistic cosmic views. (*CE* 5.147)

That last sentence is critical, although Lovecraft would shed the "pessimism" that he found in the cosmic viewpoint. As the title of this essay makes clear, Lovecraft used both the discovery of pre-Christian literature and the discovery of science as supports for the religious skepticism that he maintains developed as early as the age of five. In later years he was not shy in declaring himself an atheist (see *SL* 4.57), and he was endlessly fond of twitting pious associates such as Maurice W. Moe, who plaintively asked Lovecraft what he had against religion, to which he replied that his chief objection was that "the Judaeo-Christian mythology is NOT TRUE" (*SL* 1.60).

Lovecraft came to maturity at a time when the findings of nineteenth-century science—notably Darwin's theory of evolution, which was seen by many as destroying the last remaining intellectual support for the notion of an omnipotent deity in its implicit refutation of the "argument from design"—were being synthesized by a wide range of philosophers and scientists who, following Thomas Henry Huxley and Friedrich Nietzsche, were becoming increasingly bold in advancing purely secular theories both of cosmic origins and human motivations. Lovecraft came upon both Huxley and Nietzsche before 1920, and later absorbed Freud, Bertrand Russell, and many other secularists; but his chief bulwark remained astronomy, and in 1917 he made the pungent declaration:

> A mere knowledge of the approximate dimensions of the visible universe is enough to destroy forever the notion of a personal godhead whose whole care is expended upon puny mankind, and whose only genuine and original Messiah was dispatched to save the insignificant vermin, or men, who inhabit this one relatively microscopic globe. Not that science positively refutes religion—it merely makes religion seem monstrously improbable that a large majority of men can no longer believe in it. (*SL* 1.44)

Lovecraft may be guilty of a category error here, for there is no intrinsic reason why the size of the universe (a matter of *quantity*) should necessarily imply the insignificance of humanity (a matter of *quality*); but it becomes clear that he is relying on the argument from probability, since there now seems no particular reason why a god should have singled out this tiny corner of the unbounded universe for his special interest and concern. Elsewhere in this same letter Lovecraft flatly declares that "Life, animal and vegetable, in-cluding human life, is a mode of motion which ceases absolutely upon the death of the body containing it," and appeals to several sciences for further support for this destruction of the myth of the "soul":

> . . . sooner or later the relation betwixt organic and inorganic life will be discovered. It will be clearly demonstrated how carbon, hy-drogen, oxygen, nitrogen, and other elements combine to form sub-stances possessing vital energy. Probably the chemist or biologist will be able to create in his laboratory some very primitive sort of animal or vegetable organism. This will be the death knell of super-stition and theology alike . . . (SL 1.44)

In this as elsewhere, Lovecraft exaggerates the ability of the average person to absorb scientific information and also the influence of even generally diffused scientific knowledge in the religious and moral spheres; but it is evident that the advance of science had the effect of destroying forever any belief Lovecraft himself may have had in the human soul, in the existence of a deity, and in the role of that deity in guiding human affairs. Lovecraft could well be said to have been one of the most secular temperaments in modern litera-ture and thought.

II. Cannibals and Aliens

It is not my place here to trace the manifold ramifications of science upon Lovecraft's philosophical thought. More to the purpose is the role of science in Lovecraft's own literary work, particularly his fic-tion. It will become manifest that science provides the intellectual backbone of nearly all his short stories; but at the same time Love-craft seems to suggest that that science will itself will ultimately be a source of horror and destruction. Did he not write, in the early story "Facts Concerning the Late Arthur Jermyn and His Family" (1920), that "Science, already oppressive with its shocking revela-tions, will perhaps be the ultimate exterminator of our human spe-cies" (D 73)? Is this mere hyperbolic rhetoric, or an indication of Lovecraft's conflicted attitudes toward a science that was relent-lessly tearing away the remaining shreds of mystery in the cosmos?

And consider the more subtle expression of the same idea in the celebrated opening paragraph of "The Call of Cthulhu" (1926): "The sciences, each straining in its own direction, have hitherto harmed us little; but some day the piecing together of dissociated knowledge will open up such terrifying vistas of reality, and of our frightful position therein, that we shall either go mad from the revelation or flee from the deadly light into the peace and safety of a new dark age" (*DH* 125). The elucidation and contextualization of these passages may require considerable analysis, but in the course of it we may come to gain a better sense of what science actually meant to Lovecraft.

Some of Lovecraft's reliance on science is of an amusingly trivial sort. In the minor tale "The Transition of Juan Romero" (1919) he speaks in passing of a "gibbous moon," and then writes a self-important footnote: "Here is a lesson in scientific accuracy for fiction writers. I have just looked up the moon's phases for October, 1894, to find when a gibbous moon was visible at 2 a.m., and have changed the dates to fit!!" (*D* 340). Expressing early admiration for the work of Edgar Rice Burroughs, Lovecraft was nonetheless irritated at the scientific errors in both the Tarzan and the Mars stories (see *MW* 497); and he was tireless in correcting his colleagues' scientific errors, even going so far as to buy planispheres for Frank Belknap Long and Donald Wandrei "so that those young rascals won't get the constellations wrong in their future stories, as they have done in the past!" (*Essential Solitude* 2.724). All this is very entertaining, and at a minimum it shows the emphasis Lovecraft placed on rigid scientific accuracy. This kind of "realism" became a central tenet of his entire theory of weird fiction, as he explained in "Notes on Writing Weird Fiction": "Inconceivable events and conditions have a special handicap to overcome, and this can be accomplished only through the maintenance of a careful realism in every phase of the story *except* that touching on the one given marvel" (*CE* 2.177).

Science of a marginally more significant sort appears in "The Beast in the Cave"—in this case, biology, or, more specifically, the theory of evolution. This story could be said to have initiated a wide range of Lovecraft tales that feature a potential reversal along the evolutionary ladder. Here the narrator, lost in the labyrinthine depths of Mammoth Cave, feels threatened by some entity who appears to be pursuing him; upon his first sight of the creature—after a guide comes to rescue him and shines a flashlight upon the dying figure—he identifies it as "an anthropoid ape of large proportions" (D 327); of course, the creature turns out to be a man who had been lost in the cave for months or years. The reasons why the narrator thought the entity to be non-human are of interest: unable to see him, but only hearing his footsteps, the narrator becomes convinced that "these footfalls were *not like those of any mortal man*" because "*at times*, when I listened carefully, I seemed to trace the falls of *four* instead of *two* feet" (D 324; Lovecraft's emphasis). In other words, the man, in his "fallen" state, had renounced the prototypical badge of humanity—an upright gait—for the savagery of the animal.

This story immediately brings "Arthur Jermyn" to mind; for just as the narrator of "The Beast in the Cave" is struck by "the all-pervading and almost unearthly *whiteness* so characteristic of the whole anatomy" (D 327) of the hapless man, so in "Arthur Jermyn" we appear to be dealing with a "mummified white ape of some unknown species, less hairy than any recorded variety, and infinitely nearer mankind—quite shockingly so" (DH 82). This is, indeed, the ape that Sir Wade Jermyn had mated with in the eighteenth century, leading to the "subtly odd and repellent cast" (D 78) of the entire Jermyn line from that point onward. But it is not only this that leads Arthur Jermyn, a sensitive poet and last of the Jermyns, to set himself ablaze on a moor one night: rather, it is his realization that the peculiarities of his own heredity are, to a lesser degree, implicit in the entire human race: by subtle clues Lovecraft makes it clear that all humanity is derived from the "prehistoric white Congolese civilisation" (D 74) of which that white ape was a descendant. For someone of Lovecraft's well-known racialist inclinations (for which see Section IV), this would be the acme of horror; but more broadly, Lovecraft is emphasizing human "insignificance" by postulating—as he would repeatedly do in many different ways in later stories—a degrading or ignominious origin of our species.

For Lovecraft, devolution can occur in several ways: unwholesome inbreeding, psychological trauma, cannibalism, and miscegenation (interbreeding with alien species). Psychological trauma could conceivably be the reason for the degeneration of the man in "The Beast in the Cave," forced as he is to adopt animalistic behavior as a means of self-preservation (presumably he eats, without the benefit of cooking, any stray animals that cross his path). A similar trauma appears to cause the spectacular descent upon the evolutionary scale of the otherwise refined narrator of "The Rats in the Walls" (1923). Science would appear to be a critical component in this story, as at one point the narrator, Delapore, brings in a band of scientists to assist in elucidating the apparently supernatural phenomena by which his restored home, Exham Priory, is plagued: the "five eminent authorities" (DH 39) include "Sir William Brinton, whose excavations in the Troad excited most of the world in their day" (DH 40); the suggestion is that most of the five are archaeologists or anthropologists, although oddly enough one of them, Thornton, proves to be a "psychic investigator" (DH 41). And yet, the source of the horror in this story remains a bit unclear. It appears that Delapore comes upon evidence that his family, and by extension all the previous occupants of Exham Priory going back to prehistory, had practiced cannibalism, sadism, and other monstrous acts, and is so horrified that he immediately devolves from a modern, civilized man to a cannibalistic monster: after uttering wild cries in increasing ancient languages (archaic English, Anglo-Saxon, Latin, Gaelic, and what in a letter he terms "pithecanthropoid" [SL 1.258]) he is found "crouching in the blackness over the plump, half-eaten body of Capt. Norrys" (DH 45). In reality, the science in "The Rats in the Walls" is only a kind of gloss or patina that seeks to lend a vague sort of plausibility to a story that is otherwise fully in the old Gothic mode: it is, in fact, Lovecraft's "Fall of the House of Usher."

Much the same can be said for "The Picture in the House" (1920), where unnatural longevity—if not actual devolution—is attributed to cannibalism. The large old man with "abnormally ruddy" (DH 120) cheeks has not merely maintained his robust physique by devouring humans ("His height could not have been less than six feet, and despite a general air of age and poverty he was stout and powerful in proportion" [DH 120]); it is that he has extended the span of his life far beyond the normal, for it becomes evident that he was actually born in the eighteenth century. Once again, the scientific rationale for the story is relatively slight: the old man him-

self, in his crude patois, appeals to Biblical precedent when he remarks, "They say meat makes blood an' flesh, an' gives ye new life,
so I wondered ef 'twudn't make a man live longer an' longer ef 'twas
more the same" (*DH* 123), a manifest reference to "For the blood is
the life" (Deut. 12:23). But the story is worth contrasting with another one written a few months earlier, "The Terrible Old Man"
(1920): here no rationale at all is provided for the anomalous longevity of the old sea captain of the title; if anything, there is a suggestion that sorcery of some kind is involved, if those "many
peculiar bottles, in each [of which] a small piece of lead suspended
pendulum-wise from a string" (*DH* 273) are any indication: they appear to contain the souls of the old man's former crew. Can the
magic that has confined the souls of his shipmates also have helped
to give him unnatural life?

Things do not get much better, from a scientific perspective, in
"The Lurking Fear" (1922), a potboiler written to order for what
Lovecraft later called a "vile rag" (*SL* 4.170) named *Home Brew*. Here
one can assume that some sort of inbreeding caused the degeneration of the Martense family, who dwelt in a once-sumptuous mansion in the Catskill mountain region of New York State. The
narrator, seeking to learn the source of the repeated attacks upon
the outlying regions—attacks that had occurred randomly for more
than a century—in the end learns that it is not a single entity that is
responsible for the mayhem but an entire colony of "deformed hairy
devils or apes" (*D* 198) that have dug endless tunnels all through
Tempest Mountain, where the mansion stands. In a cataclysmic vision the narrator finally sees one of them clearly: "The object was
nauseous; a filthy whitish gorilla thing with sharp yellow fangs and
matted fur. It was the ultimate product of mammalian degeneration; the frightful outcome of isolated spawning, multiplication, and
cannibal nutrition above and below the ground; the embodiment of
all the snarling chaos and grinning fear that lurk behind life" (*D*
199). That final, hysterical phrase makes it clear that what Lovecraft
was seeking in this story was not a plausible scientific rationale but
merely a lurid shudder, made all the more flamboyant by the fe-
vered prose with which the entire tale is written.

If any scientific element predominates in the first decade (1917–
26) of Lovecraft's mature fiction-writing career, it is the notion of

alien races—races that, either emerging from the depths of space or nurtured in the secret corners of the earth, menace humanity from below and make our own dominance of the planet tenuous indeed. One of his earliest stories, "Dagon" (1917), involves a narrator who, having escaped from a German prison-ship and drifting in the open sea in a rowboat, awakens to find that an entire land mass has emerged from the depths of the sea. The bas-reliefs the narrator finds on a monolith depict some anomalous entities: "I think that these things were supposed to depict men—at least, a certain sort of men; though the creatures were shewn disporting like fishes in the waters of some marine grotto" (D 18). But the story ends shortly thereafter, and not much is made of this. What Lovecraft is hinting in this story is that there are not merely isolated non-human—or not fully human—entities lurking in hidden places, but entire civilizations of which we know nothing. "The Temple" (1920) conveys this idea somewhat more effectively. The commander of a disabled German submarine that is sinking to the bottom of the Atlantic comes upon evidence of an entire city on the sea-bottom; what is more, the art that the commander sees adorning an immense temple in this city "imparts the impression of terrible antiquity, as though it were the remotest rather than the immediate ancestor of Greek art" (D 67). In other words, Lovecraft is saying that Greek art—one of the greatest sources of aesthetic pride of which we as human beings can boast—is, in the end, a degraded echo of a much more refined art produced by an alien species. In "The Nameless City" (1921) an archaeologist encounters clear evidence that a forgotten city in Arabia was built by "monstrosities" (D 104) who, as he learns cataclysmically at the end of the story, are still existing. Lovecraft, however, does not seem to have thought through the physiology of these creatures particularly carefully:

> They were of the reptile kind, with body lines suggesting sometimes the crocodile, sometimes the seal, but more often nothing of which either the naturalist or the palaeontologist ever heard of. In size they approximated a small man, and their fore legs bore delicate and evidently flexible feet curiously like human hands and fingers. But strangest of all were their heads, which presented a contour violating all known biological principles. To nothing can

such things be well compared—in one flash I thought of comparisons as varied as the cat, the bulldog, the mythic Satyr, and the human being. Not Jove himself had so colossal and protuberant a
forehead, yet the horns and the noselessness and the alligator-like
jaw placed the things outside all established categories. (*D* 104)

All this is very piquant; but, if these creatures were the products of
terrestrial evolution, how could they have gained such anomalously
hybrid features? Analogous entities are found in "The Festival"
(1923): "They were not altogether crows, nor moles, nor buzzards,
nor ants, nor vampire bats, nor decomposed human beings; but
something I cannot and must not recall" (*D* 215). That last comment
is particularly unhelpful, and one would never know that, as Lovecraft would admit years later (see *SL* 4.297), this broodingly atmospheric story—which chiefly seeks to evoke the antique atmosphere
of Marblehead, Massachusetts—was even in part inspired by Margaret A. Murray's controversial anthropological treatise, *The Witch-
Cult in Western Europe* (1921), which advocated the theory (now
regarded as highly unlikely) that the medieval witch-cult was the
product of a pre-Aryan race of stunted human beings who retreated
into caves and other secret places but managed to carry on their ne-
farious practices. Lovecraft, who had just encountered the Welsh
writer Arthur Machen, whose horror fiction embodies an approximately similar conception in its use of the legends of the "little people," found the apparent scientific confirmation of the idea fatally
enticing, and he repeated it as proven fact to the end of his life.

It is evident that, although science peeps out here and there in
many early Lovecraft tales, it is largely used as a makeshift to en-
hance the *aesthetic* plausibility of the scenarios, which remain over-
whelmingly supernatural in their overall thrust. The best that can be
said for these stories is that they make a *gesture* toward scientific
plausibility, as Lovecraft is coming to recognize that the standard
ghost, goblin, witch, werewolf, or vampire is no longer convincing to
a sophisticated readership that has learned too much about biology,
chemistry, and physics, and that has also shed the naïve religious belief that formed at least a part of the pseudo-intellectual support for
these entities.

All this makes us stop short in amazement when we encounter

"The Shunned House" (1924). On the surface, this appears to be nothing more than an artfully told haunted house tale set in Lovecraft's native Providence. The narrator and his uncle strive to ascertain why so many deaths—and certain other anomalies—have occurred in a house in the oldest district of the city; a house that, as a matter of fact, "was never regarded by the solid part of the community as in any real sense 'haunted'" but merely "'unlucky'" (*MM* 237). But as the narrator explores the history of the house and its occupants and seems forced to the conclusion that some vampiric entity is sucking the life out of anyone who lives there too long, we suddenly come upon this remarkable passage:

> We were not, as I have said, in any sense childishly superstitious, but scientific study and reflection had taught us that the known universe of three dimensions embraces the merest fraction of the whole cosmos of substance and energy. In this case an overwhelming preponderance of evidence from numerous authentic sources pointed to the tenacious existence of certain forces of great power and, so far as the human point of view is concerned, exceptional malignancy. To say that we actually believed in vampires or werewolves would be a carelessly inclusive statement. Rather must it be said that we were not prepared to deny the possibility of certain unfamiliar and unclassified modifications of vital force and attenuated matter; existing very infrequently in three-dimensional space because of its more intimate connexion with other spatial units, yet close enough to the boundary of our own to furnish us occasional manifestations which we, for lack of a proper vantage-point, may never hope to understand. . . .
>
> Such a thing was surely not a physical or biochemical impossibility in the light of a newer since which includes the theories of relativity and intra-atomic action. One might easily imagine an alien nucleus of substance or energy, formless or otherwise, kept alive by imperceptible or immaterial subtractions from the life-force or bodily tissues and fluids of other and more palpably living things into which it penetrates and with whose fabric it sometimes completely merges itself. (*MM* 251–52)

A treatise could be written on this passage. That first sentence brings to mind the earlier tale "From Beyond" (1920), a florid and confused tale whose only interest lies in its embodiment (as I have demonstrated elsewhere [see Joshi, "Sources"]) of certain principles found in Hugh Elliot's *Modern Science and Materialism* (1919), a major source for Lovecraft's views on science and philosophy. In essence, "From Beyond" is a kind of horrific instantiation of the common fact that all material entities are in fact largely composed of the empty space between atoms and molecules. The histrionic scientist in that story, Crawford Tillinghast, declares pompously: "What do we know . . . of the world and the universe about us? Our means of receiving impressions are absurdly few, and our notions of surrounding objects infinitely narrow" (*D* 91). Tillinghast has invented a machine that can *"break down the barriers"* (*D* 91; Lovecraft's emphasis) that prevent our seeing what the universe is "really" like; accordingly, the narrator sees a succession of hideous entities "brushing past me and occasionally *walking or drifting through my supposedly solid body"* (*D* 95; Lovecraft's emphasis).

Far more interesting in "The Shunned House" is the reference to "relativity and intra-atomic action." The remarkable thing about this is that, just a year previously, Lovecraft felt that his entire worldview was in tatters because recent eclipse observations had confirmed the truth of the Einstein theory:

> My cynicism and scepticism are increasing, and from an entirely new cause—the Einstein theory. . . . All is chance, accident and ephemeral illusion—a fly may be greater than Arcturus, and Durfee Hill may surpass Mount Everest—assuming them to be removed from the present planet and differently environed in the continuum of space-time. There are no values in all infinity—the least idea that there are is the supreme mockery of all. (*SL* 1.231)

Lovecraft snapped out of this naïve response to Einstein fairly quickly, although many other intellectuals saw in relativity the downfall of much of the nineteenth century's cocksure materialism. Lovecraft rebuked such careless thinkers in a late letter:

> Although these new turns of science don't really mean a thing in relation to the myth of cosmic consciousness and teleology, a new brood of despairing and horrified moderns is seizing on the doubt of all positive knowledge which they imply; and is deducing there-

from that, *since nothing is true*, therefore *anything can be true . . .* whence one may invent or revive any sort of mythology that fancy or nostalgia or desperation may dictate, and defy anyone to prove that it isn't "emotionally" true—whatever that means. This sickly, decadent neomysticism—a protest not only against machine materialism but against pure science with its destruction of the mystery and dignity of human emotion and experience—will be the dominant creed of middle twentieth century aesthetes . . . (*SL* 3.53)

What Lovecraft is saying, in essence, is that Einstein's devising of the precise formula for the transformation of matter into energy does not make the archaic notion of "spirit" (i.e., "soul") any more plausible than before; indeed, as he says in another letter:

For matter, it appears, really is exactly what "spirit" was always supposed to be. Thus it is proved that *wandering energy always has a detectable form*—that if it doesn't take the form of waves or electron-streams, *it becomes matter itself;* and that the absence of matter or any other detectable energy-form indicates *not the presence of spirit, but the absence of anything whatever.* (*SL* 2.266–67)

This is all very clever, and pretty much on the mark. Lovecraft had a bit more difficulty with quantum theory, and the one passage I have found in his correspondence where he discusses it (*SL* 3.228) reveals a fundamental misunderstanding of it: Lovecraft wants to maintain that the "uncertainty" in regard to the action of sub-atomic particles is an *epistemological,* not an *ontological,* uncertainty; that is, it is only our human inability to predict the movement of sub-atomic particles that causes the uncertainty, and that the uncertainty is not inherent in nature. This conclusion is erroneous, but Lovecraft can be pardoned for not fully grasping this highly complex theory—which many thinkers seized upon as spelling the downfall of all causality, a conclusion that is itself highly likely to be erroneous, and is certainly erroneous where atomic or molecular action is concerned.

What we have in "The Shunned House," then, is, for the first time in Lovecraft's literary career, a coherently conceived scientific rationale that reinterprets the standard myth of the vampire and recasts it into something much more complex—and, as it happens, much more mysterious and horrifying. The appeal to advanced science is also an appeal to the scientific method—the method of keeping an open mind in regard to phenomena that may appear bizarre or even contrary to nature, but which may in the end be incorporated into an expanded conception of the universe that is still predominantly materialistic. And whereas the conventional vampire could be dealt with by such hackneyed means as a crucifix or exposure to the light of day, the vampiric entity in "The Shunned House" is a far more redoubtable creature; and it requires nothing less material than "six carboys of sulphuric acid" (*MM* 260) which, when poured upon the entity, elicits a "hideous roar" (*MM* 261) heard throughout the city.

III. The Brain in the Canister

The rest of Lovecraft's fiction shows a constant if unsystematic attempt to embody scientific principles as an intellectual substratum, even if some of them radically exceed the bounds of the known laws of nature. Moreover, it is in the stories of his last decade of writing that we finally come upon an extensive use of those sciences—especially chemistry, geology, and astronomy—that Lovecraft professed to have been his first loves, and which, taken as a whole, fostered the sense of "cosmicism" that is his defining characteristic as a fiction writer. Even though cosmicism was stated as an aesthetic principle at least as early as 1921 ("Man's relations to man do not captivate my fancy. It is man's relation to the cosmos—to the unknown—which alone arouses in me the spark of creative imagination" [*MW* 155]), it is embodied in relatively few tales prior to 1926. "Dagon," "Beyond the Wall of Sleep" (1919), and "The Temple" only hint at cosmicism; perhaps Lovecraft's most interesting treatment is found in the prose poem "Nyarlathotep" (1920), which powerfully suggests the decline of human civilization as a corollary to the collapse of the entire fabric of the universe.

All that changes with "The Call of Cthulhu" (1926). This story is important not so much for its introduction of the so-called Cthulhu Mythos (a term never coined by Lovecraft), but rather for its coherent and plausible use of the theme that would come to dominate his subsequent tales: alien races dwelling on the underside of the known world. And because these alien races are now postulated as having emerged from the depths of space, they evade the dilemma (found in various ways in "Dagon," "The Temple," and "The Nameless City") of incorporating these entities within the scope of terrestrial evolution.

The stories of this type—"The Colour out of Space" (1927), "The Dunwich Horror" (1928), "The Whisperer in Darkness" (1930), *At the Mountains of Madness* (1931), "The Shadow out of Time" (1934–35)—are all of such length and complexity as to preclude detailed analysis; but some hints as to their distinctive features can be made here. In a sense it could be said that Lovecraft is choosing the easy way out by hypothesizing an extraterrestrial origin for his various alien species, thereby obviating the need to harmonize them within the known laws of terrestrial biology and physics; but the mass of circumstantial detail Lovecraft provides shows how much thought he took in fashioning his creatures, and in rendering them simultaneously plausible and *outré*. He is careful not to make them *too* bizarre, *too* defiant of the known laws of nature; for he knows (as he states in his discussion of the ramifications of the Einstein theory) that the universe within the scope of our knowledge

> *isn't big enough* to let relativity get in its major effects—*hence we can rely on the never-failing laws of earth to give absolutely reliable results in the nearer heavens.* . . . If we can study the relation of a race of ants to a coral atoll or a volcanic islet which has risen and will sink again—and nobody dares deny that we can—then it will be *equally possible* for us, if we have suitable instruments and methods, to study the relation of man and the earth to the solar system and the nearer stars. The result will, when obtained, be just as conclusive as that of a study in terrestrial zoölogy or geology. (*SL* 2.265; Lovecraft's emphasis)

Accordingly, the only physical anomaly revealed by the baleful entity Cthulhu is his (its?) ability to recombine disparate parts of himself after they have been scattered. Old Castro, who "remembered bits of hideous legend" about Cthulhu and his "spawn," states that they "were not composed altogether of flesh and blood. They had shape . . . but that shape was not made of matter. When the stars were right, They could plunge from world to world through the sky;

but when the stars were wrong, They could not live. But although They no longer lived, They would never really die" (*DH* 140). All this is expressed in a deliberately mystical fashion, for Castro is a naïve and ignorant worshipper of Cthulhu and his minions; but underneath this language one can see Lovecraft *stretching*—but not *breaking*—the laws of nature to accommodate the existence of an alien species just outside the bounds of the known. That Cthulhu is made up of a substance not quite material as we recognize it; that there is some obscure connection between him and the stars of the outer cosmos; that his manner of existence is somewhere between "life" and "death" as we are accustomed to understand them—all this is hinted, and no more than hinted, in Castro's maunderings.

"The Colour out of Space" is perhaps Lovecraft's greatest triumph in the depiction of an extraterrestrial entity. The creature (or creatures?) that came in the meteorite that landed in a central Massachusetts farm cannot be analyzed by chemical means: the substance of the meteorite itself, when collected by scientists from Miskatonic University, "had faded wholly away when they put it in a glass beaker" (*DH* 58) and, when another specimen was gathered, it failed to respond to numerous tests—water, hydrochloric acid, nitric acid, carbon disulphide, and several others (*DH* 58). Lovecraft's chemical experiments, conducted from the age of eight onwards, certainly stood him in good stead here. But more significantly, it is the *psychology* of the nebulous entities that is least amenable to human analysis; whereas an obviously malevolent motive is at one point attributed to Cthulhu ("After vigintillions of years great Cthulhu was loose again, and ravening for delight" [*DH* 152]), the entities in the meteorite are utterly inscrutable as to their goals or purpose. Lovecraft effectively conveys both their physical and their moral incomprehensibility in the simple words of the dying farmer Nahum Gardner: ". . . the colour . . . cold an' wet, but it burns . . . dun't know what it wants . . . it beats down your mind an' then gits ye . . . it come from some place whar things ain't as they is here . . ." (*DH* 71–72).

From this perspective, "The Dunwich Horror" and even "The Whisperer in Darkness"—the latter a masterful evocation of the terror to be found in the remote backwoods of Vermont—represent a regression; for the entities in these tales are all too obviously intent on harming human beings and perhaps even in dominating them. "The

Dunwich Horror," indeed, is in many ways a reprise of the short novel *The Case of Charles Dexter Ward* (1927), which in its use of alchemy and witchcraft can be said to be the pinnacle of Lovecraft's work in the old-time Gothic mode; it is, in effect, his *House of the Seven Gables* in its tracing of a curse that spans the generations. "The Dunwich Horror" is remarkably similar in many details. The cosmic entity Yog-Sothoth has mated with a backwoods farm girl, Lavinia Whateley, and spawned twin monsters—one of them, Wilbur Whateley, approximately human, and the other, his twin, quite otherwise. Although Wilbur reveals some interesting physiological traits when his dead body is analyzed, the science here is merely a sop to plausibility in a tale that otherwise is entirely dependent on the supernatural and on sorcery (three professors from Miskatonic University destroy the twin by the use of incantations). More to be censured is the obvious good-vs.-evil scenario that Lovecraft sets up between the valiant Professor Armitage and the Whateley clan; at one point he speaks wildly and bombastically of a "plan for the extirpation of the entire human race and all animal and vegetable life from the earth by some terrible elder race of beings from another dimension" (*DH* 185), and then emits a self-important lecture at the end: "We have no business calling in such things from outside, and only very wicked people and very wicked cults ever try to" (*DH* 197).

In "The Whisperer in Darkness" Lovecraft seems to dance nervously around the issue of what the fungi from Yuggoth are actually after. Once again, a lone farmer, Henry W. Akeley, is besieged by extraterrestrials—they come from Yuggoth (Pluto), although Lovecraft is careful to specify that "Yuggoth . . . is only the steppingstone" and that "the main body of the beings inhabits strangely organised abysses wholly beyond the utmost reach of any human imagination" (*DH* 240). This is no doubt why they cannot be photographed by ordinary cameras. But the critical issue of motive emerges when a correspondent of Akeley's, Albert N. Wilmarth, comes up to Vermont for a visit at Akeley's urging, finding that Akeley has unexpectedly taken ill and can hardly speak except in a whisper, and is otherwise wrapped from head to foot in blankets. Akeley tells him of the remarkable abilities of the aliens ("The Outer Beings are perhaps the most marvellous organic things in or beyond all space and time—members of a cosmos-wide race of which all other life-forms are merely degenerate variants" [*DH* 239]), and especially of their surgical skill—they can extract a human brain, encase it in a canister, and take it on cosmos-wide voyagings where it can perceive all the wonders of the universe, "with elaborate instruments capable of duplicating the three vital faculties of sight, hearing, and speech" (*DH* 257). At one point Wilmarth finds such a prospect intoxicatingly exciting: "To shake off the maddening and wearying limitations of time and space and natural law—to be linked with the vast *outside*—to come close to the nighted and abysmal secrets of the infinite and the ultimate—surely such a thing was worth the risk of one's life, soul, and sanity!" (*DH* 243). But in the end he draws back in fear and flees the place—perhaps because he has come to realize that the letter inviting him up to Vermont was written not by Akeley but by the aliens themselves, and that the whispering figure he saw in the dimly lit room of the farmhouse was one of the aliens in disguise. Hence, the statement in the letter—"The alien beings desire to know mankind more fully, and to have a few of mankind's philosophic and scientific leaders know more about them. . . . The very idea of any attempt to *enslave* or *degrade* mankind is ridiculous" (*DH* 239)—would seem to carry the very opposite connotation.

The contradictions in Lovecraft's depiction of alien races seems to have been resolved in his two great science fiction stories, *At the Mountains of Madness* and "The Shadow out of Time." In these tales there is not only an enormously elaborate anatomical description of the alien species, but a careful working out of their psychology, morality, and even politics. Both works were, fittingly, published in the science fiction pulp magazine *Astounding Stories*. One passage in the former tale is of surpassing interest. As the protagonists decipher the bas-reliefs of the ancient Antarctic city of the barrel-shaped Old Ones, they discover that these semi-vegetable, semi-animal creatures had had encounters with both the "Cthulhu spawn" and the fungi from Yuggoth (here termed the "Mi-Go" because of their apparent resemblance to the "Mi-Go, or Abominable Snow-Men"):

> It was curious to note from the pictured battles that both the Cthulhu spawn and the Mi-Go seem to have been composed of matter more widely different from that which we know than was the

substance of the Old Ones. They were able to undergo transformations and reintegrations impossible for their adversaries, and seem therefore to have originally come from even remoter gulfs of cosmic space. The Old Ones, but for their abnormal toughness and peculiar vital properties, were strictly material, and must have had their absolute origin within the known space-time continuum. (*MM* 68)

This is exactly the distinction Lovecraft was emphasizing in his letter discussing the ramifications of the Einstein theory.

At the Mountains of Madness is significant because it appears to be the first tale written by Lovecraft after he had formulated a momentous new theory of weird fiction—one that took far more cognizance of the advance of science than any theory he had previously articulated. The canonical utterance occurs in a letter to Frank Belknap Long dating to February 27, 1931, only three days after he had begun writing his Antarctic novel:

The time has come when the normal revolt against time, space, & matter must assume a form not overtly incompatible with what is known of reality—when it must be gratified by images forming *supplements* rather than *contradictions* of the visible & mensurable universe. And what, if not a form of *non-supernatural cosmic art*, is to pacify this sense of revolt—as well as gratify the cognate sense of curiosity? (*SL* 3.296–97)

The context of this utterance is worth examining. Lovecraft, fresh from a reading of Joseph Wood Krutch's *The Modern Temper* (1929), had agreed emphatically with Krutch's belief that (as he expressed it) "some former art attitudes—like sentimental romance, loud heroics, ethical didacticism, &c.—are so patently hollow as to be visibly absurd & non-usable from the start" (*SL* 3.293). The advance of knowledge—and this includes not only our understanding of the universe but our understanding of our own psychologies—had destroyed many of the intellectual foundations that had supported previous "art attitudes," and there was a danger that weird fiction itself—especially fiction that still relied on outdated concepts like the ghost or the vampire—would cease to be of any relevance to the knowledgeable and sophisticated reader. The only recourse, as Lovecraft saw it, was the notion of *supplementing* rather than *defying* known natural law—

a principle he had perhaps unconsciously observed since "The Call of Cthulhu," but one that now became conscious. *At the Mountains of Madness* is one of his most vigorous expressions of this new aesthetic: nothing in the story—even the final emergence of the loathsome shoggoth, a fifteen-foot protoplasmic entity that the Old Ones had created as a beast of burden, but which had ultimately overthrown its masters—stretches the bounds of credulity to the breaking point, as, say, the mating of Yog-Sothoth with a human being in "The Dunwich Horror" does. The enormous care that Lovecraft took in establishing the scientific basis for the entire scenario—employing the sciences of geology, paleontology, biology, and physics in particular— and the slow, gradual accumulation of convincing detail make this novel a triumph of scientific realism. And of course, one cannot fail to quote Lovecraft's celebrated praise of the Old Ones, as the protagonists come to express the highest admiration for their courage and perseverance in traversing the cosmos, colonizing the earth, and establishing a rich and flourishing civilization: "Scientists to the last— what had they done that we would not have done in their place? God, what intelligence and persistence! What a facing of the incredible . . . Radiates, vegetables, monstrosities, star-spawn—whatever they had been, they were men!" (*MM* 96).

"The Shadow out of Time," while featuring many of the same elements of scientific verisimilitude, also represents the culmination of a theme that we can detect throughout Lovecraft's work—the theme of mind- or personality-exchange. In this novella an alien species termed the Great Race has "conquered the secret of time" (*ST* 48)[1] by its ability to send its minds forward (and, more rarely, backward) in time, displace the mind of some member of another species, and inhabit that mind for shorter or longer periods, learning everything about that species and its historical period; in the meantime, the captive mind is thrust into the body of its captor, and writes the history of its own time for the immense archives of the Great Race. Eventually, a reversal is effected, and the two minds occupy their own bodies once again. Lovecraft, while initially por-

1. I cite the Hippocampus Press edition of "The Shadow out of Time" because it is the only edition that prints the corrected text of the story, derived from the recently discovered autograph manuscript.

traying the idea as existentially terrifying, later suggests that the prospect is not at all to be despised:

When the captive mind's amazement and resentment had worn off, and when (assuming that it came from a body vastly different from the Great Race's) it had lost its horror at its unfamiliar temporary form, it was permitted to study its new environment and experience a wonder and wisdom approximating that of its displacer. With suitable precautions, and in exchange for suitable services, it was allowed to rove all over the habitable world in titan airships or on the huge boat-like atomic-engined vehicles which traversed the great roads, and to delve freely into the libraries containing the records of the planet's past and future. This reconciled many captive minds to their lot; since none were other than keen, and to such minds the unveiling of hidden mysteries earth—closed chapters if inconceivable pasts and dizzying vortices of future time which include the years ahead of their own natural ages—forms always, despite the abysmal horrors often unveiled, the supreme experience of life. (*ST* 49)

The scenario of this story is a vast expansion and subtilization of the scenario found in the early tale "Beyond the Wall of Sleep," where the notion was handled in a sadly bungled manner. There, a cosmic entity had been trapped in the body of a backwoods farmer named Joe Slater, and only manages to escape its human prison upon Slater's death. But Lovecraft has not thought through *why* or *by what means* this entity had ended up in the body of this uncouth individual, and the story collapses of its own absurdity.

What is more interesting is that Lovecraft has employed the notion of mind-exchange as a means of obviating both the scientific and the philosophical difficulties involved in the traditional idea of psychic possession, especially in the highly conventionalized form of possession by a demon or by the Devil himself. Lovecraft the atheist could of course never utilize the trope in that form, but earlier tales do make use of it in a relatively standard manner. *The Case of Charles Dexter Ward* is frequently thought to involve psychic possession, but, if it occurs at all, it does so in a manner somewhat more covert than many commentators believe. It is not that the seventeenth-century alchemist Joseph Curwen literally possesses the soul or mind of his twentieth-century descendant, Charles Dexter Ward; rather, it is that Ward, after stumbling upon his relation to Curwen, manages to revive him *bodily* (by the gathering of his "essential saltes" and the use of suitable incantations), whereupon Curwen kills Ward (whose double he proves to be) and tries to pass himself off as Ward. But psychic possession from a different angle may come into play, as it is suggested that the very interest that Ward initially takes in his relation to Curwen was a result of the latter's exercise of mental powers beyond the grave.

This scenario is roughly duplicated in the late story "The Thing on the Doorstep" (1933), which is an anomaly in its reversion to a traditional Gothic mode in the midst of Lovecraft's period of scientific realism. Here a college student named Asenath Waite seems to have an anomalous power of hypnosis: "By gazing peculiarly at a fellow-student she would often give the latter a distinct feeling of *exchanged personality*—as if the subject were placed momentarily in the magician's body and able to stare half across the room at her real body, whose eyes blazed and protruded with an alien expression" (*DH* 281). Sure enough, she does exactly that with the man she marries, the weak-willed Edward Derby; and her power also extends beyond the grave, for she manages to switch minds with Derby even after he has killed her; in turn, Derby's mind is flung back into her decaying corpse.

All this is delectably ghoulish, but the handling is crude and obvious, and "The Thing on the Doorstep" is one of the most disappointing of Lovecraft's later tales. And yet, it becomes clear that he has duplicated its basic scenario in "The Shadow out of Time," although introducing the notion of *mind-exchange over time* and, of course, rendering the entire conception far more plausible and compelling. There is, however, one philosophical issue that Lovecraft does no more than skirt in all these tales of mind-exchange: exactly what is being exchanged? In the early story "Herbert West— Reanimator" (1921–22), a flamboyant and possibly self-parodic account of a mad scientist's repeated attempts to reanimate the dead, the narrator states that Herbert West believed "with Haeckel that all life is a chemical and physical process, and that the so-called 'soul' is a myth" (*D* 134). The reference is to Ernst Haeckel (1834– 1919), the German biologist and naturalist whose vigorous support of the theory of evolution is embodied in several works, notably *Die*

Welträthsel (1899; translated into English in 1900 as *The Riddle of the Universe*), a book that markedly influenced Lovecraft when he read it around 1920. If, with Haeckel, Lovecraft had dispensed with the notion of an immaterial "soul," how then could he envision a (presumably material) mind cast out of its own body and thrust into that of another? He never really addresses the issue in the tales in question, and perhaps we are to believe that he retained this conception, even in such a purely science-fictional tale as "The Shadow out of Time," as the one supernatural "safety-valve" in a work that otherwise rigorously observes every known scientific principle.

IV. Shuddering Physical Repugnance

The one major late story I have not studied so far is "The Shadow over Innsmouth" (1931). This can readily be seen to be the culmination of Lovecraft's recurrent theme of miscegenation—the denizens of the Massachusetts coastal city of Innsmouth have become physically and mentally corrupted through interbreeding with a hideous race of fish-frogs, the Deep Ones, who appear to have underwater colonies throughout the world—but this supremely masterful evocation of urban decay is perhaps worth studying from a very different context: the context of Lovecraft's racism.

It is scarcely to be denied that H. P. Lovecraft was a racist for the whole of his life. Initially deriving his views from familial influence and from his upbringing in an old Yankee town that was, in the opinion of the once-dominant Anglo-Saxons, already being overrun by such "foreigners" as Italians, Poles, and Portuguese, Lovecraft became a systematic racist who maintained resolutely that African Americans were biological inferior to Caucasians, that Jews represented an "alien" force in American culture, and that the "the one supreme race is the Teuton" (*SL* 1.18). Perhaps from the influence of younger colleagues who objected to his doctrinaire views, Lovecraft grudgingly came to abandon the notion of *biological* superiority or inferiority (except where African Americans were concerned) and posited an extreme notion of *cultural disharmony*, maintaining that even a tiny admixture of a foreign culture produced incompatibilities that could potentially lead to the downfall of civilization. The formulation he evolved late in life—"a real friend of civilisation wishes merely to make the Germans *more German*, the French *more French*, the Spaniards *more Spanish*, & so on" (*SL* 4.253)—sounds superficially laudable, but it is based upon this notion of the radical incompatibility of even the smallest presence of "foreign" blood or culture in a predominantly homogeneous society.

The tracing of the intellectual origin of these views is a vexed issue. Certainly, the unprecedented influx of immigrants into the United States from 1890 to 1920 inspired not only the severe immigration restriction laws of 1917, 1921, and 1924, but also an unprecedented wave of pseudo-scientific defenses of racism in the teens and twenties. How much of this literature Lovecraft read is a difficult question. One of his earliest surviving poems is the embarrassing "De Triumpho Naturae: The Triumph of Nature over Northern Ignorance" (1905), a vicious attack on African Americans ("The savage black, the ape-resembling beast, / Hath held too long his Saturnalian feast" [*AT* 14]), is dedicated to one William Benjamin Smith, author of the racist treatise *The Color Line* (1905), which Lovecraft clearly read and relished. The early essay "The Crime of the Century" (1915) appeals to Thomas Henry Huxley for its division of mankind into separate racial groups, and no doubt Lovecraft may have picked up some hints from Friedrich Nietzsche, whom he read around 1919. Neither Huxley nor Nietzsche can be termed racists in any simple or obvious sense, although it is possible to read some of their writings in that way. Whether Lovecraft ever read Madison Grant's best-selling treatise *The Passing of the Great Race* (1916) is difficult to ascertain; I myself doubt it, in spite of the odd coincidence of Lovecraft's using the term "Great Race" twenty years later in "The Shadow out of Time." I similarly find no evidence that Lovecraft read another popular work, Lothrop Stoddard's *The Rising Tide of Color Against White World-Supremacy* (1920), although no doubt he would have sympathized with its message.

The plain fact is that Lovecraft believed he had scientific support for his racial views. In arguing with his old friend James F. Morton, who had written a brief tract called *The Curse of Race Prejudice* (1906), Lovecraft pontificates: "The black *is* vastly inferior. There can be no question of this among contemporary and unsentimental biologists—eminent Europeans for whom the prejudice-problem does not exist" (*SL* 3.253). Lovecraft, always eager to pick up information second-hand from reviews, newspapers, and magazine articles, does not cite any of these "eminent Europeans," but he was correct in believing that a fair number of scientists were still harboring racist beliefs well into the 1920s. It required generations of pioneering work by the anthropologist Franz Boas (1857–1942) and his students to persuade even biologists and anthropologists to discard racist presuppositions, and, as we are all aware, it has taken even longer for racialism to become intellectually and morally discreditable to the general public.

The incursion of racist presuppositions in Lovecraft's fiction is in large part covert, but it becomes visible once we realize the extent to which he ascribed to such views. Many of the tales of miscegenation now take on racial overtones: the mating of a distinguished, even aristocratic, Caucasian clan with apes in "Arthur Jermyn"; the unwholesome inbreeding that leads to degeneration in "The Lurking Fear"; even the mating of a white woman (however backward and degraded) with a "god" in "The Dunwich Horror," with the monstrosities that result. A more purely racialist story is "The Horror at Red Hook" (1925), written in the depths of Lovecraft's despair during his two miserable years (1924–26) in New York. This is nothing but a hostile snarl at the "foreigners" infesting the city that, in his view, had been established by Anglo-Saxons for the use of Anglo-Saxons; one of the worst parts of the city, the Red Hook district of Brooklyn, had now become "a maze of hybrid squalor" whose "population is a hopeless tangle and enigma; Syrian, Spanish, Italian, and negro elements impinging upon one another, and fragments of Scandinavian and American belts lying not far distant" (D 247). Lurid, pulpish, and confused, "The Horror at Red Hook" possesses only biographical importance as a sign that Lovecraft was near the end of his psychological tether in a city he had come to despise—a city in which, ironically, he felt himself to be an "unassimilated alien" (SL 2.176).

With "The Shadow over Innsmouth" we are in very different territory. The existence of racialist elements does not detract from the aesthetic supremacy of this tale, which in its skillful mingling of external horror (the horror of an alien species impinging upon our civilization) and internal horror (the narrator, after struggling so valiantly to escape the aliens' clutches, finds that he is, by heredity, himself related to them) may stand at the very pinnacle of Lovecraft's artistic achievement. And yet, the racism certainly enters into the tale. The narrator is first repelled by the physical anomalies of the Innsmouth people; of the bus driver who takes him into the city from Arkham, he writes:

> He had a narrow head, bulging, watery blue eyes that seemed never to wink, a flat nose, a receding forehead and chin, and singularly undeveloped ears. His long, thick lip and coarse-pored, greyish cheeks seemed almost beardless except for some sparse yellow hairs that straggled and curled in irregular patches; and in places the surface seemed queerly irregular, as if peeling from some cutaneous disease. His hands were large and heavily veined, and had a very unusual greyish-blue tinge. (*DH* 314)

How can we not think of the "Arab with a hatefully negroid mouth" (*D* 258) found in "The Horror at Red Hook," or, even more pertinently, Lovecraft's admission in reference to Jews that "On our side there is a shuddering physical repugnance to most Semitic types" (*Letters from New York* 269)—a clear reference to what Lovecraft took to be the anomalies of the Jewish physiognomy.

When the narrator of "The Shadow over Innsmouth" is compelled to spend a night in the seedy Gilman Hotel, further details unnerve him. Outside the hotel he is unnerved to hear that the passengers from a bus "shambled to the sidewalk and exchanged some faint guttural words with a loafer in a language I could have sworn was not English" (*DH* 341); the point is repeated once he flees the hotel and is being pursued by the Innsmouth denizens: "a large crowd of doubtful shapes was pouring [out of the Gilman House]—lanterns bobbing in the darkness, and horrible croaking voices exchanging low cries in what was certainly not English" (*DH* 350). It is probable that the presence of "foreigners" in conservative New England backwaters of this type was still uncommon in Lovecraft's day, but the emphasis he puts on the matter—as if the use of a foreign language is indicative of some kind of cosmic abnormality—is extraordinary. Lovecraft does not say that the language used by the inhabitants was not "human"—something that would indeed be productive of acute horror; rather, it was not "English."

It should, incidentally, be pointed out that Lovecraft's desire for homogeneity of culture is not intrinsically objectionable, just as the

current tendency toward multiculturalism is not intrinsically virtu-
ous. Lovecraft realized that there were virtues and drawbacks to
both these forms of social organization, and he simply preferred the
former. Where he is to be censured is (a) his refusal to take cognizance of the advances in anthropology and other sciences that had
destroyed the racialist presuppositions on which he relied throughout his life, and (b) his assumption—on no compelling evidence—
that even the tiniest admixture of "foreigners" would produce cultural chaos. As a social critic Lovecraft made many keen points, and
his screeds on the baleful dominance of machinery, on the need to
abandon *laissez-faire* capitalism for moderate socialism, and on the
benefits of broadened education to yield an intelligent electorate
and to foster civilized values have much to recommend them; but
in his racial theories Lovecraft comes up short both as an intellect
and as a compassionate human being. It is the one black mark
against his otherwise admirable character.

Epilogue: The Big Kick

This essay hardly exhausts the use of science in Lovecraft's fiction. I
have not even touched upon "The Dreams in the Witch House"
(1932), which elegantly reinterprets ancient witchcraft legendry by
means of higher mathematics, as a seventeenth-century witch develops the ability to enter into hyperspace (the fourth dimension);
but Fritz Leiber's comprehensive discussion of this tale (see Leiber,
"Through Hyperspace") leaves little for later commentators to say.

What I wish to do is to return, at last, to a query I raised earlier.
How can Lovecraft, the supreme scientific rationalist, still find himself able to say (albeit in fiction, not in essays or letters) that science
"will perhaps be the ultimate exterminator of our human species," or
that its findings might initiate a "new dark age"? Does this not indicate a hostility to science starkly at odds with his general philosophy?

Two points can be made in extenuation of Lovecraft's remarks.
In the first place, it is possible that what Lovecraft is suggesting is
not that science, as such, is dangerous, but that its results can produce *psychological* trauma in sensitive temperaments. Lovecraft
does in fact seem to have had an unusually low opinion of humanity's ability to deal with unpleasant truths; as early as 1918 he wrote:

"In many cases the truth may cause suicidal or nearly suicidal depression" (*SL* 1.65). The stories exemplify this sentiment over and over again, preeminently "The Call of Cthulhu." Here we learn that Cthulhu's underwater city, R'lyeh, emerged by accident as a result of an earthquake, but—presumably because the "stars were not right"—it sank shortly thereafter, taking Cthulhu back down to the depths of the sea. As a result, the earth is presumably spared any reemergence of the loathsome entity for the foreseeable future; and yet the narrator, having now become aware of the mere existence of such an appalling contradiction to known laws of entity, writes plangently: "I have looked upon all that the universe has to hold of horror, and even the skies of spring and the flowers of summer must ever afterward be poison to me" (*DH* 154).

From another perspective, Lovecraft's "attack" on science can be seen as part and parcel of his aesthetic (as opposed to his metaphysical) enterprise. In other words, Lovecraft used weird fiction to create "the *illusion* of some strange suspension or violation of the galling limitations of time, space, and natural law" (*CE* 2.176; my emphasis); but he knew that such a gesture was not to be confused with an actual acceptance of the *reality* of a suspension of natural law. Convinced, to his own satisfaction (in spite of the findings of Einstein, Planck, and others), of the invariability of natural laws, Lovecraft nonetheless enjoyed giving himself the *frisson* of contemplating—at least for the duration of a story—the *possibility* that natural laws had been suspended or subverted. To suggest that science did not have *all* the answers to the universe was critical to his ability to preserve the sense of wonder and awe that he believed all weird writers must retain. To adapt his own terminology, the suggestion of the limitations of science was not a *contradiction* of his materialist philosophy, but a *supplement* to it. In 1930 he wrote:

> I get no kick at all from *postulating what isn't so*, as religionists and idealists do. That leaves me cold . . . My big kick comes from *taking reality just as it is*—accepting all the limitations of the most orthodox science—and then permitting my symbolising faculty to *build outward* from the existing facts; rearing a structure of *indefinite promise and possibility* whose topless towers are in no cosmos or dimension penetrable by the contradicting-power of the tyrannous

and inexorable intellect. But the whole secret of the kick is *that I
know damn well it isn't so.* (*SL* 3.140)

The point about religion is of interest, for Lovecraft believed it was
exactly the error of religionists to take *literally* what could only have
a *symbolic* reality: "religion itself is merely a pompous formalisation of
fantastic art. Its disadvantage is that it demands an *intellectual* belief
in the impossible, whereas fantastic art does not" (*SL* 4.417–18).

Lovecraft the scientific rationalist, then, produced a literature in
which the boundaries of rationalism and science are pushed to their
limits; but he could only get the "kick" he wanted by adhering to
the most rigid and up-to-date findings of that science, which to him
was the arbiter of all truth. And yet, science was in no way a hin-
drance to the functioning of the imagination; indeed, quite the re-
verse: "The more we learn of the cosmos, the more bewildering
does it appear" (*SL* 4.324).

Works Cited

Joshi, S. T. "The Sources for 'From Beyond.'" *Crypt of Cthulhu* No.
    38 (Eastertide 1986): 15–19.
Leiber, Fritz. "A Literary Copernicus" (1949). In *Lovecraft Remem-
    bered,* ed. Peter Cannon. Sauk City, WI: Arkham House, 1998.
    455–66.
———. "Through Hyperspace with Brown Jenkin: Lovecraft's Con-
    tribution to Speculative Fiction" (1966). In *Lovecraft Remembered,*
    ed. Peter Cannon. Sauk City, WI: Arkham House, 1998. 472–83.
Lovecraft, H. P. *Essential Solitude: The Letters of H. P. Lovecraft and
    August Derleth.* Edited by David E. Schultz and S. T. Joshi. New
    York: Hippocampus Press, 2008. 2 vols.
———. *Letters from New York.* Edited by S. T. Joshi and David E.
    Schultz. San Francisco: Night Shade Books, 2005.
———. *The Shadow out of Time.* Edited by S. T. Joshi and David E.
    Schultz. New York: Hippocampus Press, 2001. [Abbreviated in
    the text as *ST*.]

Reviews

H. P. LOVECRAFT and ROBERT E. HOWARD. *A Means to Freedom: The Letters of H. P. Lovecraft and Robert E. Howard.* Edited by S. T. Joshi, David E. Schultz, and Rusty Burke. New York: Hippocampus Press, 2009. 1004 pp. in a two-volume set (not sold individually). $100 hc. Reviewed by Martin Andersson.

The story of the correspondence of H. P. Lovecraft and Robert E. Howard is a story of the fickleness of fate. It is a sad fact that it was cut brutally short after a mere six years; and it is a tragedy that Lovecraft's side of the correspondence was accidentally destroyed; but it is also extremely fortunate that Howard spotted Lovecraft's lazy scholarship in "The Rats in the Walls" (borrowing a line of Gaelic from Fiona Macleod's "The Sin-Eater" and dropping it into a setting where it did not belong linguistically); and it is extremely fortunate that August Derleth and Donald Wandrei of Arkham House were perceptive enough to realize the literary excellence of Lovecraft's letters and have large excerpts of them transcribed.

And what does it matter that this exchange lasted only six years? Into this brief time the scholarly gentleman of Providence and the master tale-spinner of Cross Plains crammed enough learning, anecdotes, and heated discussions to last most other people a lifetime. On a foundation of deep mutual admiration for each other's writing talents, they built a friendship that persevered in the face of their fundamental differences. Indeed, as Lovecraft noted on November 7, 1932: "All my favourite major correspondents are persons with whom I differ on some subject or another—usually many subjects." And Lovecraft saved all of Howard's letters to him, an indication of his high opinion of Howard, since his living quarters were cramped and he did not have the space to save everything. Likewise did Howard save all of Lovecraft's letters to him, and it was only after his death that they were accidentally destroyed, during his father's move to Ranger, Texas.

The topic on which the two most obviously disagreed was the relative merits of barbarism and civilization. Some of the longest, most scintillating letters of the present collection center on this subject, and it is a shame that there are gaps because of missing letters from Lovecraft. However, Howard's letters are clear evidence that he was Lovecraft's equal—at the very least—in presenting and refuting arguments, which obviously delighted Lovecraft, who never missed an opportunity for intellectual exchange but who was seldom seriously challenged. Sometimes Howard spots holes—real or apparent—in Lovecraft's arguments with embarrassing ease:

> You said war is merely a hangover from barbarism. According to that, modern wars are planned and instigated by those among us who are least civilized, according to the intellectual standard. Yet I hardly think that the facts would prove that our wars are caused by day-laborers, cowboys, prize fighters, soda jerkers, farmers, and other despised types. As near as I can figure it out, they are planned and started and carried out by the men who represent the very highest type of civilization—statesmen, politicians, kings, lords of finance, and diplomats.

But Lovecraft just as easily pokes holes in Howard's romantic view of life on the frontier. As Rusty Burke has observed in his excellent article on the Howard/Lovecraft letters ("The Lovecraft/Howard Correspondence," *The Fantastic Worlds of H. P. Lovecraft*; James Van Hise, 1999), it is a wonder "in light of the way these two would go at one another hammer-and-tongs in these debates" that they remained on friendly terms.

Lovecraft's letters display the usual wide-ranging interests, understated humor, gift for narrating his journeys, and willingness to discuss—at length!—everything between heaven and earth, things that we have previously seen in, for example, *O Fortunate Floridian*. His letters to Howard are indubitably among the most interesting letters he ever wrote. Yet it is, in this reviewer's opinion, Howard's letters that are the crown jewels of the present collection. He is passionate in his views; he argues his beliefs with admirable clarity and reflection, being very concrete in his examples where Lovecraft is often abstract; and his extraordinary gift for story-telling shines through in virtually everything. His description of the death of Billy the Kid is imbued with color and vitality in spite of the fact that he certainly did not witness it:

> The Kid, wary as a wolf, flashed his gun, though, and backed into Pete's room which opened on the porch. There he halted short—in the shadows he made out vaguely a dim form that should not be there—someone he knew instinctively was neither Pete nor one of Pete's servants. Where was that steel trap will of the Kid's that had gotten him out of so many desperate places? Why did he hold his fire then, he who was so quick to shoot at the least hint of suspicion? Azrael's hand was on him and his hour was come. He made his last mistake, leaping back into the doorway where he was clearly limned against the sky. He snapped a fierce enquiry—and then Death bellowed in the dark from the jaws of Pat Garrett's six-shooter.

He also pulls off the incredible stunt of narrating a game of football in a way that makes it interesting and exciting even to people whose interest in sports is zero or less, such as this reviewer. In Howard's typewriter, this game turns into an epic battle of heroic proportions, comparable to any battle in the Conan or Bran Mak Morn stories.

It is evident that Howard occasionally indulges in a bit of harmless fun at Lovecraft's expense. I cannot help feeling that Howard's anecdote of the school in Coleman County, where "the teacher kept a sixshooter in his desk and a mirror on the wall behind him so the scholars wouldn't shoot him in the back when he turned towards the blackboard," may have been embellished in the time-honored tradition of the tall tale in order to pull the genteel Yankee's leg.

The correspondence as presented in this two-volume set consists of 129 letters and postcards (for the sake of completeness, missing letters are included in this total as well). An appendix adds two more texts by Howard, "With a Set of Rattlesnake Rattles" and "The Beast from the Abyss," and four letters written by Howard's father to Lovecraft. A glossary of frequently mentioned names, a detailed bibliography, and an index round off the set.

The editors have done a tremendous job annotating the letters and arranging them in their proper order—Howard usually did not date his letters, so that the correct order must be determined from internal evidence. (I *think*, however, that letter #69 was written in response to #66, since Lovecraft responds to Howard's questions in #67.) My one complaint is that the editors have respected their source material too highly, presenting the letters as written, warts and all. These warts include typos, dropped words, habitual misspellings, and arbitrarily used apostrophes. While I can see the point of presenting letters the way they looked to the recipient, it makes reading more difficult than is necessary, and contrary to what is asserted on p. 12, it cannot be assumed that a particular error is in the original—this is particularly true of the Lovecraft letters, the originals of which we do not have. For most readers, it is probably of no interest that, for example, neither Howard nor Lovecraft could spell "accommodate" to save their lives; these mistakes could—and should—have been quietly eliminated, as was mostly done in *The Collected Letters of Robert E. Howard* (which, by the way, are a very good complement to this set), published by the Robert E. Howard Foundation.

When all is said and done, however, the fact remains that this is one of the most important correspondence cycles in the lives of both writers involved. In their mutual admiration they boosted each other when they most needed it; in their differences they challenged each other's ideas, forcing themselves to refine their own thinking on a number of subjects. So it lasted for only six years? Yes, but those were six years of epistolary glory, and the worlds of Lovecraftiana and Howardiana are both the richer for it.

S. T. JOSHI. *H. P. Lovecraft: A Comprehensive Bibliography*. Tampa: University of Tampa Press, 2009. xx, 682 pp. $50.00 hc, $30.00 tpb. Reviewed by Donald R. Burleson.

One scarcely knows where to begin, reviewing such a work as this. Indeed, it is questionable whether it is even possible to "review" this kind of volume in the sense in which one might review a novel or a volume of critical commentary. But make no mistake—this bibliography speaks to the creative process every bit as eloquently as do those other sorts of books, both because this massive compilation is an act of creation in itself and because it pays magnificent *de facto* tribute to a literary life that now stands as one of the most remarkable such lives of the twentieth century.

S. T. Joshi wisely includes, in this new volume, the original introduction to his *H. P. Lovecraft and Lovecraft Criticism: An Annotated Bibliography* (1981), because that introduction is of historical importance, having first appeared at the very time when Lovecraft was beginning to secure his place in the world of literature. But one has to read the opening paragraph of that introduction with an awareness (which one would have, from reading the preface) that the piece's significance is precisely historical. I say this because the opening paragraph, speaking of Lovecraft, refers to "the ambivalent nature of his critical acceptance," whereas there is no longer the ambivalence on that score that existed in 1981. Sometimes an assessment like that can become happily obsolete, and the very appearance of the present volume is bountiful proof of that fact—Lovecraft has come of age. Or (perhaps more accurately) the world of readers and mainstream literary critics has done so. Lovecraft's genius was always in evidence, for some of us, but it took time for the larger literary world to see it.

The sheer inclusiveness of this bibliography must be an eye-opener even to many who have long been used to thinking of H. P. Lovecraft as a worthy figure in literature. To attempt to convey any genuine idea of how much material is represented here would be like trying to convey an adequate idea, sight unseen, of a desert sunset—you just have to see one for yourself.

In any substantial bibliography, organization is everything of course, and the organization here is first-rate. One may consult several indexes in the back and then find the item of interest quite easily, as the outline headings appear at the tops of the pages for quick reference. (The listing for my own essay "A Note on Metaphor vs. Metonymy in 'The Dunwich Horror,'" for example, is located at the coordinates III-D-iii-37, and took me only seconds to find.) The broad categories are: I. Works by Lovecraft in English (broken down into four subdivisions, each with its own further subdivisions); II. Works by Lovecraft in Translation (two major subdivisions, further divided); and III. Works about Lovecraft (seven major subdivisions, further divided). Joshi provides cross-referencing throughout the volume to aid the researcher in making connections; e.g., in the case of essays listed both individually and as parts of books. One certainly senses the controlling presence of eminently capable organizational judgment in the whole fabric of the work;

but this should surprise no one, as Joshi is a veteran bibliographer, to say the least.

Even the most casual glance through the *Bibliography* will suffice to convince the reader, should a reader need convincing, of one salient fact: that Lovecraft's importance as a figure in literature is by now wholly undeniable. One finds, for instance, no fewer than twenty-five published translations listed for the story "The Call of Cthulhu," translations into languages as diverse as Spanish, Hungarian, and Danish; and the whole listing of fiction translations alone runs to thirty-three closely spaced pages with many hundreds of entries. If anyone had any doubt that Lovecraft has earned a global readership, these listings should put that doubt to rest. Likewise, the critical responses to Lovecraft have (visibly, now) mushroomed into a global wealth of material stunning to behold.

I have to look at this phenomenon from a personal viewpoint that makes it feel to me that over my life I have now witnessed a truly revolutionary development of Lovecraft's acceptance as a literary *artiste*. I first read him in 1955; in those days, I could seldom find anyone else who had. When I first visited Providence, Rhode Island, around 1970 and spoke with people at the Rhode Island Historical Society, asking why there were no plaques or historical markers at such sites as Lovecraft's birthplace on the corner at 454 Angell Street, I was met with polite incomprehension. Pretty much, the response was: "H. P. *who?*" At that point, Lovecraft was known to a handful of pulp-fiction readers with tenacious memories, but to virtually no one else. The very notion of a bibliography of the sort I am discussing here would have been beyond imagining for most people; at that point in time I hardly would have imagined it either, having largely resigned myself to the feeling that Lovecraft was a highly specialized literary taste that I might never find myself sharing with many similarly inclined readers.

The coming into his own of such a writer is a fascinating process, one full of complex dynamics. While obviously a compilation like the *Bibliography* would scarcely be possible without the material that it lists in such quantity and variegation, the compilation itself will of course prove to be another strong impetus in Lovecraft's growing fame as a writer of merit, presaging more material to compile in future bibliographies—rather, future editions of this one, which will remain definitive. The forces that establish a writer's acceptance are forces that feed upon each other; the success, for example, of stories and novels leads to screenwriting and the appearance of motion pictures, which, in turn, will set movie audiences to reading Lovecraft when they might otherwise not have done so with any alacrity.

And the place of S. T. Joshi in this literary landscape is likewise multivalent.

While the book editions and story translations and critical articles and books of commentary have had to be there for Joshi to find such a treasure trove to bibliographize, I would go so far as to say that the converse is true as well—that Joshi's tireless work over the years (aided by critical analysis done by others as well) is in a very real sense responsible for the very existence of many of those publications listed in the *Bibliography*. Without a certain critical mass of capable commentary, biography, and other work relating to Lovecraft, many of these editions, translations, and movie adaptations would in all likelihood never have come to be. (Ask yourself: for how many of Lovecraft's fellow contributors to *Weird Tales* and other magazines in the 1920s and 1930s have such bibliographies been compiled, and how many of those other writers have enjoyed anything remotely like Lovecraft's impact on world literature?) Success begets success, but sometimes it needs help in doing so. For several decades, S. T. Joshi has provided the very sort of scholarship and leadership necessary to conduce to the effect we are now seeing—the unassailable place of the Gentleman from Providence in a world of literature he himself would no doubt never have imagined himself as significantly inhabiting.

Joshi's *Bibliography* is monumental. Everyone seriously interested in Howard Phillips Lovecraft needs to have it in hand.

S. T. JOSHI. *I Am Providence: The Life and Times of H. P. Lovecraft.* New York: Hippocampus Press, 2010. 1,276 pp. $100.00 (2 vols. hc). Reviewed by Steven J. Mariconda.

I can say with confidence that S. T. Joshi's new biography, *I Am Providence*, is the finest three million characters ever concatenated regarding H. P. Lovecraft. But that would be too easy, and not very funny. I could also say, "S. T. Joshi has written a great book"—but that also would be too easy, and not very newsworthy: he counts many great books among the nearly three dozen he's written. *The Weird* Tale (University of Texas Press, 1990), in particular, comes immediately to mind.

So, a bolder and more accurate statement: *S. T. Joshi has written a classic.*

Or, more precisely, he has re-re-written a classic. The background is this: Joshi knows Lovecraft better than most people know the members of their own nuclear family, and surpasses his subject as a scholar of literature, philosophy, and history. Joshi originally wrote Lovecraft's biography fourteen years ago in 708 pages. The limited edition hardcover went out of print almost immediately and fetches prices exceeding many HPL first editions. A glance on the Internet shows today's market prices. *Dagon and Other Macabre Tales* by H. P. Lovecraft, selected and with an introduction by August Derleth; Arkham House, Sauk City, WI, 1965; 1st ed.; condition, fine in a fine dust jacket: $250.00. *H. P. Lovecraft: A Life* by S. T. Joshi; Necronomicon Press, W. Warwick RI, 1996; 1st ed.; condition, fine in a fine dust jacket: $600.00.

Necronomicon Press, humanely, issued a paperback edition of *H. P. Lovecraft: A Life* in 1996 for $29.95. Five years later, Joshi abridged and revised the original work in a 432-page book published in the UK by Liverpool University Press as *A Dreamer and a Visionary: H. P. Lovecraft in His Time.* Now we have the dreadnought version—nearly 1,300 pages—in which Joshi adds material omitted from the first two versions and provides considerable revision and updates.

The baseline reason the book is so excellent, of course, is that Joshi is an expert on the artist and his work. But more than this, he has done outstandingly well in consolidating a massive amount of information and writing a book that reads as easily and fascinatingly as a novel. It is, as the subtitle *The Life and Times of H. P. Lovecraft* states, not just about the author. What the reader gets is not only a biography but also a rich history of the incredible cultural, political, and literary upheavals that occurred between 1890 and 1937.

Lovecraft, like many authors, did not live an outwardly eventful life. He never held a job, instead living off a small inheritance and sporadic income from stories sold to pulp magazines and revision work. Nor was he a prolific writer—he composed only 60 or so tales over the three decades of career. Most of his time was spent reading and writing letters (at one point had had nearly 100 correspondents). He liked to walk around in search of colonial architecture and landscape vistas, and took advantage of public libraries and historical society collections to become something of a specialist in New England history.

It could make for a boring book, but this is far from the case here. Joshi, first of all, is strong on the work—deft in summarizing and explicating the fascinating weird tales that bring us to this book. When the reader closes the covers, he or she will have a much-enhanced appreciation of these stories—the finest supernatural horror tales of the twentieth century, a matchless blend of science fiction, fantasy, and existential terror.

Secondly, Joshi has done tremendous research on the context of Lovecraft's life, which divides cleanly into several phases: birth until at age 14; 15 to 23, when he progressively became the reclusive "invalid" (Lovecraft's term) of popular lore; 24 to 32, when he became a minor celebrity in the small world of amateur journalism; 33 to 36, when he made a failed attempt at marriage and workaday employment in New York; and the final decade of his life after his retreat to Providence, when he lived with an aunt, wrote, and did some traveling around the east coast. The biographer is tremendously adroit in using these phases as a framework upon which to interweave Lovecraft's activities, his personal life, his art, his influences, and his thought on political, philosophical, literary, and contemporary happenings. So the book is not only a compelling portrait of the artist, but also a liberal education on the early twentieth century.

Lovecraft's life is one of the most well documented in literature: for most of his adult life he wrote multiple letters—many of which were preserved by correspondents—every day. In addition to this, we have synoptic diaries Lovecraft intermittently kept—for example, a 1925 pocket agenda with multiple telegraphic entries for each day (he used this as a mnemonic aid in writing letters home to his aunt). So we have a clear idea (perhaps too clear) about his day-to-day activities—when Lovecraft woke up, what he had for breakfast, when he went out, and when he returned; when he slept, what he read, and who he saw. Joshi, happily, does a good job of blurring out the minutiae without losing the essence of the man.

It is doubtful that a more complete, accurate, and fluent biography will ever be written. The only thing left for discussion, then, is interpretation; and, as Joshi notes, "judgments of [Lovecraft] will differ in accordance with individual temperament" of the reader. Accordingly, I will mention three areas where future biographers may diverge from Joshi's assessments.

Many a literary biography has been ruined by armchair psychoanalysis. Joshi treads lightly here, but too much so. By the age of eighteen, Lovecraft had experienced a series of personal tragedies that I believe crippled him emotionally even as they provided the themes and the compelling affect that make his fiction powerful.

Joshi paints a candid picture of the really horrifying demise of Lovecraft's father—insanity, confinement, and slow death from tertiary syphilis. The biographer dwells little, however, on the effects this event likely had on young Lovecraft's mental health and the subsequent course of his life. Lovecraft had multiple "nervous breakdowns" prior to age twenty-one, the first at age eight. Joshi does, in fact, mention that the latter might have been related to the circumstances of the father's illness. But there must be more to it than this. Lovecraft was an extraordinarily bright and sensitive child; intellectually curious, and unusually aware of his surroundings (he claimed to have memories going back to before two years old.). He was nearly three years old when his father was bought to Providence's Butler Hospital under confinement from a business trip to Chicago. Lovecraft would have been mindful of household whispers—the affect of shock, shame, and guilt, if not the substance of the matter. Certainly he knew his father was alive, but absent (apparently the child was told his father was unconscious in a coma); nearby, but not available to visit. The five years that passed before Winfield Lovecraft finally died must have seemed a lifetime for the boy Lovecraft, knowing that his father was lying abed only one mile from his house.

Joshi rightly points out that Lovecraft fondly recalled his childhood, and had a grandfather and uncle as strong father figures. But after the father's confinement Lovecraft's care was left largely to his progressively psychotic mother, who told neighbors her son's face was "hideous." (There is no debate that Lovecraft's later relationships with women were problematic; and Joshi bluntly calls his treatment of his wife "shabby.")

Lovecraft's childhood, too, was overshadowed by other deaths: grandfather George (d. 1895); grandmother Robie (d. 1896); cousin Marion Gamwell (d. 1900); and grandfather Whipple (d. 1904). The latter's demise (at home, apparently) of a sudden apoplectic stroke was followed by the sale of the huge Victorian mansion—complete with stable, outbuildings, carriages, servants, and livestock—in which Lovecraft grew up. The fourteen-year old boy who considered himself an "aristocrat" and his mother removed to a humble duplex about a block away. As a coup de grace, Lovecraft's much-loved black cat—his best and perhaps only friend—ran away; he never had another pet.

Joshi is correct in giving Lovecraft tremendous credit for going far in overcoming these early issues. But the effects are clearly manifest in much of the author's eccentric behavior, and even more pronouncedly in the stories that speak to the horrors of being abandoned in an uncaring universe and the horrors of existence itself. Another biographer might have used a heavier hand delineating these matters, while still hewing to the facts.

Joshi, to his eternal credit, does not pull any punches on issue of Lovecraft's racism, which he calls "without question, the one true black mark on his character." However, some readers will feel the biographer backs off a little too much at the end of the book when he asserts that "one's final picture of Lovecraft must be based largely upon the last ten or so years of his existence; for it was at this time that he shed many of the prejudices and dogmatisms that his early upbringing and seclusion had engendered. . . . In those ten years I see very little to criticise and very much to praise." A stroll through the last volume of the Arkham House *Selected Letters* tends to refute this. A random example: Lovecraft "would advocate the improvement of backward groups through education, hygiene, & eugenics—nor do I think it especially naïve or ultra-idealistic in me to prefer these conscious & scientific methods to the blind, brutal, & accidental methods of primitive nature, in which real advances are merely the casual by-products of aimless, wasteful forces" (*SL* 5.323). There are others.

Lovecraft, however, did hit the bull's eye when he announced the death of capitalism and predicted the cultural wasteland that

American would become:

> Unsupervised capitalism is through. But various Nazi & fascist compromises can be cooked up to save the plutocrats most of their spoils while lulling the growing army of the unpropertied with either a petty programme of *panem et circenses*, or else a system of artificially created & distributed jobs at starvation wages on the C.C.C. or W.P.A. idea. A regime of that sort, spiced with the right brand of hysterical flag-waving, sloganeering, and verbal constitution-saving, might conceivably be as stable & popular as Hitlerism—& that is what the younger & more astute Babbitt's of the Republican party are quietly & insidiously working toward. (*SL* 5.326)

Regarding that last jab—Joshi permits himself a few editorial comments that reveal him as firmly with Lovecraft on the far left. This editorializing is sometimes intrusive, and begs the question as to whether it is simplistic to blame conservatives for problems that stem from not one political party but from a systemically corrupt system of business executives, lobbyists, government insiders, and elected officials from both sides of the aisle (see, for example, Janine R. Wedel's recent *Shadow Elite* [Basic Books, 2009]).

A topic that gets little space in the 1,300 pages is Lovecraft's sense of humor—or, more accurately, Lovecraft's sense of play. I believe this came from his very solitary childhood, during which he learned to amuse himself in a distinctive way. His sense of humor was truly ludic (the Latin "ludere" means "to play"). One might even go so far as to say that Lovecraft perceived reality itself to be ludicrous.

Lovecraft's unique perspective was complemented by an equally unique way of expressing himself, verbally and in writing. He became interested in the drama at six years of age; he set up a little toy theatre with hand-painted scenery, and played Shakespeare for weeks. He was taken to many productions at the Providence Opera House. Later Lovecraft expanded his tableau-play by devoting a large tabletop to a scene, which he "would proceed to develop as a broad landscape . . . [and] construct some scene as fancy—incited by some story or picture—dictated, & then to act out its life for long periods—sometimes a fortnight—making up events of a highly melodramatic cast as I went. . . . I kept this up till I was 11 or 12." Lovecraft always had a fondness for *histrionics* in all forms; he en-

joyed re-enacting scenes from plays with a fervor that once startled
neighbors, and liked to read his own works aloud adding outlandish
voice characterizations for what little dialog he used. He was also a
skilled mimic, particularly of speech patterns and dialect (one un-
fortunate manifestation is found in the last *Letters* volume, as Lovecraft uses Yiddish to mock a local fifteen-year-old "Jew boy" fan).
Lovecraft found tremendous joy and pleasure in language itself, and
we see a great deal of stylistic play in all the prose he wrote. There
is very little difference, prosodically, across Lovecraft's stories, letters, and essays. They all use the same bizarre ideolect. Memoirs tell
us he spoke the same way.

Similarly, Lovecraft looked at the world around him with a sense
of play, constantly on the alert for *prima materia* for his stories. All
fiction writers draw upon personal experience in their work; but
Lovecraft was exceptional in both the depth and breadth of details
he used for the weft of his stories, and the distinctive warp (I use the
word advisedly) he placed upon those details. He liked to make fun
of himself in his stories. He looked upon everything with a kind of
fascination. He often used in-jokes of which he—or he and a single
disinterested friend—only might be aware. In "The Colour out of
Space," for example, Lovecraft used real family names (for example,
Nabby Gardner) from the area around Prescott, Mass. But only his
friend W. Paul Cook, an amateur journalist with no interest in weird
fiction, might have known this. Similarly, his narrator is based upon
Frank E. Winsor, who from 1915 to 1926 was chief engineer for the
Scituate Reservoir in Rhode Island; it was announced on the front
page of the *Providence Journal* for October 1, 1926, that Winsor was
resigning to become chief engineer of the Quabbin Reservoir, fea-
tured in the story Lovecraft wrote five months later. But only his
aunt might have known this. Joshi, David E. Schultz, and Peter Cannon have all contributed to excellent annotated editions of Lovecraft's fiction, thick with examples of this on every page. This
factitious transmutation of the real, set side by side *with* the real, is
another reason why Lovecraft's tales have such impact.

But these are all matters of interpretation and emphasis. The
book may be complemented by other perspectives, but not ex-
celled on its factual completeness, level-headed assessments, and
sparkling narrative. Joshi—who was influenced by Lovecraft's

thought in youth but stands now as his own person, an intellectual equal—is sympathetic to his subject, but not too sympathetic. I leave it to future commentators to speculate on how biographer and subject might have gotten along had they the chance to meet. Each iconoclastic, extremely bright, and extremely opinionated, they might have been fast friends, or mortal enemies.

Briefly Noted

Kenneth W. Faig, Jr., continues his pioneering biographical research on Lovecraft with the publication of *George Elliott Lovecraft: Lost Scion of the House of Lovecraft* (Moshassuck Monograph Number 14), a fascinating look at Lovecraft's little-known second cousin. This Lovecraft (1866/67–?) was born in Rochester, NY, and appeared to live in the New York City area for many years—at least until 1933–34, when all trace of him disappears. H. P. Lovecraft was dimly aware of his second cousin, referring to him as "that lost western grandson of Joe Junior" (*SL* 3.361)—i.e., the grandson of Joseph Lovecraft, Jr. (1810–1879). The print run on this monograph is very limited, but it can be ordered for $12.50 (for delivery by media mail in the US) or $20.00 (for delivery by air mail in the rest of the world) from Kenneth W. Faig, Jr., 2311 Swainwood Drive, Glenview, IL 60025-2741.

Original fiction in the Lovecraftian tradition continues to appear in abundance from a variety of publishers. Ellen Datlow's *Lovecraft Unbound* (Dark Horse, 2009) contains a multitude of fine stories by such leading writers as Caitlín R. Kiernan, Laird Barron, Marc Laidlaw, and Joyce Carol Oates. S. T. Joshi's *Black Wings: New Tales of Lovecraftian Horror* (PS Publishing, 2010) contains original tales by Kiernan and Barron as well as Michael Shea, Nicholas Royle, David J. Schow, Jonathan Thomas, Donald R. Burleson, and many others. Joshi has also edited a largely reprint anthology, *Spawn of the Green Abyss* (Mythos Books, forthcoming), that contains three original stories. Darrell Schweitzer's *Cthulhu's Reign* (DAW, 2010) features original tales by Fred Chappell, Will Murray, Matt Cardin, and many others. Joshi is at work on a *Black Wings II*, scheduled for 2012.

www.ingramcontent.com/pod-product-compliance
Lightning Source LLC
Chambersburg PA
CBHW051824090426
42736CB00011B/1643